The Urban Response to Internationalization

Peter Karl Kresl
Bucknell University

Earl H. Fry
Brigham Young University

Edward Elgar
Cheltenham, UK • Northampton, MA, USA

Published by
Edward Elgar Publishing Limited
Glensanda House
Montpellier Parade
Cheltenham
Glos GL50 1UA
UK

Edward Elgar Publishing, Inc.
136 West Street
Suite 202
Northampton
Massachusetts 01060
USA

A catalogue record for this book
is available from the British Library

ISBN 1 84376 414 8

Typeset by Manton Typesetters, Louth, Lincolnshire, UK
Printed and bound in Great Britain by MPG Books Ltd, Bodmin, Cornwall

Contents

Figures

Tables

The authors

Peter Karl Kresl has been Professor of Economics and International Relations at Bucknell University (USA) since 1969. His teaching and research interests are in European and North American economic integration, urban economics and globalization, and cultural policy. He has published, among others, in *Urban Studies*, *The Journal of European Integration*, *The American Review of Canadian Studies* and *Ekistics*. He authored *Urban Economies and Regional Trade Liberalization* in 1994 and co-authored, with Sylvain Gallais, *France Encounters Globalization*, which was published by Edward Elgar in 2002. He has edited *Seen from the South*, Brigham Young University, 1989, and co-edited, with Gary Gappert, *North American Cities and the Global Economy*, Urban Affairs Annual Review 44, Sage Publications, 1995.

Earl H. Fry is Professor of Political Science and Endowed Professor of Canadian Studies at Brigham Young University in Provo, Utah. He is the author or editor of: *Mapping Globalization Along the Wasatch Front* (2002), *The North American West in a Global Economy* (2000), *The Expanding Role of State and Local Governments in US Foreign Affairs* (1998), and *The New International Cities Era: The Global Activities of North American Municipalities* (1989). He has served as a Fulbright Professor in France and Canada and was also a Special Assistant in the Office of the US Trade Representative (USTR).

Preface

The subject of the response of urban economies to the increasing pace of internationalization or, to use a word that has gained great popularity in recent years, globalization, is receiving a great deal of attention by scholars and by local officials during the past two decades. Perhaps it was the shock of the ten-fold increase in the price of crude petroleum that forced the economies both of developed and less-developed nations to comprehend that they have to restructure their economic activities on a new footing, with new power relationships and new actors in all areas of the economy. National governments imposed constraints on their capacity to intervene in their own economies on behalf of negatively affected constituents, and lower barriers to movements of capital, goods and services have made all economies vulnerable to new threats and challenges but also to new opportunities. It should be noted parenthetically that movement of workers in response to economic incentives has been limited by both national policy and the various attractions of place. In this environment cities have found themselves, on the one hand, to be the governmental entity that is most affected by these developments and, on the other hand, the governments that are most suited to formulate responses to them. This book is an examination of the several aspects of this situation in which local governments now find themselves.

First a word about terminology. We have chosen to use the word internationalization in the title rather than the obvious alternative – globalization. International firms are thought to be those which have linkages, through production, distribution and so forth in other countries or parts of the world; firms that have globalized their activities are those that have established multiple centers of activity in countries other than the firm's home country. Analogously, it must be noted that cities have established linkages to entities throughout the globe but they have not merged with foreign cities or adopted any of the other operational initiatives used by globalized firms. Hence, we prefer to conceptualize our subject matter as that of internationalization of the economic activities of urban economies. The latter term, urban economy, is also used as a general term that covers municipal economy as well as that of the several forms of city – central city, city plus suburbs and edge cities, consolidated metropolitan statistical area (CMSA) and metropolitan statistical area (MSA), although these other words will on occasion be used when it is appropriate.

Fry wrote the introductory chapter and those on municipal diplomacy and governance (Chapters 1, 3 and 5); Kresl was responsible for the other five chapters. Each of us has, of course, reviewed the entire text and the final product is indeed a joint effort.

1. Urban regions and economic globalization: an introduction

We live in the century of *homo urbanus*. For the first time in human history, half of the world's population will reside in urban regions by 2007, with the proportion of those urbanized predicted to grow to 60 per cent by 2030.[1] Indeed, the rate of growth in urbanization will nearly double that of the overall population increase between 2000 and 2030 – 1.8 per cent versus 1 per cent.[2] In contrast, a minuscule 3 per cent of the world's population was urbanized in 1800, 14 per cent in 1900, and 30 per cent in 1950.[3] In the United States, the first census conducted in 1790 estimated that 5 per cent of the population was urban, with the largest city being New York City with fewer than 50 000 people. Urbanization would increase to 11 per cent in 1840, almost 32 per cent in 1900, and about 80 per cent in 2000.[4]

As a result of global and regional transformations, intergovernmental tensions, social unrest, demographic changes, and a potpourri of other factors, cities are in a state of flux. Many are becoming quite large, especially in the so-called developing world. In terms of nomenclature, the United Nations often refers to the major Western 'industrialized' societies as the more developed countries, the middle-range nations as the less developed, and those suffering from widespread poverty as the least developed. We will use these UN terms throughout this book, although at times we will refer to developed and developing countries as nations of the North and nations of the South. In 2003, there were already 20 megacities with populations exceeding 10 million, and 16 of these were situated in less or lesser developed countries (see Table 1.1).[5]

In contrast to the 20 megacities in 2003, only New York City had exceeded the 10 million mark back in 1950.[6] Twenty-two cities now have between 5 and 10 million inhabitants, 370 between 1 and 5 million, and 433 between 500 000 and 1 million.[7] Those countries with the highest Human Development Index figures are more than 70 per cent urbanized, whereas those with the lowest rankings are only 30 per cent urbanized, although one should not overlook the fact that one-quarter to one-third of all urban households subsist in absolute poverty (see Table 1.2 for the degree of urbanization in the developed and developing regions).[8] In a press release issued by UN-Habitat in June 2001, this UN agency stressed that the 'central challenge of the

Table 1.1   The world's megacities, 2003

Tokyo	35.0	Los Angeles	12.0
Mexico City	18.7	Dhaka	11.6
New York	18.3	Osaka-Kobe	11.2
Sao Paulo	17.9	Rio de Janeiro	11.2
Bombay	17.4	Karachi	11.1
Delhi	14.1	Beijing	10.8
Calcutta	13.8	Cairo	10.8
Buenos Aires	13.0	Moscow	10.5
Shanghai	12.8	Manila	10.4
Jakarta	12.3	Lagos	10.1

Note: Population in millions.

Source: United Nations Department of Economic and Social Affairs, 2004.

Table 1.2   Urban population as a percentage of total population

	1970	1995	2013
Least developed countries	12.7	22.9	34.9
All developing countries	24.7	37.4	49.3
Developed countries	67.1	73.7	78.7

Source: UN Development Program, 2000.

twenty-first century will be how to make globalization and urbanization work for all the world's people, instead of benefiting only a few.' It noted that one billion urban inhabitants live in inadequate housing. In Africa, only one-third of all urban households have direct access to potable water, and in Asia and the Pacific, only 38 per cent of households are connected to sewerage systems.[9] Europe and North America were, respectively, 75 per cent and 77 per cent urbanized in 2000, with these percentages expected to increase to 83 per cent and 84 per cent by 2030.[10] Bigger is not necessarily better, and more Americans have chosen to live in suburbs rather than in central cities, with the 2000 US census ascertaining that 81 million resided in central cities, 119 million in suburbs, and 26 million in 'shadow' areas which are just beyond but not directly connected to the suburbs. Half of all Europeans also live in distinct communities ranging in size from 1000 to 50 000 inhabitants.

Without any doubt, the linkages between the local and the global have never been as extensive nor as profound as currently exist in the first decade of the new millennium. UN-Habitat asserts that the 'focal point' of globaliz-ation 'has invariably been the city, a place of deals and decisions, take-offs and landings – a place less concerned with the rhythms of nature, where everything can be bought or sold, especially one's ideas and labor.' This UN group adds that 'cities no longer stand apart as islands. They are the nexus of commerce, gateways to the world in one direction and focus of their own hinterland. Tied together in a vast web of communications and transport, cities are concentrations of energy in a global field.' Optimistically, UN-Habitat concludes that 'in a real sense, the world is completely urbanized, as this force field has the power to convert all places and all people into a productive, constantly adapting unity.'[11] As a classic example of how cities are affected by aspects of globalization, New York City's population grew by about 1 per cent per year during the 1990s, but this gradual increase masked very dramatic demographic fluctuations as about one-seventh of the popula-tion exited the city, only to be replaced by an equal number of overseas immigrants. Today, 36 per cent of New York City's population is foreign born and almost 48 per cent of the population over the age of five speaks a language other than English at home. Some other US cities have even higher concentrations of non-English speakers. For example, Santa Ana, California, which has the fifth largest public school district in that state, has a population composed of 74 per cent who speak Spanish and another 6 per cent who speak a language other than English.[12]

Cities around the world and of all sizes are subject to the vagaries of globalization, and this influence will increase noticeably over the next few decades. The purpose of this book is to examine the economic challenges and opportunities facing urban centers in the first quarter of this century as a result of growing globalization and regionalism, and then to provide some policy insights which will assist urban leaders to enhance for their constitu-ents the positive features of globalization while mitigating, as much as possible, the potentially harmful dimensions.

THE GLOBALIZATION PHENOMENON

Globalization has been referred to as 'the most important phenomenon of our time.'[13] It connotes a growing interconnectedness among people and societies around the planet. In the book *Global Transformations*, the authors state that globalization 'may be thought of initially as the widening, deepening and speeding up of worldwide interconnectedness in all aspects of contemporary social life, from the cultural to the criminal, the financial to the spiritual.'[14] Nye and Keohane describe globalization as the buzzword of the 1990s, just as 'interdependence' was the buzzword of the 1970s. They define globalization as 'a state of the world involving networks of interdependence at multi-continental distances. These networks can be linked through flows and influences of capital and goods, information and ideas, people and force, as well as environmentally and biologically relevant substances (such as acid rain or pathogens).'[15] Nye and Keohane insist, however, that globalization does not imply universality nor is it rendering nation states obsolete. Kenichi Ohmae disagrees, arguing that the nation state is giving way to region-states, many of which have populations between a few million and 10 to 20 million and are developed around a major urban center.[16]

Various aspects of globalization can be quantified. Since the 1950s, global trade has been growing at about three times the rate of individual national economies, with 6.2 trillion dollars in merchandise trade and an additional 1.5 trillion dollars in commercial services' trade achieved in 2002.[17] Foreign direct investment (FDI), which provides investors in one country with a controlling interest in a company in another country, has been growing even more rapidly than international trade, with FDI flows topping 1.2 trillion dollars in 2000 alone and with the stock of outward FDI catapulting from 1.7 trillion dollars in 1990 to 6.6 trillion dollars in 2001.[18] The number of multi-national corporations (MNCs) in the world, entities which account for a major segment of trade and FDI globally, has also expanded dramatically from 7000 in the 1960s to roughly 65 000 today. These 65 000 MNCs control 850 000 affiliates which employ 54 million workers worldwide (up from 24 million in 1990) and were responsible for producing 19 trillion dollars in annual sales in 2001, almost three times the value of total international trade.[19] The foreign affiliates of MNCs currently account for about one-tenth of the world's GDP and one-third of global exports.[20] Add to this the record levels of international portfolio investments, plus international currency trans-actions in the range of 1.5 trillion dollars per day, and one begins to understand what economic globalization means in concrete terms. Today, both the inter-national system of production-sharing and stock markets are 24-hour phenomena, following the sun as it rises and sets and beginning with eight hours in Asia and the Pacific, moving on to eight hours in Europe and Africa, and then completing the quotidian cycle with eight hours in the Americas. For example, Sequence Design, a company that produces software to design computer chips, has its headquarters in the United States but maintains other facilities in Japan, India, and the United Kingdom. It maintains a 24-hour production cycle, and as its CEO iterates, 'only time zones are boundaries in my head anymore. There are no geographical boundaries.'[21]

In addition, the movement of people across national borders is at unpre-cedented levels. In spite of the tragic events of September 2001, international tourism returned to record levels in 2002, with 703 million people visiting other countries and spending over 474 billion dollars, compared with 456 million visitors in 1990 who spent 264 billion dollars.[22] The Madrid-based World Tourism Organization expects the number of international tourists to top the one billion mark by 2010 and the 1.5 billion level by 2020.[23] Immigration and refugee flows are also without parallel, and at least 175 million people currently reside in countries different from their place of birth, more than double the figure of 1975.[24] Immigrants living in other countries constitute 3 per cent of the world's population, and that figure increases to almost 9 per cent in the more developed nations.[25]

Figures 1.1 and 1.2 indicate the degree to which international trade and direct investment activity has increased over the past several decades. Figure 1.3 illustrates the substantial increase in international tourism, and Tables 1.3 and 1.4 show the growth in international immigration and how immigrants have become a much more substantial part of many societies. Figure 1.4 indicates that globalization goes far beyond the economic dimension and is affecting local populations in myriad ways. As James Wolfensohn, President of the World Bank, emphasizes: 'There is no wall. We are linked by trade, investment, finance, by travel and communications, by disease, by crime, by migration, by environmental degradation, by drugs, by financial crises and by terror.'[26]

To illustrate this growing interdependence and its impact on local populations, there is no doubt that individual nations are capable of taking concrete steps toward controlling the use of substances within their respective borders which contribute to ozone deterioration or global warming (Fig.1.4). However, unless other nations, many of which may be located

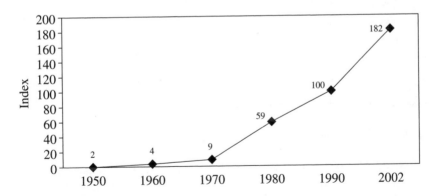

Note: 1990 = 100

Source: World Trade Organization (2003).

Figure 1.1 *World merchandise exports in current US dollars, 1950–2002*

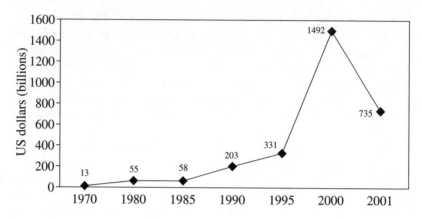

Source: UNCTAD (2002).

*Figure 1.2   Annual inflows of foreign direct investment, 1970–2001, billions
of US dollars*

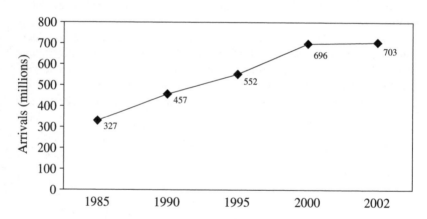

Source: World Tourism Organization (2003).

Figure 1.3   International tourism, 1985–2002, millions of arrivals

thousands of miles from affected local communities, enact similar measures, the ozone layer will continue to deteriorate and global warming will intensify, leading to harmful effects on residents in urban areas everywhere, even those whose national governments have attempted to combat environmental degradation.

The United States has long been considered as one of the most self-sufficient nations in the world, and its exports as a percentage of gross domestic product

Table 1.3   *Growth in the number of immigrants, 1990–2000*

	1990	2000	Number	Per cent
World	154.0	174.8	20.8	13.5
More developed countries	81.4	104.1	22.7	27.9
Less developed countries	72.5	70.7	−1.8	−2.6
Least developed countries	11.0	10.5	−0.05	−4.9
Africa	16.2	16.3	0.1	0.03
Asia	50.0	49.8	−0.02	−0.04
Europe	48.4	56.1	7.7	15.8
Latin America	7.0	5.9	−1.1	−15.0
North America	27.6	40.8	13.2	48.0
Oceanic	4.8	5.8	1.0	22.8

Note: Figures are in millions.

Source: United Nations Population Division, 2002.

Table 1.4   *Immigrants as a percentage of a nation's total population, 2000*

United Arab Emirates	74
Kuwait	58
Jordan	40
Israel	37
Singapore	34
Saudi Arabia	26
Switzerland	25
Australia	25
New Zealand	23
Canada	19
United States	10

Source: United Nations Population Division, 2002.

(GDP) were only about 10 per cent in 2001, compared with 43 per cent in Canada, 35 per cent in Germany, 29 per cent in France, 27 per cent in Great Britain and 11 per cent in Japan. The stock of FDI in the United States in 2000 was the equivalent of about 12 per cent of its GDP, compared with 34 per cent in Great Britain, 28 per cent in Canada, 25 per cent in Germany, 21 per cent in France, and 1 per cent in Japan.[27] Nonetheless, when measured in dollar terms, the United States is the world's leading importer, exporter, foreign direct inves-

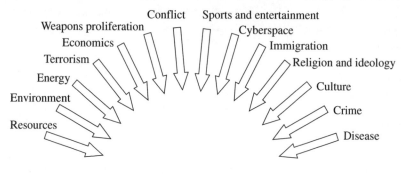

Figure 1.4   *International events transforming life in urban regions*

tor, recipient of FDI, provider of international tourists, and leading recipient of spending by foreign visitors (see Table 1.5). It is the world's only superpower, but it is incapable of building a jet fighter or an automobile or a computer without substantial component parts and resources provided by many other nations around the world. The Department of the Treasury issues US dollars, but once in circulation, two-thirds of the currency finds its way to individuals and governments located outside the United States.[28] The movement of motor vehicles and aircraft and the heating of homes and offices would also be extremely difficult without other countries providing more than 50 per cent of all petroleum products used in the USA each year. Vaclav Smil stresses the need for the world community of nations to develop alternative energy sources such as solar and wind power. He points out that solar radiation reaching the earth every year is equal to nearly 14 000 times the current global total primary energy supply, and the ability to convert one per cent of all wind energy would be ten times greater than the total installed in all fossil-fuel, nuclear and hydroelectric stations in 2000. Unfortunately, the technology allowing these conversions to be made in mass quantities may still be decades away, and humanity remains highly dependent on non-renewable fossil fuels for energy, with less than 5 per cent of the global population situated in the United States expending about 27 per cent of annual primary energy usage worldwide.[29] In the entertainment sector, Hollywood would also be in dire financial straits without the nearly 60 per cent of box office revenues which are generated outside US borders.[30]

Americans are also painfully aware about how unrest and grievances abroad can be translated into carnage and death in New York City or the Washington,

Table 1.5   The United States and globalization

World's leading importer
($1.41 trillion in 2002)

World's leading exporter
($973 billion in 2002)

World's leading foreign direct investor
($1.52 trillion in 2002)

World's leading host nation for foreign direct investment
($1.35 trillion in 2002)

World's leading holder of foreign assets
($6.4 trillion in 2002)

World's leading host nation for foreign-owned assets
($8.8 trillion in 2002)

World's leading source of international tourists
(56.4 million in 2002 vs. 60.9 million in 2000)

World's number three recipient of international tourists
(41.9 million in 2002 vs. 51.0 million in 2000)

World's leading nation for spending by foreign tourists
($66.5 billion in 2002 vs. $82.4 billion in 2000)

World's leading host nation for immigrants
(one million documented and undocumented per year)

DC area. Terrorism and international crime affect most villages, towns, and neighborhoods around the planet, with organized crime alone accounting for perhaps 3 per cent or more of total annual global production. Jeffrey Robinson estimates that international drug trafficking alone accounts for 2 per cent of global GDP, and this does not even include child prostitution, money laundering, gambling, racketeering, counterfeiting, arms trafficking and other illicit activities associated with organized crime.[31] Diseases are also no respecter of national or regional political boundaries. Many of the major diseases now inflicting humanity were not even identified three decades ago, including AIDS, the HIV virus, Ebola, Hepatitis C, SARS, and the West Nile virus, and just in the period 1976–98, the World Health Organization (WHO) identified nearly 40 new diseases in humans.[32] Most of these diseases had their origins in some of the remotest and rural parts of the planet, but within months or years they had spread to most of the world's major cities, piggybacking on the record movement of goods and people across national boundaries. As Richard Preston points out, 'a hot virus from the rain forest lives within a 24-hour plane flight from every city on earth.'[33] In his emphasis on 'global life systems,' Robert P. Clark documents the complexity and interconnectedness of ecosystems, emphasizing that the European expansion after 1500 helped to globalize the gene pool of humans, food and diseases, and that humans today share 65 diseases with dogs (including whooping cough), 45 to 50 with cattle (including small pox, tuberculosis and measles), 46 with sheep and goats, 42 with pigs, 35 with horses and 26 with poultry.[34] Some diseases, including many that began initially in animals, have had horrific effects on human society, with the influenza pandemic of 1918–19 claiming over 20 million lives globally, and AIDS responsible thus far for 28 million fatalities and 40 million additional infections, with 5 million new HIV cases identified in 2003 alone.[35] As André-Jacques Neusy suggests, in

> a world where people and economies are increasingly interdependent, health risks are not self-contained. Consequently, the health in both high and low-income countries is increasingly dependent on how global health issues are managed in the world. These issues include control of infectious and chronic diseases, rising social inequalities and humanitarian crises caused by warfare, biochemical terrorism, environmental hazards and mass-migration to urban areas.[36]

The information and communication technologies (ICT) revolution is also accelerating the process of globalization. The human information base may be doubling every half decade. The School of Information Management and Systems at the University of California at Berkeley, in a report entitled 'How Much Information?,' has calculated that humanity stored about five exabytes (a billion gigabytes) of new information on paper, film, and optical or magnetic media in 2002, double what was stored just three years earlier. These five exabytes are equivalent to all the words ever spoken by humans since the dawn of civilization.[37] Alvin Toffler has postulated that illiteracy will not be the major challenge of the twenty-first century; rather, the ability to learn, unlearn, and relearn will be the major task facing societies around the world.[38] With transformations in human society occurring so rapidly, many are worried that they or their children will be unable to keep pace, and are concerned that ultimately they will be counted among the digital 'have nots' instead of the digital 'haves.'

Globalization, when combined with unprecedented technological change identified with the New Economy, has provoked rather ambivalent feelings among both urban and rural dwellers around the world. Without any doubt, the notion of the pervasive influence of the New Economy was greatly exaggerated during the period of the rapid increase in the value of 'dot.com' companies. However, the following statement made by the New Economy

Task Force is still credible: 'The information technology revolution has expanded well beyond the cutting edge high-tech sector. It has shaken the very foundations of the old industrial and occupational order, redefined the rules of entrepreneurship and competition, and created an increasingly global marketplace for a myriad of goods and service.'[39] For example, the creation and expansion of the World Wide Web was a phenomenon of the 1990s, and the first US web page was not even created until 1992. The impact of the Internet has increased exponentially since that time and has had a profound impact on many societies around the world.[40] As an illustration, the 'e-choupals' project in India is currently serving 18 000 villages and provides a computer and Internet service in a central location in each village, permitting local farmers to check futures prices globally and locally before taking their commodities to market. They are also given immediate access to local weather conditions, new soil-testing techniques, and other expert knowledge intended to increase their productivity.[41]

In an extensive 2003 survey conducted by the Pew Research Center for the People and the Press, a majority of respondents in 35 of the 44 nations covered had a favorable view toward at least four aspects of globalization: (1) growing trade and business ties; (2) faster communications and travel; (3) growing availability of foreign culture; and (4) the wide variety of products available from different parts of the world.[42] In more than half of these nations, six of every ten respondents deemed globalization to be good or somewhat good. In 41 nations, majorities perceived trade and business ties as good for their countries and good for their families, including 96 per cent of respondents in Vietnam, 93 per cent in the Ivory Coast, and 90 per cent in Nigeria.[43] Thomas Friedman observes that India and China, with two-fifths of the world's population, have staked their futures on globalization, emphasizing education, infrastructure modernization and international trade, among other priorities. He predicts that by 2010 there will be many more Internet users in those countries than in the United States.[44] According to the Pew survey, young people are more likely to be favorable toward globalization, whereas those over 50 are more opposed or at least more skeptical. On the other hand, many perceive that globalization helps certain countries more than others, 'foreign' is still viewed as a negative word by many of those surveyed, and immigration to one's country is rarely viewed in positive terms.[45] Broadly speaking, as underlined by A.G. Hopkins, the

> advocates of capitalism and free trade see globalization as a positive, progressive force generating employment and ultimately raising living standards throughout the world. Those opposed to globalization perceive it as a means of expropriating the resources of poor countries by drawing them into debt, encouraging the use of sweated labor, and accelerating environmental degradation

all within a contemporary world in which one-fifth of humanity takes home four-fifths of its income.[46]

Critics of globalization are to be found both on the political left and the political right. On the left, Maude Barlow and her compatriots in Canada lament the loss of national sovereignty and the subjugation of the environment and workers' rights to the demands of powerful MNCs.[47] On the right, Patrick J. Buchanan in the United States laments that free trade and liberal immigration policies have cost millions of jobs for native-born Americans and are relegating the nation to a 'developing-country' status.[48] Similar arguments have been rendered by leftist groups in Europe and by right-wing proponents such as Jean-Marie Le Pen in France and the Northern League in Italy. The political left also tends to identify globalization with the United States and contends that US political and business leaders are intent on exporting the American way of life and homogenizing culture worldwide so that it reflects American values and generates profits for US-based corporations.

Globalization also has a distinctly political dimension and is affecting the ability of local elected officials to shape the futures of their municipalities. At the beginning of 2004, 148 nation states were members of the World Trade Organization (WTO), and 184 were affiliated with both the World Bank and the International Monetary Fund (IMF). An additional 30 nations or territories have also been granted 'observer status' at the WTO. In the name of freer trade and investment, national governments have agreed to adopt measures which limit the policy prerogatives of their regional and local governments. This is an especially sensitive issue in federal systems where intermediate governments such as states and provinces, as well as some local governments, operate within their own constitutionally guaranteed areas of jurisdiction.

Similar restrictions are found when national governments become members of regional groupings such as the European Union (EU) and the North American Free Trade Area (NAFTA). The EU can trace its roots back to the 1950s and expanded from six to nine members in 1973, from nine to 12 between 1981 and 1986, from 12 to 15 in 1995, and from 15 to 25 in May 2004. NAFTA has only three members, the United States, Canada, and Mexico. It went into effect in 1994 and will be fully implemented in 2008. A major controversy has erupted in North America as NAFTA's Chapter 11, which is intended to provide corporations with the right of establishment and 'national treatment' in Canada, the United States, and Mexico, has repeatedly attempted to limit what state, provincial, and local governments in North America's three federal systems can do in exercising authority to protect the workplace and the environment.

Jagdish Bhagwati posits that there are two great forces characterizing the twenty-first century: globalization and the growing civil society. The big question is whether they can coexist in partnership or face continuing confrontation. The other question is how well prepared municipal governments are to articulate the interests of civil society in protecting and enhancing the interests of their local constituents.[49] James Rosenau adds that we live in an era of shifting boundaries, weakened states and proliferating non-governmental organizations, and over time we have developed local, provincial, national, transnational, international, and global 'levels of community.' Within this complicated setting, there are growing interactions of globalizing and localizing forces and divergent tendencies leading at times to integration and at other times to fragmentation. In effect, there is a plurality of governing actors and new patterns are evolving concerning interactions between governments and society.[50] With this in mind, the impact of international and regional pacts on the decision-making latitude of municipal leaders is likely to increase in light of the expansion of the EU from 15 to 25 member-states in 2004, the anticipated completion of the WTO's Doha Development Round in 2005, and the targeted implementation of the Free Trade Area of the Americas (FTAA) in 2005.

Joseph Schumpeter's notion of creative destruction is also more relevant in the current period of globalization than when he was writing about it many decades ago. During the past several years in the United States, roughly 550 000 to 600 000 new businesses have been created annually, but almost as many close down each year. Approximately 30 per cent of private sector jobs in the United States may also change dramatically each year, either being newly created, terminated, or requiring a substantial change in job requirements and expectations. Manufacturing in the 1950s employed up to 35 per cent of the US private sector workforce, a figure which had dwindled to little more than 11 per cent by mid-2004.[51] This drop in manufacturing jobs as a percentage of overall employment is even more significant because in 2001, salaries and benefits per full-time worker in manufacturing averaged 54 000 dollars, versus only 45 600 dollars for the private sector in general.[52] In the period between August 2000 and December 2003, 2.8 million manufacturing jobs were lost, primarily attributable to a slow-growing economy, outsourcing, and the relocation of corporate jobs overseas.[53] Unionization rates have also plummeted from the 35 per cent range in the early 1950s to 13.2 per cent of all jobs in 2002 and only 8.5 per cent of jobs in the private sector.[54]

The fortunes of individual communities may also vary significantly, with the Silicon Valley region in northern California enjoying a ten-fold increase in jobs in the period between 1980 and 2000, whereas manufacturing jobs in Detroit, Newark, St. Louis and various other metropolitan regions decreased alarmingly during the same period. Joel Kotkin adds that the New Economy in the United States has not only been unkind to a broad array of places, but also a number of economic sectors such as ranching, lumbering, fishing, farming, textiles, automobiles, and manufacturing in general.⁵⁵ Even in Silicon Valley, often viewed worldwide as the 'model' for local economic development in an era where the ITC sector is becoming much more prominent, fortunes can change rapidly. In 2001, the unemployment rate dipped into the one per cent range in Silicon Valley, but two years later Santa Clara County, the heart of Silicon Valley, was suffering from an unemployment rate well above 8 per cent, far higher than the national and California averages.⁵⁶ At the same time, residents of the area faced housing prices which were among the highest in the world, clogged freeways, a deteriorating public school system and municipal and state government fiscal problems unparalleled since the end of the Second World War. State, provincial and local governments from other parts of the United States and Canada have also been 'poaching' in Silicon Valley, attempting to convince companies to move their operations or at least expand elsewhere in order to lower their costs of doing business. However, this poaching is not limited to the boundaries of North America, for many high-tech jobs in Silicon Valley and its counterparts elsewhere in the Western world have been relocated to India, China and other nations which can provide skilled labor in rich abundance but at relatively low wage rates. Forrester Research, a US consultant firm, predicts that 3.3 million US jobs and 136 billion dollars in wages will be moved offshore over the next 15 years to countries such as India, China, Russia and the Philippines, with the ICT sector leading the initial exodus overseas.⁵⁷

In effect, cities around the world are involved in inter-urban competition, especially in the economic domain.⁵⁸ Some of this competition may be healthy, but some is also very short-sighted, duplicative, and wasteful. Whether they like it or not, cities have been tossed into the cauldron of creative destruction. For centuries, many of the important cities of Europe and the Middle East rose to greatness because of the power base of their respective nation states, combined with their favorable location along seas, rivers, or caravan routes.⁵⁹ Location near oceans or other waterways is no longer nearly as important, even though cities continue to engage in 'place' marketing. Distance, time and location have become less important in an era of unprecedented transportation and communication innovations. Even the smallest of cities in Western countries are no more than one or two airplane stops from most other major urban areas around the world. Satellite and Internet connections have also theoretically equalized the gathering and dissemination of critical information between a New York City and a Moose Jaw, Saskatchewan. Cities have become entrepreneurial zones, with the largest being the nodes for international finance, but some also represent what Saskia Sassen terms 'a new geography of centrality and marginality,' especially in the United States.⁶⁰ The so-called best and brightest in a society are to be found within blocks of some very disadvantaged people, especially those with little formal education, recent immigrants and those facing a variety of physical and emotional challenges. In New York City, a world-renowned municipality with tremendous aggregate wealth, 44 per cent of families have few or any assets at all, three times the national average in the United States.[61] As UN-Habitat points out, there are often lines of stratification between people in major cities, with the costs and benefits of globalization unevenly distributed both within and between cities. It adds that 'homeless people are living in cardboard boxes on sidewalks of gleaming corporate sky-scrapers, whose budgets exceed those of many countries.'[62] Many would argue that the success of cities in the future cannot be measured in terms of total metropolitan production and spending, but rather on overall income distribution and the quality of life of its residents.

CITIES IN HISTORY

As indicated earlier, most of the world's population through history has been rural-based. Although humans have been around for millions of years, the first noteworthy urban settlements probably occurred in Mesopotamia and around Jericho a few thousand years ago, and the Greeks may have been the first to engage in systematic urban planning. Paul Bairoch estimates that cites emerged two to three thousand years after agriculture was first established by humans.[63] Edward Soja postulates that Jericho may have been the first urban area capable of self-generated growth and development, with the roots of the city's development dating back as far as 8350 BC.[64] Although cities were very small by today's standards back in medieval Europe, once they were developed they tended to have staying power, with an estimated 93 per cent of the cities with populations over 20 000 in 1800 already in existence in 1300.[65] Hohenberg and Lees add that most of the major cities in Europe were actually founded by 1300, signifying that urban Europe was 'functionally made' many centuries ago.[66] Between 1000 and 1500, cities had the major role in the diffusion of knowledge and began to draw from the countryside both people and food, much as is occurring in the developing world today. As people began to pour into European cities after 1750, terrible living conditions, a lack of proper sanitation, horrendous pollution, inadequate food supplies and the easy spread of disease among people living in close proximity resulted in deaths in these cities actually outnumbering births until the latter part of the 19th century.[67] Yet in spite of unspeakable living conditions for many residents, cities remained the centers of creativity and innovation. As Peter Hall concludes:

> Cities were and are quite different places, places for people who can stand the heat of the kitchen: places where the adrenalin pumps through the bodies of the

people and through the streets on which they walk; messy places, sordid places sometimes, but places nevertheless superbly worth living in, long to be remembered and long to be celebrated.[68]

The Industrial Revolution stands out as a true 'break with the past' and helped to foment a tremendous growth in urbanization.[69] Bairoch estimates that the number of urban residents in the world doubled between AD 1 and 1300, then doubled again between 1300 and 1800. In contrast, between 1800 and 1980, urban dwellers increased twenty-fold and we are now in the midst of another remarkable urban explosion in the developing world.[70] Indeed, David C. Thorns predicts that the 'twenty-first century is likely to be dominated by urban living in a way that we have not experienced before,' adding that almost 90 per cent of the world's total population growth through 2025 will be concentrated in urban areas.[71]

CHALLENGES FACING THE WORLD'S CITIES

Cities on a regional, national, and global basis are competing against one another to attract businesses, manufacturing enterprises, research and development facilities and head offices in an effort to provide well-paid jobs for local residents and in hopes of developing world-class clusters, whether these clusters be related to the auto industry, steel, textiles, energy, transportation, ICT, biotech or emerging fields linked to nanotechnology.[72] Some of these cities are also formidable or potentially formidable global economic actors. A study sponsored by the US Conference of Mayors in 2001 compared the annual production in metropolitan areas in the United States with the gross domestic products of nation states. The study revealed that if city/county metro economies were individual nation states, 47 of the world's 100 largest 'national' economies and 85 of the top 150 would be situated in US metropolitan areas.[73] Major cities such as New York City, with an annual local government budget approaching 45 billion dollars, also spend more annually than many national governments.

Cities are not only expanding population-wise but also territorially. Pudong near Shanghai and Shenzhen near Hong Kong were transformed over the course of a couple of decades from small towns into large metropolises with populations of 1.7 million and 7 million respectively. The average territorial size of the 100 most populated cities in the United States in 2000 was 168 square miles, more than triple the land size of the top 100 in 1950. As an example, Phoenix, Arizona was the ninety-ninth most populated US city in 1950 with 107 000 people living within city limits measuring 17 square miles. Fifty years later, Phoenix ranked as the seventh largest city with 1.3

million people living in boundaries encompassing 475 square miles.[74] Between 1982 and 1997, 25 million acres of farmland and open spaces, about the size of the state of Indiana, were developed by metropolitan governments, representing a 47 per cent increase in their territorial size. This physical expansion may boost overall urban production but may also contribute to urban sprawl, growing suburbanization, a further weakening of the central core, and a deterioration of older communities within the core and the so-called 'near' suburbs.[75]

Cities are at the crossroads of both globalization and the New Economy.[76] Change is occurring so rapidly and various factors will affect cities in the future. Peter Drucker asserts that northern nations now live in a post-capitalist knowledge society which is far different from recent human history. He points out that during the twentieth century there was a rapid decline in the sector which had dominated society for 10 000 years: agriculture. In 1900, agriculture was the largest contributor to GDP and to jobs, in stark contrast to the year 2000 when its contribution in both categories had become marginalized.[77] Manufacturing in developed countries has been following the same road in terms of its contribution to jobs, and to a lesser extent, GDP. In 1900, most people in the North worked with their hands, but this fell to 50 per cent by mid-century and to less than 25 per cent at the beginning of the twenty-first century. Ageing will be yet another challenge in the more developed nations, with those over age 65 expected to constitute over half of the adult population in Japan and Germany by 2030, and with many other European societies approaching that level over the next three decades.[78]

Most global trade, investment, and the movement of people are funneled through major cities. As UN-Habitat suggests, 'a country's global success rests on local shoulders.'[79] In the United States, 84 per cent of the nation's employment is concentrated in 319 metro areas. In Canada, the second largest nation in the world territorially, over half of the population and jobs is concentrated in only four broad metropolitan regions mostly sequestered close to the US border: Toronto and the Golden Horseshoe region of southern Ontario, Montreal, Vancouver and the lower British Columbia mainland, and the Calgary–Edmonton corridor. This concentration in four major centers has prompted one commentator to label Canada as primarily 'a handful of city-states.'[80] Many municipal leaders believe in the adage 'think globally and act locally,' while others are trying to implement 'glocalization' strategies which meld global trends with local particularities. The term glocalization may be traced to the Japanese expression 'dochakuka' which literally means global localization.[81] In other words, the world is becoming more homogeneous in certain ways, but it is also becoming more heterogeneous in other ways, and global–local linkages and interaction may differ rather substantially from one city to the next.[82] As Malcolm Cross and Robert Moore point out, features of what they call 'globalism' in the cultural domain do include McDonald's, Coca-Cola, pop singers, Hollywood film stars, sports heroes and filmmakers who are known throughout the world and whose appeal transcends both language and nationality. So, to a certain extent, globalism spreads 'Americanization' in the cultural realm, but it does not mean the homogenization of culture. Rather, regional, ethnic, religious and local cultures can still 'flourish in the face of globalism.'[83] The same is true in other aspects of life as well.

Most international immigrants also gravitate to large cities. In the United States, half of the foreign-born population resides in the Los Angeles, New York City, San Francisco, Miami and Chicago metro regions which together account for 21 per cent of the total US population.[84] Forty per cent of the current residents of Miami and 31 per cent of Los Angeles' are foreign born.[85] In Canada, 73 per cent of immigrants arriving between 1990 and 2000 settled in Toronto, Montreal, or Vancouver, and almost 44 per cent of all the residents of the Toronto metropolitan region were born outside Canada.[86] The United States now relies on foreign-born labor for about one-sixth of its private-sector workforce, Switzerland nearly one-fifth and Australia almost one-fourth.[87] In the US, new immigrants plus children born to recent immigrants accounted for almost 70 per cent of total population growth between 1990 and 2000, and high percentages are also found in Canada, Australia, and some European nations.[88]

In addition, many New Economy jobs are concentrated in larger cities, and some of these new immigrants have been instrumental in the transformation of local economies, such as the influence of Indian and Chinese-born entrepreneurs in Silicon Valley. In Canada, the high-technology revolution has been disproportionately centered in the very largest cities where, coincidentally, immigrants tend to congregate.[89] One of every six jobs created in Canada during the 1990s was in the high-tech sector, but this increased to four of every 10 jobs in the largest cities. In 1990, 63 per cent of Canada's ICT jobs were in cities with populations close to or exceeding one million people, and this increased to 70 per cent in 2000, compared with 45 per cent of the total workforce in 1990 and 43 per cent ten years later.[90]

Globalization, the ICT revolution, and creative destruction have all combined in the 21st century to greatly complicate governance and economic development in cities around the world. How cities react to the challenges highlighted by Drucker and others will probably differ from continent to continent, or even sub-region to sub-region. As Patrick Le Galès asserts, there are already noticeable policy differences between major European and US cities, with municipal leaders in the USA having greater faith in finance-driven capitalism and European municipal leaders leaning toward stronger social citizenship and relative equality among local residents.[91]

These phenomena, as well as policy alternatives available to municipal leaders, will be discussed in much greater detail in subsequent chapters. Chapter 2 will examine urban competitiveness, Chapter 3 the evolving field of municipal diplomacy, Chapter 4 the condition of urban economies and the role of new technologies, Chapter 5 new challenges to urban governance, and Chapter 6 the development of new international structures. Chapter 7 will then delve into the complicated process of strategic planning, and the final chapter will ponder both the exigencies of a world in a period of unprecedented transformation and the capacities for response available to urban governments. The global community is without a doubt becoming more interdependent, interconnected and intertwined, but much of its success or failure in bringing about greater prosperity, sustainability, and economic and political justice for the earth's inhabitants will depend on what transpires at the grassroots' level in cities around the world. 'Think globally and act locally' will certainly be recognized as one of the most enduring concepts of the 21st century.

NOTES

1. UN Human Settlements Program, 2001, p. 6.
2. UN Department of Economic and Social Affairs, 2001, p. 5.
3. Population Reference Bureau, 'Human population: Fundamentals of growth patterns of world urbanization,' 2003, www.prb.org.
4. Ibid.
5. UN Human Settlements Program, 2001, p. 6.
6. UN Department of Economic and Social Affairs, 2001, p. 6.
7. Ibid.
8. Ibid., pp. 10 and 18.
9. Ibid.
10. Ibid., p. 8.
11. UN Human Settlements Program, 2001, p. 6.
12. US Census Bureau, 2002, and *Washington Times*, 28 January 2003.
13. Micklethwait and Woolridge, 2000, p. viii.
14. Held *et al.*, 1999, p. 2.
15. Joseph S. Nye, Jr. and Robert O. Keohane, 'Introduction,' in Nye and Donahue (eds), 2000, p. 1.
16. Ohmae, 1995, pp. 100 and 143.
17. World Trade Organization, 2003, p. 10.
18. Ibid., p. 7.
19. UNCTAD, 2002, pp. 1 and 4.
20. Ibid.
21. Sappenfield, 2003.
22. World Tourism Organization, 2003, pp. 1–2.
23. Speech by Francesco Frangialli, Secretary-General of the World Tourism Organization, on the occasion of the inauguration of the ITB, Berlin, 16 March 2002.
24. UN Department of Economic and Social Affairs, Population Division, 2002, p. 1.
25. Ibid., p. 11.
26. *International Herald Tribune*, 13 March 2002.

27. These export and FDI statistics were compiled by the Organisation for Economic Co-operation and Development (OECD) in cooperation with various UN-affiliated agencies.
28. This estimation is made by the US Federal Reserve Board. See the *Washington Post*, 18 January 2000, p. E1.
29. Smil, 2002, pp. 126–32.
30. *Los Angeles Times*, 27 July 2003.
31. Robinson, 2000, p. 337.
32. *Wall Street Journal*, 8 July 2003, p. B1.
33. Clark, 2001, p. 106.
34. Ibid., pp. 102 and 104.
35. UNAIDS/WHO, 2003, p. 3.
36. Neusy, 2003, p. 3.
37. Klinkenbourg, 2003.
38. Toffler, 1970.
39. Progressive Policy Institute, 1999, Introduction.
40. Berners-Lee, 1999.
41. *New York Times*, 1 January 2004.
42. Pew Global Attitudes Project, 2003.
43. Ibid.
44. 'Terrorism may have put sand in its gears but globalization won't stop: Interview with Thomas L. Friedman,' *YaleGlobal*, 30 January 2003.
45. Pew Global Attitudes Project, 2003.
46. A.G. Hopkins, 'Introduction,' in Hopkins, 2002, p. 9, and *International Herald Tribune*, 13 March 2002, p. 6.
47. Barlow and Clarke, 2001.
48. Buchanan, 2002.
49. Bhagwati, 2002, pp. 2–7.
50. Rosenau, 1999, especially pp. 287, 293, and 295.
51. Bureau of Economic Analysis, US Department of Commerce (2004).
52. Popkin, 2003, p. 17.
53. US National Association of Manufacturers, and *New York Times*, 3 January 2004.
54. US Bureau of Labor Statistics (2004).
55. Kotkin, 2000, pp. 9 and 184.
56. *Los Angeles Times*, 8 August 2003.
57. Gongliff, 2003.
58. Camagni, 2002, pp. 2395–411, and Jensen-Butler *et al.*, 1997.
59. Rugman and Moore, 2001, p. 65.
60. Sassen, 1998, p. xxv.
61. Kotkin, 2000, p. 23.
62. UN-Habitat, 2001.
63. Bairoch, 1988, pp. 74 and 493.
64. Soja, 2000, p. 27.
65. Bairoch, 1988, p. 153.
66. Hohenberg and Lees, 1985, pp. 1 and 340.
67. Bairoch, 1988, pp. 240–42.
68. Hall, 1998, p. 989.
69. Bairoch, 1988, pp. 500–501.
70. Ibid., pp. 501–502, and 510.
71. Thorns, 2002, p. 1.
72. Uldrich, 2002, p. 16, and Aeppel, 2000, p. R40.
73. US Conference of Mayors, 2001.
74. US Department of Commerce, census 2000 data.
75. *Wall Street Journal*, 9 July 2001, pp. A2 and A17.
76. Agarwal, 2000, p. 6.
77. Drucker, 2003, p. 199.
78. Ibid., p. 201.

79. UN Human Settlements Program, 2001.
80. Francis, 2002.
81. Czarniawska, 2002, p. 12, and Kantor, 1995, p. 24.
82. Czarniawska, 2002, p. 14, and Bairoch, 1988, pp. 515–17.
83. Malcolm Cross and Robert Moore, 'Globalization and the new city,' in Cross and Moore (eds), 2002, p. 2.
84. 2000 US census data featured in the *Los Angeles Times*, 7 February 2002, p. A11.
85. US Department of Commerce, census 2000 data.
86. Statistics Canada, census 2001 data, and McIsaac, 2003, p. 59.
87. *Economist*, 31 March 2001, p. 15.
88. Camarota, 2001.
89. *National Post*, 28 September 2002.
90. Statistics Canada, *The Daily*, 31 July 2003.
91. Le Galès, 2002, p. 275.

2.   Urban competitiveness

Toward the end of the 20th century the role of urban economies in their own economic futures expanded dramatically; as we enter the 21st century this role seems to be developing even more.[1] The forces that have induced this during the past quarter century continue to exert their influence and they have been joined by yet other forces. One of the primary concerns for urban economies is that of the durability of these forces – are they short term adjustments to one-time shocks or will they endure for decades to come? It is most likely that they are a mixture of both, but that the residual or net effect will be to continue to place cities at the center of questions having to do with the viability of certain economic activities in certain locations, and with the evolution of economies, whether urban, regional, or national. National economies are, after all, composed of regional and urban economies and the performance of the nation is a function of the efficacy of research and development, and of the production and distribution of the wide array of goods and services in the component sub-national levels of aggregation that make up the national economy. A closer look at these forces that are changing the role of urban economies will clarify this situation.

We will start by explaining how some of these forces that are promoting the role of cities or urban economies are subsumed under the heading of globalization. In an operational sense we identify globalization as being composed of three primary forces: changes in technology, trade and market liberalization, and developments in the role of the nation state. These three forces have dramatically altered economic space and the factors that determine the location of various economic activities; each warrants a separate discussion. Then we will examine other recent developments that have affected the role of urban economies in the global economy. Finally, we will examine the work that has been done on economic competitiveness at the level of the nation and the urban economy.

MARKET LIBERALIZATION

The primary policy phenomenon has been the liberalization of international trade and investment. At the end of the Second World War, tariffs of industrial nations averaged about 45 per cent, remnants of the protectionist years of the Great Depression. Through a series of rounds of trade liberalization under the aegis of the General Agreement on Tariffs and Trade (GATT) these tariffs have been reduced to about 4 per cent today. Economic theory tells us that the consequence of this will be an increase in specialization in all nations, a reduction in the lines of production everywhere, an increase in production efficiency, higher per capita incomes and an increase in the exposure of all productive entities to competition from other nations and continents. In addition to this global or multilateral trade liberalization, regional groupings such as those in Europe and North America have reduced barriers to the free flow of goods and services even further. The *Financial Times* recently published a map of the world with scores of bilateral and regional trade agreements indicated.[2]

Whether this phenomenon is a complement or an alternative to global free trade is yet to be determined. While the North American Free Trade Agreement has limited the liberalization among Canada, Mexico, and the United States to the exchange of goods of their own production, the integration process of the European Union has progressed beyond the original customs union to an economic union and, for most of its members, a monetary union. Regional trade agreements of various forms have also been adopted by nations in Africa, Latin America and Asia. In addition, most countries have negotiated bilateral trade liberalization agreements with any number of other countries, for economic, strategic or cultural reasons. While the Multilateral Agreement on Investment (MAI) was not adopted, liberalization of financial flows and direct investment has been promoted through a vast number of *ad hoc* bi-national and regional agreements.

The increasing openness of international economic interaction has increased the stakes for the private and public sector leaders of all urban economies. Protectionist measures have always limited the vulnerability to local economies to competition from foreign firms, but now every firm in traded-goods sectors is confronted by a new set of challenges consisting of threats to existing activity and opportunities of greatly expanded markets. For cities that are dominated by one major industry or that are centers of a cluster of firms in the same line of production, this can create a situation of life or death. As we will argue below, cities that react intelligently and quickly to this situation have the chance of maintaining their level of economic activity – jobs and incomes, while those that are passive run the risk of marginalization and decline. A moment's reflection on urban economies that were historically important centers of steel or textile production will make this point clearly.

TECHNOLOGICAL CHANGE

Changes in technology in production, transportation, and communication have re-shaped the geography of the location of economic activities. Advances in production technology have led to increased efficiency of small units of production and this has posed a challenge to the notion that economies of scale are an important part of competitiveness. Steel is now made in mini-mills scattered throughout economic space, rather than in traditional sites such as Gary, Pittsburgh, the Ruhr, and the English Midlands. Just-in-time inventory management has diminished the need for suppliers to be located within a few miles of an auto production facility. With advances in transportation and logistics, goods can be moved greater distances at lower cost so the advantages of proximity to the market, to sources of raw materials or to ports have given way to other factors such as proximity to universities and research centers or to lifestyle amenities for workers. Finally, with fiber optics, information technology, wireless communication and so forth, it is now possible to site production and control or management and all other activities of the firm where each can be done most efficiently and effectively rather than cluster them in one location. This is a topic of such importance that it will be examined in detail in Chapter 4, on cities and new technologies.

Advances in technology have effects on urban economies that are quite similar to those of market liberalization. In each instance, the economic base of a city can be destroyed or eroded, or exciting new opportunities may be developed. The primary difference is that market liberalization is a policy change that is introduced by the national government and is a phenomenon over which the urban economy has little or no influence or control. The only thing the city can do is react as appropriately as it possibly can. This reaction is a topic that will be examined more closely later in this chapter and in Chapter 7, on strategic planning. Advances in technology are the result of research and development that is undertaken by firms and other entities in all countries of the world. The challenge to city leaders is to make the local economy one that can participate in the development of technology and to integrate these advances into its activities. The actions that can be taken relate to the education of the local labor force, provision of the appropriate infrastructure, close cooperation between the private and public sectors, and doing what can be done to make the local fiscal and regulatory climate as congenial to this activity as possible.

DEVELOPMENTS IN THE ROLE OF GOVERNMENTS

Concurrent with the two forces just discussed, there has been a reduction in the ability or capacity of national governments to intervene in their own economies to protect or subsidize economic activities, workers, and regions. While some see this as an unwanted consequence of globalization and something that has been forced on national governments, it is more realistic to comprehend it as the desired result of actions taken at the level of the national government. Market liberalization is, after all, a process that national governments have pursued relentlessly since the end of the Second World War. They created the GATT and participated in the series of trade liberalization rounds that have brought tariffs to their current low level and have made subsidization, quotas and other forms of protection increasingly unavailable to them. The freer movement of goods, services, and capital has been a continuing policy objective of industrial country governments, but now of those of Third World countries as well. Rather than the death of the nation state, as many observers have suggested, it would be more accurate to speak of the dormancy of this institution. Nation states have lost neither their desire nor their capacity to intervene in the current round of WTO negotiations in the interest of their farmers, labor, or companies. In Europe, the conflict between the growth and stability pact of the Monetary Union and rising unemployment in France, Germany and Italy has resulted in these three nation states thumbing their noses at the requirement that the budget deficit does not exceed 3 per cent of GDP. When push comes to shove, nation states awaken from their slumber and assert themselves as they always have and, most likely, always will.

The self-imposed limitation on the action of national governments has shifted the responsibility and the capacity for development of the economy to lower levels of government. In Europe the subnational level of departments, *Länder*, autonomous communities, and so forth, have certainly gained legitimacy through the Council of Regions of the EU; however, there as in North America, it remains the case that these entities are divided in their attention between urban and rural interests. In the United States, one thinks of New York City and up-state New York, of Chicago and down-state Illinois, and of Pennsylvania being, as James Carvell rather famously said, Pittsburgh and Philadelphia separated by Alabama. The same tension is played out in Quebec, Bavaria, Aquitaine, and Andalucia. A coherent and consistent long-term effort to enhance the vitality of urban economies is difficult to do at the subnational level of government. Thus, when it comes to the economic future of the urban economy, both the national and subnational levels of government fail; only the city administration and its private sector actors can be trusted to pursue the interest of the urban economy. This relationship and responsibility will be developed in detail during the remainder of this book.

OTHER RECENT FORCES

During the 1990s another force, initiated in the previous decade by Republican and Conservative governments in the United States and the United Kingdom, began to have its impact throughout the industrialized world. Neo-liberalism argued that the smaller government was the better, the lower taxes were the better, individuals should be left to fend for themselves in the capitalist market economy, and social support for those who were not able to do so should be reduced or removed altogether in the interest of providing an incentive to work and become self-reliant. In the United States this was coupled with a run-up of defense expenditures, and the budget deficit and national debt soared – the latter almost quadrupling to over four trillion dollars during the dozen years of the Reagan and Bush administrations. The huge debt was designed by neo-liberal hard-liners to be a mechanism that would constrain any subsequent progressive government in its allocation, redistribution and stabilization efforts, as was made clear during the Clinton administration during the 1990s.[3] Canada quickly got the message, as did much of Europe, albeit more slowly.

Fiscal constraint at the national level was accompanied in North America by the imposition by the national government of unfunded mandates on subnational governments. Thus in both Canada and the United States provincial and state governments were increasingly stressed by the actions of their national government until today there is a fiscal crisis in most of these subnational governments. On the one hand, this signals a withdrawal of the national government from many traditional responsibilities for social programs, education, health care, and economic development while, on the other, it has the effect of forcing a concomitant withdrawal of subnational governments from some of their traditional responsibilities in the same areas. The net effect is to increase both the financial burden on cities and their programmatic responsibilities for looking after their own economic futures. In brief, cities have been forced to become more active and aggressive about the design of their future economic vitality and the specific structure of that future economy.

The progress of economic integration in Europe is another development that has had its impact on urban economies elsewhere. The adoption of the Euro by 12 of the 15 EU member states, prior to the recent expansion to 25 members, means that if costs rise in Germany relative to its principal trading partners, German firms are not likely to reduce their costs by locating production facilities in, say, Spain or Italy, since exchange rate movements between strong and weak EU economies will no longer take place and relocation to another EU country is less likely to afford cost relief to the firm. In fact, the Euro may fall or rise *vis-à-vis* the dollar or other currencies and any cost-based relocation of production would be between Germany and the USA or Canada rather than another Euro-land economy. Thus the economic consequences of cost developments, or uncertainty or lack of stability in Europe, may be transferred to urban economies in North America or elsewhere. While this will usually be a rather minor factor for most cities, it is nonetheless one more aspect of the changes that are occurring in the global economy that affect them.

Finally, in the post-September 11 era, concerns about security with regard to borders, access to traditional markets and free movement of goods and people have become paramount. The negative consequences of this have been seen rather dramatically in cities along the Canada–US and Mexico–US borders. For major industries such as automobiles, especially those with highly integrated production systems such as just-in-time inventory management, the economic importance of the cross-border flows will be such that the pressures for some accommodation by national governments will be enormous, if not always overwhelming. But for less significant industries, citing various activities in the vertical structure of production may prove to be too unreliable and firms may find it necessary to locate all their facilities on one side or the other of the border. In this game, some cities will be gainers and others will be losers. Various innovations in logistics – certification, tracking, and inspection – may reduce the importance of this factor but many of these innovations are still in the planning stage.

THE STUDY OF THE COMPETITIVENESS OF ECONOMIES

For as long as economic activity has involved something other than tilling the soil and grazing animals, cities have been at the center of the economy.[4] During the past few centuries the most highly developed nations have experienced a rural to urban migration that has given explicit recognition of the growing importance of urban economies in the nation's economic life. Typically these economically important cities have owed their central place in the economy to locational features related to transportation nodes such as a good harbor or a branching of two rivers, a topographical feature such as a mountain pass or a defensible position, or access to some resource. Each of these cities had a monopoly on some economically important feature. Out of this set of cities emerged an urban hierarchy of centers that ranged from primary centers of government through regional centers to rural market towns, with an appropriate allocation of economic and cultural activities. As agriculture gave way to manufacturing and services and as the traditional gave way to the modern and post-modern, the traditional locational advantages lost their power and gave way to new, less obvious attractions for economic activity.[5]

In the 17th century the nation state rose to prominence as the focal point of governance and of economic power. The role of the economy was to provide a basic livelihood for the population and to enhance the power of the nation. Cities were still the locus of much economic activity – shipping, commerce, finance and some nascent manufacturing, but it was the national government that organized the mercantilist economy and allowed or facilitated various individual initiatives. In consonance with this, in the two centuries that followed, Adam Smith wrote of the 'wealth of nations' and Friedrich List wrote of 'the national system of political economy.'[6]

During the 20th century economic competitiveness was the provenance of two entities: the nation state and the firm. The national economy was seen as being little more than the aggregation of thousands of individual firms; therefore, if the national economy were to be considered as competitive, the government should adopt the right policies to put in place the business environment that would be conducive to the development and maintenance of companies that would be able to meet the competition from firms in other parts of the economic space in which they operate. This space might be national, continental, or global. The firms themselves were expected to look after the mundane details of succeeding in their own markets. Micro-economic theory analyzed the operations of the firm and proselytized its effectiveness as a mechanism for the achievement of both efficiency and equity. Business schools worked to prepare the next generation of managers and senior executives of these firms. It was in the United States that both micro-economic theory and business schools received the most attention from the educational establishment, and it is therefore no surprise that American firms were the most successful in most industries during the post-Second World War period.

Competitiveness of the Nation and the Firm

The competitiveness of the nation has drawn considerable interest during the past couple of decades. As early as 1985, the Harvard Business School sponsored a research colloquium on 'US competitiveness in the world economy' in which the focus was on national competitiveness and policies the national government could implement to enhance the competitiveness of key or 'sunrise' industries and sectors of the economy.[7] A decade later Industry Canada issued a study that examined competitiveness at the firm, the industry and the national levels, but said nothing about the city or urban economy.[8] In France, the *Centre d'etudes prospectives et d'information internationales* has issued a report entitled *Compétitivité des nations*.[9] More recently, the Inter-American Development Bank produced a report on competitiveness in Latin America in which the focus was on micro-economic aspects, such as factor productivity, or national policies with regard to foreign investment and industrial policy.[10] While these references are not comprehensive, they are indicative of the omission of the urban economy from major studies on national economic competitiveness. It should be noted that due to the difficulty inherent in studying the competitiveness of a subnational entity that is, as has been noted, a complex of urban and rural economies with conflicting objectives for economic development, in this book we will not provide an analysis of the competitiveness of regions.

When examining studies of competitiveness for geographic entities, rather than for firms, the first difficulty is that there is no single, widely-accepted indicator of or variable for competitiveness. Therefore, the initial task of the researcher is the specification of what will be used to measure the competitiveness of the nation, region or urban economy. This will be discussed further in the next section of this chapter, but for now we can review what has been done by those who have done research at the level of the nation.

In the earliest of the studies noted above, that of the Harvard Business School, Bruce R. Scott wrote that: 'National competitiveness refers to a nation-state's ability to produce, distribute, and service goods in the international economy in competition with goods and services produced in other countries, and to do so in a way that earns a rising standard of living.'[11] He goes on to stress the latter as the primary indicator of competitiveness. In a survey of competitiveness studies done by government agencies in nine European Union member states (Germany, Denmark, Finland, Spain, France, Ireland, the Netherlands, Portugal and the United Kingdom), Alexis Jacquemin and Lucio R. Pench found that the performance indicators most often used were GDP growth per capita, the balance of trade, the export/import ratio, and movements of foreign direct investment.[12] Donald D. McFetridge summed up these studies by stating that when looking for indicators of national competitiveness: 'There are only two alternatives. The first is to emphasize real per capita income or productivity growth. The second is to emphasize trade performance.'[13]

What can we make of these studies of competitiveness at the level of the nation? First, it is, of course, desirable to have a comparative evaluation of a nation's economic competitiveness. However, this comes with its own constraints. Obtaining comparable data for 20 to 50 national economies is not an easy task. The United Nations and the Organisation for Economic Co-operation and Development (OECD) give us many series for dozens of nations, but when one looks for any but the most general series of data one finds that even for the member states of the EU data are rather limited. It is even the case that for many subnational entities such as the German *Länder*, comparable data for the vast majority of series are not available; hence, one is limited in what one can do with national economies within the EU. When one tries to examine competitiveness from a comparative standpoint, one is quite limited in the methodology one can use at the level of the nation and the researcher is forced to focus on readily available series, such as per capita income. This would be a possible approach if one could accept the assumption that all nations take the same approach to such things as the work–leisure trade-off. However, we know that French society has chosen to adopt the 35-hour work week and that this already exists in some sectors of the German economy. American workers choose to work between 40 and 45 hours. European work-ers choose to retire at roughly 59 years of age while workers in the USA work an additional several years. This suggests that European and American workers have made quite different choices with regard to the portion of their lives they will spend at work. Would we not then expect that per capita incomes would be higher in the US than in European nations, without refer-ence to the 'competitiveness' of their national economies? If we are forced to use per capita real income in part because it is available and if the underlying assumptions that must be made are called into question, can we then take per capita income as an indicator of national economic competitiveness?

Furthermore, if all countries had the same economic structure we could look at the trade balance as an indicator of competitiveness. But the struc-tures of output of all economies are not identical; some countries specialize in traded goods while others do not. Exports are less then 10 per cent of the US economy, almost 40 per cent of the Canadian economy, and even higher for some of the smaller European countries. The USA is usually at the top of the competitiveness ranking of the World Economic Forum, although it has a massive trade deficit. This is a reflection of the distinctive role the USA plays in the global economy. So can one use trade performance as an indicator of competitiveness?

With both of these suggested indicators of competitiveness, we may be seeing the combination of some theoretical justification plus the limited availability of comparable data for a large number of national economies, rather than an ideal measure of competitiveness. The question of which series one would actually choose to use to measure competitiveness will be raised again when we consider competitiveness from the standpoint of the urban economy, but one can wonder whether the concept of national economic competitiveness is a usable concept. The primary use of this work seems to ·be in the changes of ranking that take place from year to year and the kudos that can be claimed by the leaders of those countries. From the standpoint of political economy, it also exerts pressure on governments to adopt the neoliberal policies that will, it is argued, generate success in the ranking game.

The World Economic Forum's annual study of national economic competi-tiveness, *Global Competitiveness Report* (GCR),[14] is more sophisticated in its methodology. It consists of two separate rankings, the Growth Competitiveness Index and the Microeconomic Competitiveness Index. In conducting these studies, recognition is given by the authors of the factors that have just been noted above in relation to the other efforts to examine national economic competitiveness. The latest GCR cautions that 'using publicly available information and statistics is not enough,' 'data often do not cover all the countries in our sample,' in some areas 'no reliable hard data sources exist for many of the most important aspects of an economy,' and it is necessary to supplement available data with survey evidence. Even then Egypt had to be dropped from the GCR because of the lack of survey data.[15] Beyond the difficulties inherent in obtaining comparable data for 80 national economies, there is the residual question whether one gains much from comparing the 'competitiveness' of the United States, Poland and Botswana. In what sense are they actually competitors, or 'competitive?'

None of the studies considered the firm to be the ideal level of aggregation for the study of competitiveness of a national economy, although the one for Denmark focused on the firm as a way of comprehending the obstacles in the way of enhancement of national competitiveness.[16] Policy recommendations tended to target easing of regulations and improvement in infrastructure.

The GCR does bring the firm into the picture by means of the Microeconomic Competitiveness Index. This is actually composed of two sub-indexes: one that focuses on 'the degree of company sophistication' and one that treats 'the quality of the national business environment,' although it is recognized that there is a close correlation between the two. The ultimate objective at the microeconomic level is a sustainable level of productivity that will ensure maximum creation of wealth. The two sub-indexes treat elements that are considered vital if the macroeconomic, legal and political contexts are to be optimized, and include variables such as the availability of venture capital, protection of intellectual property rights, the regulatory environment, R&D expenditures, the effectiveness of government administration and buyer sophistication. There is no recognition of the role played by municipal governments. This is understandable since the GCR is concerned with large, usually multinational firms that have multiple research, production, distribution and administrative facilities that are located in many towns and cities and in several countries – the policies of an individual urban economy get lost in the big picture. This is consistent with the literature on the competitiveness of the firm.

The literature on firm competitiveness is well developed, has been the subject of decades if not centuries of analysis, and is known to all of us; thus, it will not be developed at any length here. The theory of the firm has dwelt exclusively on cost reduction for firms in a purely competitive market structure, and marketing and product differentiation for those in an imperfectly or a monopolistically competitive structure. The monopolistic firm concerns itself primarily with cost reduction and the regulatory environment. But, again, in this literature almost no attention is given to the local government other than to argue that a congenial business, fiscal and regulatory environment is needed. In a typical text on the subject, Sharon Oster's *Modern Competitive Analysis*, marketing, strategic planning, diversification, and similar topics are covered, with the only reference to government being that of regulatory issues in Chapter 17.[17] In an examination of the operations of Asian firms in North America and Europe, *The Global Competitiveness of the Asian Firm*,[18] recognition is given to corporate and local cultures but only from the standpoint of a firm ensuring that its system or model of operation can be successfully inserted into the environment of another country. The third of the many studies that are available, and the last one that will be mentioned, is the work on 'dynamic competitive strategy' done by the Wharton School.[19] Here attention is given totally to competitive interactions with other firms and how the firms can design a strategy to meet that competition. In these studies, that are typical of the others that are available, as well as in the standard microeconomic theory of the firm, virtually no attention is given to local authorities. Only in decisions about the location of specific facilities would this level of government be given any attention, other than with regard to the local fiscal and regulatory environment. More attention will be given to this aspect in the next section of the chapter.

A treatment that was somewhat more sympathetic to urban economies is found in one of the seminal studies in this area, Michael Porter's *The Competitive Advantage of Nations*.[20] Little is said explicitly of the importance of urban economies in the study of competitiveness, but of the four points in his renowned 'diamond of competitiveness,' the importance of the local authorities is implicit and cannot be ignored. 'Demand conditions' are clearly the mandate of the national government. But 'factor conditions,' such as the quality and availability of appropriately skilled labor, are powerfully affected by the actions of municipal governments, and both 'firm strategy, structure, and rivalry' and 'related and supporting industries' are dependent upon the local business climate, and municipal tax and expenditure decisions. Hence, even when focusing on the competitiveness of the national economy, it is impossible not to give recognition to the crucial roles played by local authorities and initiatives.

It is in his work on the inner city that Porter focuses on the role of local government. As he states, the advantages of the inner city are essentially in four areas: location, local demand, integration in regional clusters, and human resources.[21] The disadvantages have to do with availability of suitable land, security, infrastructure, labor skills and building costs. Clearly municipal government has a role to play, especially with regard to addressing the disadvantages of the inner city as a location for economic activity. Porter's 'new role of government' tends to be that of other writers, that of 'creating a favorable environment for business,' but he is far more explicit with regard to what can and must be done. First, the inner city should be able to capture funds from superior levels of government for such obvious needs as security, infrastructure and environmental clean-up. Second, government must become less of a detriment to inner city investment through reduction of various charges for services and through subsidization of land preparation. Third, Porter argues that many programs and services should be channeled through the private sector – service-sector firms and financial institutions. Finally, government should avoid subsidizing economic activities and allow private firms, operating in a congenial environment, to make decisions based on profit.

While Porter opens the discussion of competitiveness to the role of urban economies, it is done implicitly or 'through the back door' in his primary work, and when focusing on the inner city his suggestions are concentrated on creation of a favorable environment for business. Competitiveness is a feature of the nation and the firm, and the city should do little more than provide whatever the firms need. What is lacking is an analysis that sees the urban economy as an entity that is active and instrumental in shaping and even creating its future economic structure and role in the larger economic space within which it must function. This is what we will now examine.

Competitiveness of the Urban Economy

As we enter the 21st century, the factors that were of importance for the previous century are far less relevant for many industries. As has just been noted, trade and market liberalization have made nations less able to intervene to shape their own national economic space. Changes in the technologies of production, transportation, and communication have greatly affected economic space, with such standard concepts as agglomeration and core-periphery being subjected to essential rethinking. It is this new locational and structural environment that has made cities so much more central to the study of competitiveness.

With the diminished importance of ports, rivers, proximity to raw materials and so forth, cities must be considered to be, at base, undifferentiated entities. It is what people, rather than nature or geography, make of them that gives them their distinctiveness. The mini-mills of the contemporary steel industry are not sited in accordance with the factors that determined plant location in the 19th century – cheap water transportation, proximity to coal, access to rail transportation to manufacturers of finished goods and so forth. Today closeness to markets or pools of specialized labor may play the dominant role. But more importantly, the economic activities that are of growing importance today are in many cases industries that either did not exist a century ago or that have been totally transformed due to changes in the technologies of production, transportation and communication. These activities of the new economy are powerfully affected by locational factors, but those factors are rarely natural endowments or gifts of nature and are more likely to be elements that have been put in place by the public and/or private sector as the purposeful policies of local leaders. The centers of high technology activity in informatics, communication, bio-technology, pharmacology, optics, aerospace and so forth are invariably located where they are because of the decisions of individuals decades ago to develop the research capabilities of one or more local universities, to design curricula that would provide the knowledge base of these emerging industries, and to introduce university policies that encouraged faculty to devote their attention to developing new technologies and products that would be the base for this industrial development. Many of these industries could have been located at any of scores of other potential sites, and would have been if the appropriate policy initiatives by local authorities/leaders had been introduced. Governments have also adopted policies that, for example, have made venture capital more readily available.

In this new environment it is necessary to see this as a situation of supply of and demand for local assets, such as urban amenities, transportation and communication infrastructure, skilled labor, venture capital, educational/training institutions, research facilities and so forth. While national and subnational governments can still do things that are positive in this regard, it is the cities or urban economies that are the suppliers of these assets, and the firms or potential new firms are the demanders. Conceptualizing the situation in this way emphasizes the capacity of local leadership to enhance positively the competitiveness of their urban economy, as well as making it clear that the responsibility rests primarily on their shoulders. Trade agreements and other market liberalization initiatives are mechanisms whereby national governments have considerably diminished their capacity to intervene in their own economies for the purposes of initiating economic activity or of protecting it from competitive forces external to the national economic space. This capacity to intervene has been given up by governments of all political philosophies in hopes of the efficiency gains that have been promised by liberal economic theory since Adam Smith.

While leaders of urban economies have responded to this challenge with varying degrees of astuteness and speed, it has become clear to all but the most self-absorbed that those who respond effectively can enormously increase the likelihood that their city will be among those that are able to respond to the exigencies of the New Economy and will be able to enhance their position in the international hierarchy of cities. Those who ignore the challenge or who respond to it ineffectively will find their cities being sentenced to stagnation and marginalization. Thus we find that many city administrations are paying increasing attention to strategic planning and to enhancement of the competitiveness of their urban economic space as a place in which to locate economic activities that are, for one reason or another, deemed to be desirable.

At the same time, firms have new freedom in the decisions to locate their various business activities. Vertical integration from the base level of manufacturing to corporate headquarters in the past meant that, except for the largest firms, one site would suffice for most of the company's activities. Certainly subsidiaries would be located in proximity to sources of inputs or to markets but the decision-making core of the firm would be centrally sited. Today, the benefits from this sort of agglomeration have in many cases given way to the advantages of siting each corporate activity in the location that best suits it. The optimal combination of site assets will most likely differ for each activity. The headquarters, manufacturing, assembly, warehousing/storage, marketing, and finance functions for the firms need no longer be located in the same general area. This is explicitly the case in North America where many firms have located various functions in the United States, Canada and Mexico. None of this is done because of the competitiveness of the three national economies, but rather because of the local assets that can be made available by individual urban economies and utilized by the firm.

More recently attention has been given to this third party when it comes to economic competitiveness – that is the city or the urban economy. After all, in every national economy over a period of decades, some regions of the national economic space will be in recession or are being marginalized while others are booming. Research tells us that while with regional free trade agreements per capita incomes of the member national economies usually converge, with the low income countries growing more rapidly than do the high income countries, within member countries income levels of subnational regions do not converge but grow farther apart.[22] This can be seen at the global level as well. So while one notes that at the World Economic Forum the United States is usually one of the top two countries in competitiveness, as the Forum defines it, it is never the case that all regions of the country are doing this well. The industrial heartland crashed in the 1970s and 1980s, but then boomed in the 1990s; while the reverse was true of the two coastal economies and the South. Wisconsin booms while Connecticut suffers from double-digit unemployment. Furthermore, certain regional economies in the USA, such as the Mississippi Delta, Appalachia, the Four Corners area of the Southwest and parts of the Great Plains, have been depressed for decades while others, such as California, the New York City region and the industrial Midwest, have been wealthy for at least as long. In China today, Shenzhen booms but what of more peripheral cities in the center and western parts of the country? In Canada, the Atlantic Provinces have been recipients of regional equalization payments for decades and Alberta and Ontario have been contributors for the same period of time. It is similarly the case within the EU and within member countries from Sweden to Spain, regional economic differences and per capita income gaps are substantial and seemingly as intransigent as they are in Canada or the USA. Thus, to understand and analyse actual competitiveness we must direct our focus somewhere other than on the nation.

In countries all over the world, a variety of forces such as advances in agricultural technology, political instability, lack of capital for small farmers, the lure of the big city and so forth are driving a rural to urban migration of extraordinary proportions. In some countries, such as those of Europe, this migration has taken place for hundreds of years; in others, it is a more recent phenomenon, as some regions and urban areas of traditional societies have given way to modernity during the past decades or the past century or so while others have not. Recent political events such as the creation of the European Economic Community and European Union, the fall of the barriers between Central and Western Europe, NAFTA, and conflicts and wars in Africa, the Middle East, Southeastern Europe, Asia and Latin America have unleashed powerful forces of push and pull that have resulted in massive migrations of people, often to cities in safer countries and with more robust economies. In many industrialized countries, 75 or 80 per cent or more of the population are now city dwellers. With this rapidly growing urbanization of most national economies, the economic role and vitality of urban areas has concomitantly called for greater attention.

In subsequent chapters we will examine what city governments have done with regard to diplomacy or international engagement, the development of new technologies, the requirements for new models of municipal governance, initiatives of networking and cross-border relationships, and strategic planning. Policies aimed at the enhancement of urban competitiveness, the subject of this chapter, provide the basis on which many of these other areas of city activism are grounded.

In industrialized countries most cities are experiencing the typical dynamic of development of the urban center, then the move to the suburban area, then the deterioration of the city centers, then the development of edge-cities, and finally a rediscovery of the advantages of the city center. In developing countries' cities, their inevitable growth in population is followed by increasing traffic congestion, pollution, inadequate housing and demands for improved infrastructure such as sewage treatment, safe drinkable water, electricity and so forth. For all of these cities planning for management of these two sets of problems becomes imperative. The growth of population brings both an increase in the labor supply and demands for social and other services. At some point the quality of the jobs created becomes an issue and all cities must undertake an effort at economic planning; one of the primary objectives of this economic planning must be that of the enhancement of the urban economy's competitiveness. Planning for enhancement of urban competitiveness will be examined in detail in Chapter 7.

Advances in the technologies of transportation and communication have made it no longer possible for a city to focus only on its immediate economic space. Economic space was enlarged during the 19th century for many countries with the introduction of canals, then railroads, and finally road transportation. Some cities found they were not able to meet the challenges of the new technologies, as is attested to by the many abandoned or 'ghost' towns, or by the many cities that have suffered long-term decline, unemployment, out-migration and social pathologies. Others, of course, were either favored by these changes or able to adapt the structure of their economic activity and their comparative advantage in ways that brought them an improved position in the continental or global urban hierarchy.

For cities today the challenges are even more crucial. With growth no longer privileging cities located near sources of raw materials or ports or crossroads of transportation routes, no city can assume it will have a thriving, competitive economy that will meet the needs and aspirations of its citizenry a decade or two from now. Competitiveness assessment and pro-active economic planning are no longer exotic luxuries; they are the tools of survival for any urban economy. And to return full circle, we can see that healthy, competitive cities are the base for a healthy, competitive national economy.

Research on urban economic competitiveness

This increased importance of urban economies has made the study of their competitiveness all the more important. A small number of researchers in a small number of countries has begun to do empirical work on urban competitiveness in their country. One of the important constraints on research in this area is the limited data that are available for large numbers of cities. Given the different definitions of economic and social variables in each country, accurate comparative analysis is, as was noted above, very difficult and the analysis is in part determined by what data are available. In many countries subnational entities gather much of the data, according to their own definitions and requirements, so analysis at the national level is also difficult. The EU should be a prime entity for quantitative research on urban competitiveness, but, as we shall see, this is not the case. Even a large country such as Germany, with a sufficient number of large cities for good quantitative research, presents daunting difficulties as much of the data is provided by the subnational states, the *Länder*, not all of which use the same definitions of variables, time periods and so forth. Canada simply does not collect and make available the statistical series that are required, as was noted recently by Stephen Clarkson.[23] Mexico and China are two other possibilities for quantitative research, and they will be discussed below. Only in the USA is there readily available data for scores of relevant series for a sufficient number of large cities. For example, the *State and Metropolitan Data Book* presents data for 245 Metropolitan statistical areas, 17 consolidated metropolitan statistical areas and 58 primary metropolitan statistical areas, and 12 New England county metropolitan areas.[24] Additional data are given for every city and every county in the country in the *County and City Data Book*.[25] Each is issued every five years. Other data are available from other government sources. This opens the intriguing possibility that the quantitative research that is done on US urban economies could be taken as suggestive of what one would find with regard to cities in other industrialized economies. For this to be methodologically acceptable, one would have to accept the notion that in a global economy that is marked by market liberalization, deregulation, decisions made by the same large multinational corporations using the same criteria everywhere, and subject to the same disruptive forces of technological development and the same external shocks so that one could accept results from research on US urban economies as a first approximation to what would be found in other industrialized countries in which the data are not available or in which there is not a sufficiently large number of large cities to allow for good statistical analysis.

In reviewing the research that has been done on urban economic competitiveness, we will begin with what has been done in Europe, then in some other countries, and finally in the USA. Paul Cheshire in the UK has published several articles in which he examines the condition of European cities from the standpoint of the presence or absence of urban problems. He and his co-authors put the issue in terms of 'urban decline and growth' and performance, which could be considered to be an indirect approach to the question of urban competitiveness. In two papers, the first with Gianni Carbonaro and Dennis Hay, 101 European cities are ranked according to the presence or absence of 'problems.'[26] The indicators used are income, unemployment, migration, and business and tourist travel demand. While the focus is not directly on competitiveness, we can examine whether this does get us to a measure of urban competitiveness. Travel demand would appear to be the best variable for a measure of competitiveness, but each of the others is problematic. Income can be sustained, in non-competitive cities, by transfers from the national or subnational government rather that being reflective of competitive economic activity. Migration will be greater the less economically viable is the rest of the national economy or the more proximate the city is to an area of conflict or deterioration – some Italian and German cities have experienced large inflows of people from the Balkans or Central Europe, without regard to their competitiveness in the context of other cities in the EU. Finally, high unemployment may be a consequence of factors such as the inward migration that has just been mentioned or a process of transition in which new competitive industries that are expanding are less labor intensive than the older industries that are declining, the net result of which is unemployment. Cheshire and his co-authors were not attempting to measure urban competitiveness, but examination of their approach suggests some of the difficulties in the study of urban competitiveness. The literature in Europe on declining or lagging cities and regions is extensive, and developed rapidly during the 1990s when it became clear that the rising sea of EU economic growth was not lifting all regions and urban economies.[27]

In the United States the interest in declining urban economies began a bit earlier, probably due to the impacts on the industrial heartland of the country of the increases in the price of energy following the actions of OPEC in 1973 and 1979. Cynthia Negrey and Mary Beth Zickel related urban development to changes in population and manufacturing employment. In their schema there were cities in which either of the two variables could be increasing while the other was increasing or decreasing and the growth in population could be greater or below the national average.[28] This suggests the possibility of the concern expressed in the previous paragraph about high unemployment being an indicator of anything specific. Their cities were in one of the following five categories: de-industrializing, in stable transition, an innovation center, a new services center or a new manufacturing center. Change in one and/or the other of the variables could put the city in a category that was descriptive rather than evaluative. That is, growth of some services or manufacturing activities could equally be indicative of either increased or diminished competitiveness. Another approach was taken by Jane Pollard and Michael Storper who classified US cities as centers of 'intellectual capital' industries, 'innovation-based' industries and 'variety-based manufacturing.'[29] They conclude that: 'The most consistent pattern we detect is the link between specialization in innovation-based employment and overall regional employment growth.' But they also note that: 'This empirical exercise suggests a multiplicity of pathways to regional growth,' and they call for 'clearer hypotheses about such pathways.' Employment growth is not acceptable as an indicator of competitiveness, as has been noted above, but the caution about the multiplicity of ways to achieve it, or some other policy objective, holds equally strongly with regard to the study of urban competitiveness.

This European and American literature on declining or advancing urban regions is extensive but, since it is not directly related to urban competitiveness, exploring it more closely would take us far afield. More directly related to the topic are two publications from the United Kingdom: in 1999, an issue of *Urban Studies* was devoted to the subject of urban competitiveness,[30] and three years later Iain Begg edited a book, *Urban Competitiveness*, with a dozen contributions by scholars on the subject.[31] The papers in these two collections clarify both the contribution to our understanding that recent research has made and the difficulty encountered in developing an analysis that will be of use to city officials seeking to enhance the competitiveness of their economy. There is, of course, no single variable that captures competitiveness, so researchers have to develop one or more proxies for it. Most of the papers that evaluate competitiveness rely on two alternative approaches. The first is to measure outcomes such as employment growth, growth of output, reduction in unemployment, or the growth of some sector of activity that is asserted to be a sector that will be important in the economy of the near future. The second is to evaluate the economic base or the competitive assets of that urban economy.

The problem with the first approach is that we are often as interested in specifically what is growing as we are in how rapidly growth is taking place. Some jobs are low skill and low pay, the growth of which may not indicate a competitive economy but rather one that is deteriorating over time. The same can be said of output. If a city is perceived to be one that is on the move, it may become a target for migrants and the rate of unemployment may actually increase rather than decline. This could be the result of an inward movement of unemployable workers or because the new high skill jobs are filled by migrants and the original workers are now unemployed. The problem with the second approach is that any set of urban assets will be most appropriate for a specific sort of economy: a manufacturing economy needs a different set of assets than does a tourist-culture center or a financial center or a research and development center. In privileging one set of assets, the research is implicitly asserting that one path to competitiveness is superior to others, and this may not, as Pollard and Storper suggest, be the case.

An example of the first approach is a paper by Iain Begg, Barry Moore and Yener Altunbas in which they evaluate 87 UK cities and 22 'new and enlarged towns' from the standpoint of employment growth.[32] Each of the cities and towns is then characterized as either steadily growing, steadily declining, recovering, backsliding or unstable. For their analysis of population growth and unemployment trends, they lump cities and towns in seven categories: conurbations, free-standing, 'northern' smaller, 'southern' smaller, expanded, new towns and coastal. With regard to population growth, they find migration patterns are from northern to southern cities and from conurbations to smaller cities and towns. Unemployment has been a problem for large cities, coastal cities and free-standing cities while improvement has been experienced by smaller cities. The decline of traditional industries, residential preferences and proximity to London seem to be the primary causal factors in these shifts.

The urban assets approach is followed by Bill Lever, who starts from the well-established understanding that the knowledge base is increasingly important for the economic future of any city and then examines the various indicators of the knowledge base of 12 to 15 cities throughout the world. He includes the telecommunications infrastructure, R&D activity, the number of students in higher education, airport activity, conventions and exhibitions and published research papers (aggregate and per capita).[33] As Lever notes, one of the difficulties with this approach to urban competitiveness is that it does not really give good guidance to local officials, as most of these assets are out of their control. Some of the most important are the responsibility of the national government and each city must struggle with other cities to get the attention of national leaders. Furthermore, even if the knowledge base can be developed, it is notoriously uncertain that the main economic benefits will be captured by that city. Firms may do research in one city and then locate the job-creating production facilities in other cities. Finally, it should be noted that without an ordering or prioritizing of these assets, local authorities will find it difficult to know exactly what they should do for maximum impact – they cannot be expected to mount their horses and ride off in all directions.

The two approaches are linked in a model developed by Iain Deas and Benito Giordano. In this 'assets-outcomes model,' 'competitive assets' are grouped in economic, policy, environmental, and social contexts, and are interactively linked to firm-based and area-based 'competitive outcomes.'[34] This approach explicitly adds qualitative 'economic, social, political, and environmental circumstances' to the quantitative measures that are so much more easily dealt with. The result is a rather nuanced evaluation not only of the competitiveness of a city's urban assets but of how effectively these assets are being utilized. The linkage between the assets and the outcomes consists of the effectiveness of local government, of the mobilization of local actors, and the suitability of the development plan that is adopted.

Interesting work on urban competitiveness has been done in other countries as well. In Mexico, Jaime Sobrino presented his research on the same topic at Foro 2025, a strategic planning forum for the state of San Luis Potosi that was held in September 2002.[35] Sobrino examined Mexico's 24 largest cities according to their 'industrial competitiveness.' The dependent variable in his regression analysis is the increase between 1988 and 1998 of the gross value of industrial production of the city as a share of that of the nation. Presumably this would capture production in manufacturing, mining and petroleum, and construction, but would exclude finance, government (including health and education), transportation and other services as well as agriculture and fishing. Thus he does not treat urban competitiveness in a way that would recognize the competitiveness of cities focusing on the financial, health, education or tourism sectors, even though his concept of competitiveness refers to the ability of the urban economy to penetrate markets, generate economic growth and improve the quality of life of its residents. Sobrino's ranking of the Mexican cities is dependent upon four constructed variables that refer to the city's absolute and relative changes in its share of national industrial output, the absolute growth of this production, and the growth in the economic and export base in relation to population growth for the same (1988–98) period. The five most competitive cities are Guadalajara, Aguascalientes, Mexicali, Puebla and Torreon.

The next step in his analysis is that of explaining the ranking; that is, what are the factors that generate the competitiveness ranking? Here Sobrino has two sets of explanatory factors, static and dynamic. The static include the capital–labor ratio, hospital beds per capita (an indication of urbanization), the local economic structure, producer services, transportation linkages and distance from markets. The signs for capital, economic structure, services and distance are negative. The dynamic include labor productivity, the share of local industrial employment that is accounted for by industrial parks, the increase in industrial concentration (1988–93), growth of per capita income and exports by local firms. All signs for the dynamic factors are positive except for industrial concentration. The selection of variables to use in an exercise such as this is usually constrained by what happens to be available for a large number of cities. Sobrino gives a good discussion of both the literature on this subject and of each of the many variables used both to give the ranking and to explain it as justification for the inclusion of the specific variables used. One has to agree with his conclusion that although it is unlikely that researchers will concur on one definitive study of urban competitiveness, studies such as his will serve well the work that is yet to be done.

In another paper, Sobrino ranks 39 Mexican cities according to their competitiveness, but this time it is done with a broader brush.[36] Urban competitiveness is now comprised of three separate aspects: industrial competitiveness, commercial competitiveness and services competitiveness, with each being the ratio of that city's to that of the nation. This gives a different and more accurate evaluation of the competitiveness of each of the cities in the study. Of the top five cities of the first study, Torreón, Puebla, and Guadalajara are ranked 1st, 2nd and 6th, while Aguascalientes and Mexicali are 13th and 20th. The strength in industrial competitiveness of each of these cities was not shown in the other two areas of competitiveness. In fact, Guadalajara was ranked 25th in services, Aguascalientes was 28th and 16th respectively in commerce and services, and Mexicali was 37th and 26th in commerce and services. This indicates clearly that the definition of urban competitiveness used is of crucial importance and must be closely related to the objective of the study. Another important aspect of this second study by Sobrino is the fact that he was able to do two time periods – 1980–98 and 1988–98. Four of the top ten cities in the longer period were not in the top ten of the shorter one, while 20 cities changed their position by less than ten spots and 19 did so by more than ten. In fact, the top two cities during 1988–98, Torreón and Puebla, were ranked 32nd and 16th for the longer period. Thus the economies of Mexican cities during the 1980s did not relate that closely to their experiences during the 1990s. Again, this suggests the sensitivity of the results of urban competitiveness studies to assumptions and methodology used.

In China, Ni Pengfei, who is part of a section of the Chinese Academy of Social Sciences that is focused on urban competitiveness, has just completed a study of the competitiveness of 24 Chinease cities.[37] In his work, Ni sets the scene by describing the situation for China's cities in recent years. He argues that many urban governments sought to increase their economic strength by rather blindly positioning themselves in accordance with the latest trend, which was to develop in the same sectors: automobiles, machinery, chemicals, medical and electronics, rather than by assessing their true comparative advantage(s). The result was excessive competition in the same industries and a serious misallocation of resources. At the same time, the cities on the eastern coast were able to grow at relatively rapid rates, while those in the interior were disadvantaged. The result has been development of regional imbalances and the attendant social problems. Ni argues that what China needs is a more scientific and analytical approach to strategic planning for competitiveness on the part of the major cities.

His contribution to this debate begins with a ranking of the 24 cities using what he refers to, in translation, as 'urban value income.' By this he means a composite dependent variable composed of: city income during a moment of time, growth of that income over a period of time, income generated per unit of cost, and some measure of urban assets (location, reputation and environmental quality). The weighting of the four is not indicated. One understands that the translation probably does not do full justice to the original text, but urban value income is essentially the ability of the city to earn income. The objective of the city's competitiveness, he argues, is that of attracting and controlling resources, gaining access to markets, creating value and providing welfare for its residents.

Having ranked the 24 cities, Ni then uses several variables to explain that ranking. He asserts that urban competitiveness is a function of 'hard' and 'soft' factors. The hard include: labor, capital, technology, environment, location, infrastructure and structural elements. The soft are: culture, management, openness and social structures. The result is a table which consists of the absolute values for each of 13 factors for each of 24 cities. He is then able to rank each of the cities with regard not only to competitiveness but to its position in relation to each of the 13 factors. While the latter is too complex to be discussed here, the top ten Chinese cities, according to Ni's notion of competitiveness and his methodology are: Shanghai, Shenzhen, Quangzhou, Beijing, Xiamen, Wuxi, Tianjin, Dalian, Hangzhou and Nanjing. This gives him the support for discussion of 15 conclusions he draws from his analysis – again, too complex to be discussed here. His paper concludes with a set of policy recommendations that researchers and practitioners in the area of urban economics would not find controversial: investment in human capital, openness to foreign investment, development of infrastructure, enhancing research and development capacity and reform of management, administrative, and market systems.

While the English translation of Ni's work is 90 pages, the Chinese text is 250 pages and it is accompanied by 110 pages of graphs and tables. Hence, one who cannot read the original is probably not getting the full value of Ni's project. Nonetheless, as is the case with Sobrino and Mexico, it is exciting to discover that economists/geographers in countries that are large enough to have a statistically significant number of large internationally engaged cities are creatively doing work on urban competitiveness. One can only hope for more of this.

Finally we will refer to work that one of the authors of this book has done with Balwant Singh on US cities and with Pierre-Paul Proulx on US and Canadian cities.[38] Since these studies have been published and should be available to the reader, we will not present the tables and will focus on the methodology and the nature of the results obtained. The approach to urban competitiveness taken here focuses explicitly on the interaction between the city and the firm. That is, the city must do what it can to make itself attractive to the firms that produce the output and the jobs that are in such demand, and it needs to enhance its competitiveness in relation to other cities that want to gain that economic activity. The first step in this approach is to create a dependent variable, since there is no single variable for the competitiveness of a city. A composite of three variables was used: the change over several years in manufacturing value added, in retail sales, and in some set of professional or business services. Each is weighted by its share of the value of the total for all three. The justifications for the elements of this composite variable are that growth in manufacturing value added suggests either that manufacturing is growing or that the local firms are moving into higher valued added activity; growth in retail sales indicates that the city is an attractive place for visitors to come for cultural or recreational or shopping activities and/or that the income of the residents is increasing; and growth in the indicated services is important because these services are necessary if the city is to reshape itself to the evolving needs of the larger economy. This index was then used to rank either 24 or 40 US cities in the Kresl–Singh studies, or 40 US and seven Canadian cities in the Kresl–Proulx study. The period of time used for the growth in the variables was a decade or 15 years. The ranking of the cities in the three studies was of interest at the time, but will not be discussed here.

The next step in the methodology was to explain the competitiveness rankings of the cities. For this a regression analysis was done using variables that had been selected through a review of the relevant literature.[39] The regression analysis resulted in eight variables being determined to be primary variables explaining the ranking, and an additional five as secondary explanatory variables for two of the primary variables. These variables related to income growth, educational attainment, research centers, categories of the labor force, cultural institutions, location, economic structure and population growth. The results are of interest, but the challenge is always to make them useful to the ultimate audience – city planners and policy makers. To this end, in each of the Kresl–Singh studies a table was constructed in which the cities were then ranked according to the 13 explanatory variables, thus making it possible to ascertain the specific strengths and weaknesses of each city. These urban strengths and weaknesses have the advantage of being determined in a process that was data-based, statistical and objective, rather than being the perceptions of individuals in the cities. The value of this approach will be made clear in Chapter 7 when we examine strategic planning.

Final comments on the study of urban competitiveness

As is clear from the discussion above, several researchers have taken different approaches to the study of urban competitiveness. The objectives of these studies should be, first, to gain an understanding of the subject itself and, second, to be able to provide useful information to practitioners and policymakers in the individual cities. In this final section of the chapter we will examine some of the principal issues that confront those doing research on urban competitiveness and what approaches have been taken to deal with them. First, one has to understand that there is no generally agreed upon definition of urban competitiveness and certainly no single notion as to how it can be measured. One approach is to assert that the exigencies of the economy of today and of the near future are such that certain assets or characteristics of a city are to be given priority. The city that positions itself best with these assets is then declared to be the most competitive city. Unfortunately, there is no agreement as to what these priority assets are. Some would argue that information technology is the key factor and that the most competitive cities will be well provided with the appropriate assets; others would focus on high technology industries such as bio-pharmaceuticals, optics, electronics or robotics. There is really no way to differentiate among these possible candidates. Of course, a city that embarks on a strategic initiative has no real assurance that the targeted 'sector of the future' will, in fact, be a sector of the future or a sector that is appropriate for that city. Ni has alerted us to the danger that city leaders may join a broad movement of cities toward adoption of the same currently trendy strategy, a strategy that may in fact be suitable for only a small number of cities. This is analogous to the caution that was given in the 1980s that national governments should not target the so-called 'sun-rise industries' and that a general development of skills and infrastructure was the best policy.

Some researchers have taken another approach to this issue by asserting a proxy for urban competitiveness. This focus is more on indicators than on assets. Sobrino, Ni and Kresl *et al.* have each done this. Again, there is no obvious 'best' single or composite indicator and the researcher is limited by the availability of data, but some attempt can be made to justify, perhaps through reference to the literature on urban economic development, the choice that is made. The idea here is that while competitiveness cannot be measured, some small set of rather general performance variables can be used perhaps in combination with a facilitator of change, as Kresl and Singh did with a set of professional or business services, to indicate the extent to which an individual urban economy is successfully meeting the aspirations of the residents of that city.

Relying on a set of outcomes as the indicator of urban competitiveness has the disadvantage of privileging one end result of competitiveness enhancement. As has been noted, each of the possible outcomes can be the result of a variety of factors that may have little or nothing to do with urban competitiveness.

The final contrast among the approaches to urban competitiveness that we have examined is the effort that is made to generate a clear strategic message to the local planners and decision-makers in each city. We will reconsider this in Chapter 7.

NOTES

1. For a European view see Le Galès and Harding, 1998, pp. 120–45.
2. *Financial Times*, 19 November 2002, p. 11.
3. The three functions of government as articulated by Musgrave, 1959.
4. This point is made convincingly in Bairoch, 1988.
5. For a broad historical review of the experience in Europe see Hohenberg and Lees, 1995.
6. Smith, 1937, and List, 1966.
7. Scott and Lodge, 1985.
8. McFetridge, 1995.
9. *Centre d'études prospectives et d'information internationales*, 1998.
10. Inter-American Development Bank, 2001.
11. Scott, pp. 14 and 15.
12. Jacquemin and Pench, 1997, p. 29.

13. McFetridge, 1995, p. 24.
14. World Economic Forum, published annually.
15. World Economic Forum, 2003, pp. xii–xiii.
16. Jacquemin and Pench, 1997, p. 30.
17. Oster, 1999.
18. Schutte, 1994.
19. Day and Reibstein, 1997.
20. Porter, 1998.
21. Porter, 1995.
22. Fagerberg and Verspagen, 1996.
23. Clarkson, 2002.
24. US Bureau of the Census, *State and Metropolitan Data Book*, various issues.
25. US Bureau of the Census, *County and City Data Book*, various issues.
26. Cheshire *et al.*, 1986 and Cheshire, 1990.
27. See, for example, Camagni, 1995, Conway and Konvitz, 2000.
28. Negrey and Zickel, 1994.
29. Pollard and Storper, 1996.
30. *Urban Studies*, Vol. 36, Nos. 5/6, May, 1999.
31. Begg, 2002.
32. Begg *et al.*, 'Cities, in Begg, 2002, pp. 101–33.
33. William F. Lever, 'The knowledge base and the competitive city,' in Begg, 2002, pp. 11–31.
34. Deas and Giordano, in Begg, 2002, pp. 191–209.
35. Sobrino, 2002.
36. Sobrino, 2003.
37. Pengfei, 2003b, pp. 252–340 and Pengfei (ed.), 2003a.
38. Kresl and Singh, 1995, Kresl and Singh, 1999, and Kresl and Proulx, 2000, pp. 282–314.
39. Kresl, 1995.

3. Municipal foreign affairs

Traditional international relations theory once inferred that relations among nations fell completely within the purview of national governments. Alas, this perception of international interactions is clearly outmoded and fails to reflect what is actually occurring in an era of globalization. At the beginning of 2004, there were 191 members of the United Nations. Almost all of these nation states have borders which are more permeable today than ever before, and all have local governments and local citizens who are tangibly affected by actions which transpire outside their nation states or decisions which are made by foreign governments and non-governmental actors. Only rarely can someone identify what is strictly 'domestic policy' and what is strictly 'foreign policy' because there is a growing overlap of these two arenas. Bayless Manning first coined the term 'intermestic' to describe policy that has both domestic and international dimensions, and the great bulk of all 21st century policy is intermestic.[1] Bruce Bueno de Mesquita has recently advised specialists in international relations to shift 'to an outlook that understands international affairs as a normal and routine aspect of ordinary domestic politics.' He adds that 'international relations is, simply put, a venue for politicians to gain or lose domestic political advantage. From this viewpoint, concepts such as the national interest, grand strategy, and international politics as a domain distinct from foreign and domestic calculations are troubling.'[2] A former Speaker of the US House of Representatives, Tip O'Neill of Massachusetts, repeatedly stressed that 'all politics is local.' One can accord a great deal of credence to this adage, but in the current century, one must give equal credence to the notion that 'local politics cannot be divorced from national and international politics,' no matter how deep the suspicion and or even the animosity some local constituents harbor toward globalization and 'things foreign.'

Most governments in large municipalities and even in some medium and small-sized cities and towns are engaged in foreign affairs, which may be defined as carrying forth with activities which transcend national boundaries in an effort to protect and enhance the interests of the constituents they represent. For example, cities may send delegations abroad in an effort to identify and solidify export leads for local companies, or they may meet with foreign-based firms in an effort to convince them to expand their operations within the territorial jurisdiction of the local government. The goal is to create more and higher paying jobs for local constituents, to assist local companies in producing globally competitive goods and services and to diversify the local economic base. With a proliferation of regional and international agreements and agencies, municipalities also want to insure that their policy prerogatives, which are often constitutionally protected within the nation state, are not abridged or even eliminated as a result of binding treaties or pacts entered into by their respective national governments. Many of the large cities within the European Union either individually or collectively lobby in Brussels in an effort to safeguard their ability to govern locally and to promote environmental, phytosanitary and other policies of special interest to the people they directly represent. They also want to insure that policymakers in Brussels and in the respective national capitals of the EU faithfully observe the notion of subsidiarity, which means allowing government entities closest to the people to develop and implement a wide variety of programs, as long as these programs can be put in place appropriately and efficiently. In North America, where the United States, Canada and Mexico are joint members of NAFTA but also maintain distinctive federal systems, state, provincial and local governments have been demanding much closer intergovernmental consultations before anything is agreed to in the future related to the expansion of NAFTA, the creation of the FTAA, or the phasing in of the Doha Round of the WTO.

There is another dimension of local–global linkages which is more controversial, and that falls within the domain of municipal foreign policy. In this case, municipal leaders attempt to engage directly in either formulating or implementing their own version of foreign policy, even if it might run counter to the foreign policy priorities of their national governments. As an illustration, a number of US municipal and county governments placed sanctions on companies which did business with South Africa during the apartheid era. Companies or banks which continued to do so were either eliminated from or heavily penalized when it came to bidding on local government contracts, or were not allowed to accept deposits of local government money. Some local governments also ordered their own law enforcement personnel to cease cooperating with federal officers who were tracking down undocumented immigrants from certain countries.

In a gray area between foreign affairs and foreign policy are found municipal actions which decry their national government's international pursuits but do not advocate breaking the law in order to protest these pursuits. For example, city and county councils from over 160 jurisdictions passed resolutions or sent letters to the national government condemning any US unilateral intervention in Iraq. This list includes councils from New York City, Washington, DC, Los Angeles, San Francisco, Chicago, Boston, Atlanta, Detroit,

Seattle, Philadelphia, Cleveland and Austin, municipalities which represent
at the local level a substantial portion of the US population.[3] The late mayor
of Los Angeles, Tom Bradley, argued that local leaders should take stances on
certain foreign policy issues because they are democratically elected and
understand the pulse of the people at the grassroots' level better than any
other elected officials. Others argue, however, that foreign policy is clearly
reserved for the national government and that too many local government
fingers in the pie would make it virtually impossible for the nation to speak
with 'one voice' on critical foreign policy issues.

The Rationale for Pursuing Municipal Foreign Affairs

Must the conduct of foreign affairs be left to the very largest cities, or can
smaller municipalities also engage in the game? As mentioned in Chapter 1,
the GDP of the ten largest metro areas in the United States exceeds that of 31
of the 50 US states. At the beginning of 2003, 37 of the states plus the
Commonwealth of Puerto Rico were operating almost 240 foreign offices.
Most governors or lieutenant governors lead international missions each year
and approximately 190 million dollars is spent annually on state-level international programs, up from 20 million dollars in 1982.[4] In Canada, Quebec
spends more on its international programs than any other subnational government in the world, with over 800 government employees working on
international activities and with the annual international budget easily surpassing 100 million Canadian dollars. The Quebec provincial government
also maintains 26 offices abroad in 18 different countries. Other Canadian
and Chinese provinces, German *Länder*, Swiss cantons, Australian states,
Spanish regions, French departments and Japanese prefectures are also actively engaged in international activities to an extent unparalleled in history.
With this in mind, it is not difficult to understand why many municipal
leaders are in the process of adopting similar international policies.

There are a number of factors which are prompting municipal leaders to
engage in foreign affairs. These factors include the following eight.

Economic globalization

International trade, investment and tourism activity are near record levels and
more local jobs than ever before are linked to the global economy. In the
United States, 12 million jobs are directly tied to export activity and one
million to international tourism. More than seven million Americans also
work for foreign-owned enterprises located on US soil. In Canada, over 40
per cent of GDP is linked to cross-border trade and direct investment, and in
many European countries a far larger percentage of jobs is tied to cross-
border activity than in the United States. Many local businesses need to be

engaged in international activities in order to expand their operations and to prosper financially, and the taxes they pay and the jobs they generate contribute substantially to the economic well-being of cities. A complacent business community, on the other hand, satisfied to service local markets and being slow to innovate and modernize, may soon lose business share to importers or to large foreign enterprises which do provide globally competitive goods and services. Under such a scenario, not only do the local businesses suffer, but so too does the tax and employment base of the municipality.

As Peter Drucker emphasizes, 'all institutions have to make global competitiveness a strategic goal. No institution, whether a business, a university or a hospital, can hope to survive, let alone to succeed, unless it measures up to the standards set by the leaders in its field, any place in the world.'[5] Local government leaders must be astute about economic globalization, encourage their business communities to be engaged in the international marketplace, and provide a world-class infrastructure and regulatory climate which will help businesses to compete internationally, while at the same time promoting policies leading to a better quality of life for all constituents.

The ICT revolution
It is easier than ever before for local government leaders to be involved internationally because of tremendous advancements in information technology, communications and transportation. It is now quite simple and relatively inexpensive for them to be in touch with counterparts and business representatives around the world via telephone, fax, the Internet and other modes of communication. Distance has been conquered in the ICT era, with a telephone call from many places in North America to many parts of Europe now costing a few pennies per minute. A three-minute phone call from New York City to London cost the equivalent of 300 current dollars in 1930, compared with less than 10 cents today, and these costs might continue to fall with the introduction of the voice-over-Internet protocol (VoIP).[6] The World Wide Web on the Internet was not even created until 1990, but it is now having a revolutionary effect on communication among households, governments and businesses in many countries. With messages traveling from one part of the world to any other in less than a second, communicating three thousand miles away is often no more difficult than communicating with someone in the same city. International transportation is more cumbersome, but costs of traveling abroad have dropped precipitously over the past few decades and international airline connections have proliferated dramatically.

The Internet has also become a useful tool to spur on economic development. Many large local governments now have websites highlighting the strong points of their cities and encouraging people from abroad to visit or for foreign companies either to invest locally or enter into joint ventures with local companies. Some, such as the Greater Seattle Alliance, have websites in multiple languages. This is a step in the right direction, because too many people in English-speaking countries perceive that a website can be exclusively in English as a result of the proliferation of the use of English around the world, especially in the business community. A better strategy is to embrace the notion that the most important language in the world is the language of existing or potential customers. Following this philosophy would lead to core information on websites being listed in at least four or five major languages.

Electoral considerations

In democratic nations where local officials are elected, being engaged internationally may determine whether or not an incumbent local leader is reelected. In most instances, the voters' perception of the state of the local economy will weigh heavily on whom they will vote for in municipal elections. With local economies being linked more than ever before to the international economy, local officials must be astute in the realm of municipal foreign affairs. A municipal official who attempts to facilitate greater export activity on the part of local companies, who encourage networking which may lead to joint distribution, joint licensing, or other types of cooperative cross-border business activity, or who helps to attract new direct investment and thus new jobs into the community, is likely to be reelected. On the other hand, too much activity in the international sector, including trips abroad to drum up new business opportunities, may be perceived by some voters as 'junketing' (an excuse to vacation and have a good time in glamorous spots around the world). Consequently, a careful balance must be reached between local and foreign affairs, and elected leaders must demonstrate that their international pursuits will eventually pay tangible benefits for local constituents.

The proliferation of national and international municipal associations

Small cities in particular are constrained in terms of what financial resources can be dedicated to international programs, but they may be able to stretch these scarce resources by participating in a few cross-border programs sponsored by national or international municipal associations. In the United States, the National League of Cities (NLC) and the US Conference of Mayors have a significant number of programs which link members of their organizations with their local counterparts around the world. The NLC, which works in partnership with 49 state municipal leagues and serves as an advocate for more than 18 000 cities, has an international task force composed of local government leaders, publishes a newsletter entitled *Globecon*, and prepares booklets for local officials which highlight the international dimension, including *Global Dollars, Local Sense: Cities and Towns in the International Economy.*[7] This latter publication includes sections dealing with strategies for globalization, resource strengths, seeking partnerships, improving workforce training, building on cultural diversity, and 'internationalizing' city hall. The US Conference of Mayors, which was founded in 1932 and represents almost 1200 cities with populations exceeding 30 000, hosted the International Conference of Mayors in June 2003 in Denver, bringing together municipal leaders from 25 countries to discuss common issues of concern over a three-day period. The Federation of Canadian Municipalities is also very actively engaged abroad and currently coordinates the International Centre for Municipal Development with ties to many cities in the developing world, including Burkina Faso, Chile, China, the Czech Republic, El Salvador, Ghana, Guatemala, the Ivory Coast, Malawi, Morocco, Nepal, Nicaragua, Palestine, Peru, the Philippines, Thailand, Uganda, Vietnam and Zimbabwe. Much of the funding for the Centre comes from the federal Canadian International Development Agency (CIDA). The Council of European Municipalities and Regions (CMER), Eurocities, Japan's Council of Local Authorities for International Relations (CLAIR), the Korea Local Authorities Foundation for International Relations and other national or regional associations sponsor similar programs, often in conjunction with their national governments. CMER, for example, was created in 1951 and currently brings together more than 100 000 local and regional authorities from 46 national associations in 33 European countries. It has been a strong proponent of inter-municipal cooperation in Central and Eastern Europe. CMER also asserts that greater influence should be accorded local governments within the European Union, stressing that the future European model must be based on subsidiarity, proportionality, partnership, consultation, participation, transparency and democracy. Moreover, CMER has demanded a stronger role for local governments in determining a common asylum policy for the EU, pointing out that most asylum-seekers settle in major urban areas.[8]

Some US municipal and state governments which are the most greatly affected by inflows of new immigrants and asylum-seekers have made similar demands to Washington, DC. The International Union of Local Authorities (IULA) and the United Towns Organization (UTO) merged in 2004 to form United Cities and Local Government (UCLG). This new organization is headquartered in Barcelona and one of its chief goals is to be the worldwide advocate and voice of democratic local governments. Its mandate is to promote the cause of municipalities around the world and to facilitate networking, the publicizing of best practices by municipalities, and the organization of conferences which address current challenges facing cities. In May 2004, UCLG invited representatives from cities around the world to a five-day conference held in Paris devoted to 'cities, local governments, and the future for development.' Six months earlier, the World Summit of Cities and Local Authorities on the Information Society was convened in Lyon to discuss (a) rethinking democracy in the era of networks, (b) changing work practices, social organizations and responsibilities, (c) freeware and local authorities, (d) community health and telemedicine services, and (e) the impact of information and communication technologies on living standards.[9]

UN-Habitat is another international organization which concentrates on the needs of cities and focuses on sustainable development, the eradication of urban poverty, the development of world-class local infrastructures, and related concerns. Its executive director, Anna Kajumulo Tibaijuka, has stressed that globalization

> is making the 21st century the century of the cities. However, because of the rate of urbanization, in many cities of the developing world, up to 70 per cent of the population lives in informal settlements without adequate shelter or basic services. The challenge is how to give the majority of people a decent life. If we are to improve the living conditions of the urban poor, partnership is the key, and we must encourage city-to-city cooperation.[10]

With support from the World Bank and UN-Habitat, Cities Alliance was formed in 1999 in an effort to eliminate slums from urban areas, fearing that inaction will lead to an additional 100 million slum dwellers by 2020.

Taylor, Catalano and Walker consider that the top cities in the world measured in terms of 'global connectivity are London, New York City, Paris, Tokyo, Singapore, Chicago, Milan, Los Angeles, and Madrid.'[11] Other scholars have come up with their own hierarchical lists, and there is little doubt that large cities have an advantage over smaller metropolitan areas in establishing a wide range of international connections.[12] However, the organizations listed in the preceding paragraphs can be tapped by leaders in even modestly sized cities in an effort to help them to engage in efficient international activities, to join international municipal networks, and to put into place programs which have been tested by cities elsewhere in the world and found to be successful. Additional information can be gleaned through the use of the Internet, phone calls and occasional travel to visit with local counterparts in other countries.

The growth in ethnic associations

With cross-border immigration at record levels, and with most immigrant groups settling in municipal areas, ethnic ties to the 'old country' represent another way for local leaders to engage in municipal foreign relations. Allen Scott and Ivan Light have documented how important such ties have been in the Los Angeles area in the development of the clothing, financial and other industries.[13] These ethnic ties provide a source of foreign funding for the establishment or expansion of individual businesses, and a source of workers and foreign markets for the finished products. Elected officials can facilitate such interactions through their own city-to-city contacts and through the creation of twinning arrangements with major cities in the ethnic groups' former homelands. Such linkages help to reflect the internal diversity of cities externally.[14]

Intrusions from above

As their national governments enter into binding accords regionally or internationally, city governments find that their policy-making latitude is being restricted without proper consideration given to their concerns and points of view. As mentioned earlier, this has occurred with the creation of the WTO in 1995 and the efforts to expand its purview under the auspices of the Doha Round; the strings attached when national governments accept loans from the International Monetary Fund; the creation of the European Union, NAFTA, the Southern Cone Common Market (Mercosur), the Association of Southeast Asian Nations (ASEAN), and other regional economic associations; and the proposed Multilateral Agreement on Investment which would establish uniform rules for the treatment of investment among the more developed nations. UN-Habitat has warned that 'in the name of a global economy, international institutions are taking steps to liberate markets from the regulatory authority of nations and their autonomous subdivisions – the provinces and cities,' intimating that this might not always be a wise policy to pursue.[15] Local governments must be cognizant of how these international agreements will affect their own local constituents and authority to govern, and must ensure that their perspectives are given proper recognition and hopefully incorporated into current and future international accords.[16]

Within the domestic context, there are at times great discrepancies in the economic fortunes of cities and regions. The per capita income of the residents of Mississippi, which was 22 370 dollars in 2002, is only slightly more than half of Connecticut's 42 829 dollars.[17] The per capita annual production base in Newfoundland and Labrador is only 60 per cent of Alberta's level, and only two of the ten provinces in Canada are deemed by the federal government in Ottawa to 'have' provinces, with the other eight designated as 'have nots' eligible for special payments from the federal government and transfer payments from the 'have' provinces.[18] Northern Italy does much better economically than the *mezzogiorno* region of southern Italy, and Paris does much better proportionally than northwest France. Even within the same state or province, the fortunes of communities can differ dramatically. In mid-2003, the unemployment rate in San Diego was about 4 per cent, but in the eastern part of San Diego County the unemployment rate approached 20 per cent. Some of the same contrast in fortunes is also manifested in major

US metropolitan areas, where the median household income in the central city is less than 75 per cent of that in the suburbs.[19]

Fortunately, it is no longer necessary for a city to be situated next to the ocean or a major waterway in order to prosper. Nor does it have to be situated in a temperate climate. Las Vegas, which is in close proximity to Death Valley, suffers from some of the hottest temperatures on earth. Within its city boundaries is to be found some of the most arid, desolate, God-forsaken land anywhere on the planet. Yet, it has been the fastest growing major metropolitan area in the United States over the past decade and has created more jobs proportionally than any other major city. It is also home to 11 of the 13 largest hotels in the world, with the number of hotel rooms in the city approaching 130 000. In addition, it has three of the seven largest convention centers in the United States with 4.1 million conventioneers visiting in 2001, compared with only 1.7 million in 1990.[20] In 2003, Las Vegas signed up more large conventions than did New York City, a metro region with a far greater population base and much higher national and international profile. Why has it done so well in recent years? The invention of air conditioning, the relatively easy access by automobile to consumers in California which has a population base larger than Canada's and a GDP larger than France's, and the city's niche specialty of gambling, entertainment, and hosting major conventions have all combined to bring about unprecedented economic growth in Las Vegas. As will be discussed later in this chapter, it is now expending significant resources on opening overseas offices and attempting to build up its international clientele, a clientele which tends to spend much more money per capita in Las Vegas than do visitors from other parts of the US.

In spite of daunting physical challenges, Las Vegas has succeeded beyond its wildest expectations. Lyon has done extremely well in spite of being part of *le désert français* in a nation dominated by Paris. Turin has prospered in a nation dominated by Rome and a northern region dominated by Milan. Calgary has been a great success in an isolated area of Canada once referred to as 'the empty quarter.'[21] As a result of very enlightened local policies, Curitiba in Brazil has been for many years a model of urban development for municipalities in developing nations, in spite of widespread national poverty and the dominance nationally of the state and city of Sao Paulo. Similar examples of urban success stories can be found in a fair number of countries around the world. In effect, local governance is critical even in an era when most nations maintain unitary systems of government and when local economic fortunes are being affected increasingly by globalization.

Competition among municipalities
Cities compete against one another to attract new companies or to convince existing companies to expand locally, and in an era of globalization, this

competitive game now crosses national borders. In a report entitled *Early Warning: Will Canadian Cities Compete?*, the Federation of Canadian Municipalities outlines how US and European cities are in much better shape than Canadian cities in funding critical infrastructure projects, suggesting that municipalities in Canada have been placed at a distinctive competitive disadvantage.[22]

The UN Division of Transnational Corporations and Investment estimates that billions of dollars in incentives have been offered over the past decade by local, state and national governments in over 100 countries in an effort to lure foreign-owned companies to their particular areas of jurisdiction.[23] With FDI increasing so dramatically up to the September 11 crisis, US and European cities in particular have been very active in putting together incentive packages for prospective overseas investors. Almost all US state, county and city governments have established economic development agencies and many fund investment incentives in the range of 50 billion dollars annually to domestic and foreign-owned companies.[24] Annual incentives offered by various levels of governments in the European Union in the mid-1990s may have totaled the equivalent of 38 billion euros or more.[25] These incentives often include the donation of land, pledges to build infrastructure to support a new facility, low-interest loans, tax rebates or tax holidays depending on the number and skill level of new jobs created, free training of workers and other public services. In their efforts to attract new investment to the metropolitan area, economic development officers in Fort Lauderdale, Florida list on the city's Internet website incentives which are available from both the state and municipal governments. This list includes (1) no state or local personal income tax, (2) no inventory tax, (3) no state ad valorem tax, (4) very low state corporate income taxes, (5) sales tax exemptions, (6) tax incentives up to 5000 dollars per job created, increasing to 7500 dollars in special enterprise zones, (7) loan guarantees, (8) some infrastructure expenses, (9) industrial development bonds, (10) assistance from state-sponsored manufacturing technology centers and (11) employee training assistance.

Perhaps the greatest municipal success story in the United States linked to foreign direct investment is found in Spartanburg, South Carolina. Thirty-five years ago, this city had 45 000 residents and its economic development prospects were poor because of an overwhelming reliance on an ageing textile industry. Leaders from the local chamber of commerce and elected officials joined together in an effort to attract FDI which would bring in new companies, diversify the city's economic profile, create new higher paying jobs and enhance tax revenues. The campaign initially focused on textile companies in Western Europe, but then spread to other business sectors. A variety of state, county and municipal financial incentives were offered to some of these companies. Today, scores of companies from Germany and several other nations have established facilities in Spartanburg and have created tens of thousands of new jobs. BMW has constructed an assembly plant within the county and well over one billion dollars in FDI has poured into the metropolitan area, transforming Spartanburg from a small, introverted city in an isolated region of South Carolina to a much more dynamic, cosmopolitan city of the 'New South.'[26]

As indicated by BMW's experience in Spartanburg, foreign automakers have been cashing in on over a billion dollars' worth of multi-year incentives provided by state and local governments in order to entice these auto giants to their areas of jurisdiction. Japanese companies especially have been major recipients of incentives offered by US subnational governments. These Japanese companies have invested 20 billion dollars in plants in the United States and now have the capacity to manufacture 2.4 million vehicles per year within US borders.[27] Volkswagen of Germany was one of the first auto companies to receive these incentives when it decided in 1976 to accept an offer worth 70 million dollars from state and local governments in Pennsylvania. VW never met its employment target and eventually closed its plant 11 years after it had been opened. Ironically, even after the plant had been closed, VW continued to collect incentives which had been phased in by the state and local governments over several years.[28] Almost 20 years after VW set up shop in Pennsylvania, another German company, Mercedes-Benz, was again willing to pit state government against state government in an investment bidding war, with Chancellor Helmut Kohl actually inviting the governors of North Carolina, South Carolina, Tennessee and Georgia to Germany in September 1993, prior to a final decision being made on where Mercedes-Benz would locate in the United States. Following these visits, executives at Mercedes-Benz decided to opt for a sweetened bid from various levels of government in Alabama, another state whose political leaders had traveled to Germany during the lengthy bidding process.[29] In terms of the costs per job of the incentive packages, they have escalated from 3550 dollars per job for VW in Pennsylvania in 1978, to 11 000 dollars for Nissan in Tennessee in 1980, and then to 150 000 dollars for Mercedes Benz in Alabama in 1993.[30] David Donovan, a partner at Wadley Donovan, a location consulting firm based in New Jersey, estimated in 2002 that in most industries, outside the auto sector, incentives average out to 5000 to 10 000 dollars per job created.[31]

Expanded capacity to be internationally engaged
Municipal governments, especially those in the countries of the North, tend to have substantial resources available to permit them to at least 'test the waters' internationally. US local governments have combined annual revenues in the range of 1.1 trillion dollars per year, and the far smaller number of Canadian municipalities generates collectively about 83 billion Canadian

dollars.[32] There were 87 525 local governments in the United States in 2002, up from 78 000 in 1972 but down considerably from the 117 000 governments in 1952 and the 155 000 in 1942.[33] Of the so-called general local governments in 2002, 3034 were counties, 19 431 municipalities and 16 506 townships. All local governments in the United States employ 11.2 million workers, of which 4.8 million are not directly involved in education.[34]

When one combines the substantial revenue and employment bases with contributions which can be made by the private sector (corporations, ethnic and civic associations, and so forth) and local colleges and universities, municipal governments can be engaged in a number of international activities. The lower costs and relative ease in using modern communications and transportation systems add to the allure of being involved internationally.

Engaging in Municipal Foreign Affairs

Many of the international activities sponsored by local governments or quasi-public organizations are intended to enhance economic development at the municipal level. These activities include developing Internet sites for international consumption, sponsoring periodic trade or investment missions which include business leaders along with a spattering of elected officials, hosting numerous delegations from abroad who have an interest in solidifying ties with local businesses, universities, or research institutions, establishing twinning partnerships with foreign cities and so on.

The most common expression of municipal foreign affairs is found in twinning relationships. Sister-cities International was created in 1956 and has helped to coordinate twinning between 675 communities in the United States and almost 1500 communities in 121 countries.[35] CMER, Eurocities, and other municipal-related organizations in Europe have also promoted greater twinning among European cities and their counterparts in developing countries, especially those which are likely candidates for EU membership over the next few years or decades. Presently, more than 8000 towns, cities and regional governments in Council of Europe countries are twinned, and the European Union actually provides financial incentives for twinning purposes to cities within its member countries.[36]

A careful examination of twinning programs around the world reveals that some of the relationships work quite well, leading to regular meetings between city leaders and ambitious agendas which often deal with economic development, cultural and educational exchanges, internships or related activities.[37] The programs also permit relatively small cities to be involved, such as Roanoke, Virginia's long-term program with Kisumu, Kenya; Sandy, Utah's program with Piedras Negras, Mexico; or Boulder, Colorado's program with Dushanbe, Tajikistan.[38] On the other hand, some of the bilateral ties are fairly tepid, have fallen into relative disuse or exist in name only. Many do not involve taxpayer funds and depend on donations of time and money from local corporations, civic groups and ethnic associations. Some lack institutional cohesion and do little to promote local economic development. One mayor of a city may be an enthusiastic supporter of the sister-city program, while his or her successor may have little interest at all. In order to survive and prosper, the relationship should have a committed civil servant spearheading the program, or at least very dedicated patrons in civil society.

Some American cities are leading the way in establishing international programs, and almost all include public–private sector cooperation. In 1986, Seattle created an Office of International Affairs, which was placed within the city's executive department. This office was given responsibility for coordinating Seattle's numerous sister-cities programs and other international activities which might impact upon economic development within the city limits. In 1991, the Trade Development Alliance of Greater Seattle was established as a public–private sector partnership to enhance the business community's role in the international economy. Ninety-five per cent of the value of the Port of Seattle's business is with the Asia–Pacific region, so the Alliance concentrates on building linkages with these nations and with neighboring Canada. Aircraft and software are the two major exports of the Seattle metropolitan area, but the Alliance recognizes that Boeing and Microsoft have little need for the Alliance's expertise or networking. Instead, efforts are concentrated on smaller firms in a wide variety of economic sectors.

Boston and Silicon Valley have established networks which function in much the same way as the Trade Development Alliance of Greater Seattle, although Boston's emphasis is on solidifying economic ties with the Atlantic Rim countries.[39] Dallas has a small Office of International Affairs and the Greater Phoenix Economic Council has taken the lead in addressing issues such as local currency exchange outlets, multilingual services, signage, appropriate meeting and conference facilities for international visitors, non-stop commercial and cargo air service abroad, and international banking, accounting, and legal expertise.[40] Officials in Charlotte, North Carolina sponsored in the mid-1990s an inventory of international businesses within that metropolitan region. They discovered that 321 foreign-owned companies were operating in the city in 1995 and that manufacturing exports from Charlotte had increased by 254 per cent between 1987 and 1993.[41] Charlotte has now established a World Affairs Council, a World Trade Association and the Mayor's International Cabinet to help coordinate the city's diverse international activities.

Other cities attempt to raise their international profiles by hosting major world conferences or events. It took Salt Lake City almost three decades before it was able to secure the International Olympic Committee's endorsement to host the 2002 Winter Olympics. The rationale for doing so was based in part on surveys indicating that most Europeans had never even heard of Utah or Salt Lake City, and if they had heard, they thought about one of three things: Mormons, mountains and the Osmonds. While the games were in progress, the governor of Utah, the mayor of Salt Lake City and other local officials would meet on an almost daily basis with international business groups who were attending the festivities. The long-range strategy was to put Salt Lake City and Utah on the global map, show to the world that the city and state could host a highly successful international event, develop a world-class local infrastructure, which in part was paid for by federal government funds earmarked specifically for the Winter Olympics, optimize the chances of international visitors coming to Utah in the future, especially for winter sports and other recreational activity, and solidify and expand international business linkages.[42] In the 18-month period following the Olympics, the governor made more foreign trips and visited more foreign countries than any other governor in the United States, almost all linked to contacts made during the Olympics. The mayor of Salt Lake City also engaged in a number of international activities following the games. Officials in Turin, Italy, view their hosting of the Winter Olympics in 2006 as an investment in that city's economic future, believing that Barcelona had benefited substantially from hosting the Summer Olympics in 1992 and Sydney from hosting the summer games in 2000, and that this success could be replicated in this northern Italian city.[43]

Other cities work diligently to become the headquarters for regional and international agencies, believing that this will enhance their international visibility and create good-paying jobs for local workers. Lyon has been very successful and now hosts Interpol and more than 40 other European and international governmental and non-governmental organizations.[44] Montreal is also home to three dozen such organizations, including the North American headquarters for the International Air Transport Association (IATA).[45] In addition, Houston provides the secretariat office for the World Energy Cities Partnership. This organization includes the 'energy cities' of Aberdeen, Baku, Daqing, Dongying, Halifax, Houston, Perth, Rio de Janeiro, St. John's, Stavanger and Villahermosa, and its mission is to engage in 'business development activity, trade missions, joint projects, and sharing of information in areas such as emergency planning, international schools, oil industry expectations, and oil industry diversification strategies.'[46]

A few cities or local metropolitan governments maintain their own offices abroad, mostly for economic development purposes but sometimes for political reasons. More than 200 regions have opened offices in Brussels, of which 30 represent the interests of individual cities or groups of cities. Another 20 offices have been opened by local authorities or city networks. Part of the rationale for these offices is to keep abreast of developments within the EU, to lobby extensively, and to increase the overall municipal influence in EU decision-making.[47] The economic development agency in Lyon has permanent offices in New York City and Tokyo, Yokohama maintains offices in New York City, Shanghai, and Frankfurt, and neighboring Osaka has a bureau within the Japan External Trade Organization's (JETRO) facilities in Chicago and Düsseldorf, plus its own separate offices in Singapore, Paris, and Shanghai.[48]

The Las Vegas Convention and Visitors Authority, which is mainly funded through a local tax on hotel guests, has an annual budget of 124 million dollars and over 500 authorized employment positions. It maintains representative offices in Japan, South Korea, Australia, the United Kingdom, France and Germany. It has also launched a 1.6 million dollar campaign to produce tourist advertisements in Spanish geared to the US Hispanic market and border communities in Mexico.[49] The Authority has also spearheaded efforts to obtain non-stop charter flights from Europe, Asia and the Americas, and is now working with some success on securing non-stop regularly scheduled overseas commercial flights. The first major success was the inauguration of regular Singapore Air flights to Las Vegas from Singapore via Hong Kong in August 2002. Unfortunately, these flights were suspended because of uncertainty surrounding international travel after the United States invaded Iraq in March 2003. McCarran Airport in Las Vegas is one of the most modern in the United States and has constructed an international facility where foreign visitors can pass through immigration and customs. In the year 2000, almost 36 million people visited Las Vegas, with a record 13 per cent coming from other countries. In 2002, however, foreign visits were down to 8 per cent of the total, in part because of September 11 but also because of more stringent border control policies put in place by the US federal government.[50]

With a far more modest budget than Las Vegas's, New Orleans promotes itself as an entertainment destination and emphasizes Mardi Gras, its historical sites, nightlife, and casinos.[51] Denver was the first US city to open an office in China, and it once had an office in London. The city has established the Mayor's Office for Economic Development and Trade and works closely with Colorado state officials in coordinating trade missions, in helping local businesses to use Colorado's overseas offices and in seeking FDI.[52] The same pattern of municipal–state cooperation exists in many other parts of the United States as well. Tucson, Arizona also maintained an office in Taipei for several years, and currently has a local office which deals exclusively with economic ties to Mexico.

Border cities in Canada, Mexico and the United States often have good working relationships with their close neighbors in the other country, exemplified by San Diego Dialogue which sponsors conferences and research projects of common interest to San Diego, Tijuana and Mexicali.[53] Such relationships are even more common among border cities in Europe. NAFTA has also spurred on inter-municipal cooperation in the three North American nations in an effort to promote CANAMEX trucking routes running from Canada in the north, through the United States and then deep into Mexico. Cities want to be along these routes in order to spur on commercial trucking and tourism-related activities. With more than 25 million Mexican and Mexican-Americans residing in the United States, and with the Inter-American Development Bank estimating that these groups sent back an estimated 14 billion dollars in remittances to their families during 2003, it is not unusual for governors and mayors in Mexico to visit California, Texas or other border states to seek funds for public projects.[54] Leaders in Oaxaca have occasionally visited the Oaxacan Foundation in Los Angeles and pledged to match every dollar sent to Oaxaca for infrastructure modernization with three dollars of local, state, and national government funding.[55] Mayors in Canada also occasionally lobby their neighboring mayors in the United States in an effort to put additional pressure on officials in Washington, DC to change policies perceived as being injurious to workers in Canada. For example, municipal leaders who were members of the Federation of Canadian Municipalities' Softwood Lumber Task Force visited seven US cities in early 2003 to lobby for an end to the 27 per cent combined duty which the US government had imposed on Canadian lumber exports.[56]

Peter Hall divides major cities around the world into three categories: (1) international or global; (2) subglobal; and (3) regional.[57] His list of global cities is relatively short and would include New York City, Tokyo, London and perhaps Paris. He places many of the other major cities in Europe in the sub-global category, and would add to this list Washington, DC for government, Chicago and San Francisco for financial services, Los Angeles for culture and entertainment, and Osaka, arguing that each competes with the global cities in certain functional areas. His final category, regional cities, usually includes urban areas with a population between 500 000 and 4 million, and would include such metropolitan areas as Lyon, Manchester, Hanover, Boston, Denver and Seattle. These cities play dominant roles within their own regions, but do not compete directly with the handful of global cities.

Even though the international pursuits of US municipalities are up dramatically over the past decade, 'place promotion,' an awareness of the importance of global trade and financial flows to the local citizenry, and a quest to be included on one of Hall's lists seem to be accorded greater importance by cities outside the United States. Part of this difference in perception is attributable to the fact that most economic activity in the United States continues to be domestically oriented, largely as a result of the huge size of the US economy, the territorial expansiveness of the nation itself, and its population of almost 300 million fairly affluent consumers. An extensive survey completed by John Kincaid for the National League of Cities, indicates that most smaller US cities continue to focus on local or regional markets and are only beginning to understand both the challenges and opportunities found in an increasingly interdependent continental and global economy.[58] To put the US domestic economy in perspective, just the growth in US GDP between 1990 and 2002, measured in nominal American dollars, was greater than the entire GDP of any other nation on earth, including Japan. Americans also tend to be among the most insular people on earth and have a relatively low knowledge level about trans-Atlantic, trans-Pacific, and hemispheric affairs. In the same vein, relatively few have been convinced of the need to become fluent in a language other than English.

In contrast, Asian cities such as Shanghai, Taipei, Manila and Shenzhen have been very energetic in place promotion and have a keen desire to be recognized as major players continentally and globally.[59] Many city governments in Asia have international or foreign affairs offices, such as Hiroshima or Chengdu municipality in China. Most major European cities also have advanced international programs, in part because of the emergence of the European Union but also in part because so many local jobs are dependent on international trade, investment and tourism activity.[60] Lyon, for example, has its own Department of International Relations, its aforementioned overseas offices in New York City and Tokyo, partnerships with 17 cities around the world, and other special linkages to another 14 cities. Lyon's Department of International Relations works to intensify economic, scientific, academic, scholastic, cultural and information exchanges with its partner cities, hosts foreign delegations and VIPs, assists the organization and management of major national and international events held in Lyon and participates in the work of inter-city networks around the world and the activities of Lyon-based international organizations.[61] The city of Montreal has emphasized international programs for over two decades and many other major Canadian cities usually have international divisions in one form or another. This is understandable because a third of all Canadian jobs are dependent on exports and other international economic activities. In the United States, about 10 per cent of the GDP is tied to exports and perhaps one job in six in the private sector is directly linked to the global economy. This dependency is certainly growing, but many municipal leaders are still rather complacent about being engaged internationally, at least in comparison to many of their counterparts in other parts of the world.

Municipal Foreign Policy

Very few local governments engage in their own foreign policy pursuits, and even those that do significantly limit the scope of their policies. Over 100 US state, county, and municipal governments did invoke sanctions on companies doing business with the apartheid regime in South Africa during the early 1990s, even after the federal government had lifted most of its sanctions. The sanctions fell into four broad categories: (1) laws requiring the divestiture or partial divestiture of public pension-fund holdings in companies doing business with South Africa; (2) a prohibition on local governments using the financial services of banks doing business with South Africa; (3) a ban on the purchase on South African-made goods by local governments; and (4) restrictions on contracting out services to any companies that continued to do business with South Africa after specified deadlines.[62] At one time or another, some local governments have placed their own sanctions on African nations such as Nigeria, Middle Eastern nations such as Israel and Saudi Arabia, Asian nations such as Myanmar, the former Soviet Union, Switzerland, Germany, and even against the United Kingdom because of its policies in Northern Ireland.[63] During the Reagan administration, 28 cities and two states adopted sanctuary resolutions for Central American refugees, especially those from El Salvador and Guatemala, actions which clearly were in violation of federal law. After the rejection of the Kyoto Protocol on global warming by the administration of George W. Bush, several states and cities have enacted mandatory policies to curtail greenhouse emissions, policies which may be tested in the federal courts to sort out the limitations on state and local government control over environmental regulations.[64]

In this arena of subnational foreign policies, state government officials often take the lead, although they are occasionally joined by county and local government officials and by representatives of state and local government employee pension funds, funds which control hundreds of billions of dollars in assets. For example, in September 2003, the Treasurer of the State of California, the New York State Comptroller, and representatives of the California Public Employees' Retirement System and the California State Teachers' Retirement System, the largest and third largest public pension funds in the USA, met with officials of Unocal, one of the major US oil companies, in an effort to persuade the company to end its investments in Myanmar.

City councils should be totally free to express their disagreement with the foreign policies of their national governments, as exemplified by the number of US cities opposed to the unilateral intervention of the United States into Iraq in 2003, and the passage of the Patriot Act following the terrorist incidents of September 2001. They should also attempt to influence public opinion in general and their representatives in the national legislature in particular.

However, direct sanctions against foreign governments or individual businesses from foreign countries, sanctions which are not approved by their national governments, represent misguided and potentially dangerous policies. Such sanctions cast doubt on the integrity of the national government's foreign policy, blatantly interfere with international and interstate commerce, openly violate the supremacy clause in the US and some other national constitutions, and invite retaliatory actions by foreign governments. In an era of globalization and an already complicated decision-making process at all levels of government, the national government must be permitted to speak with a relatively unified voice on foreign policy and not be undermined by the actions of its local governments. Nevertheless, local elected officials should feel free to drum up support from domestic constituencies and work through their elected representatives in the national legislature or through their national court systems to effectuate changes in aspects of their nation's foreign policy which they consider to be repugnant and offensive.[65]

NOTES

1. Manning, 1977, pp. 309–10.
2. Bueno de Mesquita, 2002, p. 8.
3. Hobbs, 2004 and the Cities for Peace website at www.ips-dc.org/citiesforpeace.
4. See Fry, 1998 and Edisis, 2003.
5. Drucker, 1999.
6. Chanda, 2002 and Samuelson, 2004.
7. National League of Cities, 1993.
8. Council of European Municipalities and Regions, 2003.
9. See http://www.iula.org/.
10. See www.unhabitat.org.
11. Taylor *et al.*, 2002b, p. 2372.
12. Friedmann, 1995b, p. 25.
13. Scott, 2002 and Light, 2002. See also Samers, 2002.
14. Thürer, 2003, p. 29.
15. UN Human Settlements Program, 2001, p. 19.
16. Schweke and Stumberg, 2000 and Mooney, 2001.
17. US Census Bureau, state per capita income figures for 2002.
18. Statistics Canada 2002 data on provincial production and population.
19. 'Executive summary,' in Altshuler *et al.*, 1999, p. 4.
20. *Las Vegas Review-Journal*, 4 January 2003 and *New York Times*, 5 January 2003.
21. Joel Garreau, *The Nine Nations of North America*, Boston: Houghton Mifflin, 1981.
22. Federation of Canadian Municipalities, 2001.
23. *Wall Street Journal*, 14 April 1995.
24. Olivier, 2002.
25. Ibid.
26. Earl H. Fry, 'North American municipalities and their involvement in the global economy,' in Kresl and Gappert (eds), 1995, pp. 37–8.
27. Japan Automobile Manufacturers' Association, 2002.
28. Fry, 1980, pp. 58–75 and *Wall Street Journal*, 11 April 1995.
29. Watson, 1995, p. 70.

30. Olivier, 2002.
31. Ibid.
32. US Census Bureau and Statistics Canada.
33. US Census Bureau, 2002.
34. Ibid., and US Census Bureau employment data, March 2001.
35. See www.sister-cities.org.
36. CMER, 'Brief history of European town-twinning,' at www.ccre.org/docs/jumelages/origins.html.
37. Handley (ed.), 2001.
38. See www.sister-cities.org.
39. Kantor, 1995.
40. 'An international agenda for Phoenix,' *Arizona Republic*, 5 February 1995, p. F1.
41. Chernotsky and Jennifer Watson Roberts, 'America's shifting global agendas: a case study' 1996, and Chernotsky, 2004.
42. Fry and McCarlie, 2002.
43. Brooks, 2003.
44. Lyon Area Economic Development Agency, ADERLY, at www.lyon-aderly.com.
45. Montreal International at www.montrealinternational.org.
46. World Energy Cities Partnership website at http://www.wecp.org/.
47. Schultze, 2003 and Van Hecke, 2003, pp. 55 and 71.
48. Respective websites of these cities.
49. *Las Vegas Review Journal*, 17 July 2003.
50. Las Vegas Convention and Visitors Authority.
51. Gotham, 2002.
52. *Rocky Mountain News*, 31 March 2001.
53. San Diego Dialogue, 2000.
54. *International Herald Tribune*, 29 October 2003, and *Los Angeles Times*, 1 June 2003.
55. *Los Angeles Times*, 8 July 2001.
56. Federation of Canadian Municipalities' press release, 17 February 2003.
57. Hall, 1998a, p. 24.
58. Kincaid, 1997, pp. 55–84.
59. Cartier, 2002; Wang 2003; Masahiko Henjo, 'The growth of Tokyo as a world city,' in Lo and Yeung (1998), pp. 109-131; and Yusuf and Wu, 2002.
60. Hans Thor Andersen, 'The new urban politics of Europe,' in Andersen and Kempen (eds), 2001, pp. 233–53.
61. Ville de Lyon, 'Partner cities,' at www.mairie-lyon.fr/international/ villes_partenaires.
62. Fry, 1998, p. 95.
63. Ibid.
64. 'On global warming, states act locally,' *Washington Post*, 11 November 2002, p. A3.
65. Fry, 1998, p. 65.

4. New technologies and the urban economy

The rapid pace of technological advance we have experienced since the Second World War has made powerful impacts on all aspects of our economic life. The resulting efficiencies have lowered costs of production and the prices of goods and services, redefined comparative advantage and optimal specialization for all economic entities and increased living standards for most people. But technological changes have also made many skills no longer viable in places where they had been viable for decades if not centuries, they have made individuals and firms vulnerable to competition for jobs and markets from localities thousands of miles away, and they have made the economic bases of many urban economies increasingly threatened and unsustainable. Globalization may be centered on the reduction of barriers to movements of goods and services and to the opening of these markets as well as that for financial services and flows, but it is advances in technology that enable all economic actors to realize the potential that is inherent in these liberalization policies that are enacted by national governments. Market liberalization may make it possible to think of reconceptualizing the economic space within which some activity is done but, for example, it is the advances in communication technology that make it possible for accounting, financial analysis, back office activities and other services to be outsourced from New York or London and to be done in south India.

Obviously this new environment brings many exciting opportunities for the urban economies of the industrialized world, but it also carries with it the possible destruction of many traditional activities that have provided them with the bases of their economic lives. Economists argue that these forces that emanate from technological change should be embraced for the gains in living standards they can bring, but they also stress the need to be proactive, to engage in a serious planning process to develop new activities, and to avoid protectionism. This is easier said than done, given that many of the adjustment assistance instruments are in the hands of superior levels of government and that adjustment assistance must compete with many funding possibilities that have greater political pay-off to that other government – tax cuts, military expenditures, agricultural supports and so forth.

In addition to this set of challenges and opportunities that confront urban economies, advances in technology also affect the places where people want to live and thereby generate new streams of migrants from rural to urban areas and from low income to high income countries. Cities are predominantly the location of choice for these migrants and cities thus bear the positive and negative consequences of these movements of people who are usually both workers and social service recipients. Some times this brings a net positive consequence, but at other times it may be negative, at least in the short term. In either event it is the large cities that must adopt policies to deal with the issue. Concerns about border security have been ramped up since September 11 and, as we shall see, reconsideration of national borders has impacts on the movement of goods and people and difficulties for all cities, whether they are border cities or inland cities.

Changes in technology also give rise to new industries and transform other industries with regard to the level and nature of skills required by workers. High technology industries both produce high technology products, and goods and services, and use advanced technology and technologically advanced inputs in production. The information-communication sector has expanded dramatically during the past quarter century. Knowledge- and R&D-intensive sectors such as universities, research laboratories, consultancy firms and software development and bio-pharmaceutical firms have become increasingly prominent and vital for any advanced industrial economy. Finally, financial institutions, law firms, the health sector and some parts of the entertainment industry must also be considered to be in the high technology area of the economy. One consequence of inclusion of both technology producers and users in the understanding of the high technology sector is the difficulty in coming to a generally agreed definition of the subject. In his book on the information economy, Matthew Drennan wrote that the 'information' sector accounts for 30 per cent of the US GDP.[1] However, in an article on 'knowledge-based' jobs in Canada, M. Drolet and R. Morissete tell us that firms in this sector employed 7 per cent of workers in 1999.[2] Obviously, one must be very careful to be specific with regard to definitions.

All of these changes also bring new relationships of economic and political power among the classes, economic groups, and ethnic, gender and race communities in the urban economy. It also can lead to loss of control by local entities over the local economy, and major local firms, both manufacturing and financial, are taken over by outside firms and the locus of decision-making shifts to individuals who have no connection to or interest in the welfare of that city. Since the 1970s, economists and other observers not totally enthused about globalization have rallied under the banners of global restructuring, capital flight, deindustrialization and down-sizing – today the term used both in the literature and in the 2004 US presidential campaign is outsourcing. Whatever the term used, it evokes first the loss of low-skill jobs to the USA and other industrialized economies – and then the loss of 'good, high paying' jobs. The consequences of free trade, market liberalization and technological change promise to be with us for some considerable time to come and powerfully to color our collective discourse.

Finally, these changes in the nature of economic space and in the relations among and between urban economic spaces are making it necessary for economists and economic geographers to re-think some of their long held notions with regard to things such as clusters and the economies of agglomeration, to name just two. How do changes in technology affect the economic benefits to individual firms of locating their activities in close proximity to other firms in the same industry or subsector of that industry? In which industries is the face-to-face contact that is so important for local economies that are as successful as Silicon Valley going to be a factor of importance in the information technology economy and other economies that we see developing as we enter the 21st century? Getting this right is of obvious importance for private and public sector leaders in urban economies everywhere.

Each of these is very important and collectively they certainly deserve a chapter in this book for their consideration.

IMPACTS OF NEW TECHNOLOGIES OF INFORMATION AND COMMUNICATION, TRANSPORTATION AND LOGISTICS AND PRODUCTION

These impacts have such broadly based consequences on the economy, society and polity of any country that some of them are discussed in other sections of this chapter. In subsequent sections that follow, we will examine the impacts of new technologies in the context of globalization, in the post-September 11 environment, on who in the national economy gains and loses power, and on the long-held assumptions of economists and economic geographers regarding the value of clustering and agglomeration. In this section we will limit our attention to issues that relate to the continued viability of urban economies and large cities, to probable changes in their economic structures, and to the anticipated changes in the roles of cities in general in the evolving global economy.

In the new economy of the 21st century there is little about any particular city that assures its continued importance and economic viability. The service economy is increasingly marked by products that can be produced anywhere and transported at very low cost to anywhere else. Much has been made of the transfer of jobs in financial services, for example, to India and other relatively low-cost locations from the traditional centers of this industry in

North America, Europe and Japan. Many individual cities have seen their role in this sector diminished during the past decade or two. New York and London have both suffered serious loss of jobs in some areas of the financial services industry. Second tier cities such as Pittsburgh, Manchester and Lyon have had an even worse experience. The question to be raised here is whether, beyond these and other cities, the city or the large city itself is threatened by advances in technologies.

While many cities still have significant manufacturing sectors, it is clear that this is a diminishing feature of urban economies and that they are increasingly becoming centers of service sector activities. For now, we will focus our attention on this aspect of the urban economy and leave manufacturing to the last substantive section of this chapter. One approach to the metropolitan economy and services is to argue that with improved telecommunications, someone on the twentieth floor of an office building in Manhattan is as close to a colleague in Boise, Idaho, as he/she is to someone on the twenty-third floor of the same building when it comes to business/professional communication. In this case the benefits of proximity lose their strength and the logic of locating each worker or office randomly or in accordance with some non-business amenity gains force. There are several important dimensions to the response to this question. One is the necessity of the widely discussed face-to-face contact – what sorts of things can be done by telephone and what require direct personal contact.

Some of the early futorologists, such as Alvin Toffler, were convinced that advances in the technology of telecommunications would cause both space and large cities to become irrelevant.[3] This seemed on the face of it to make immediate and intuitive sense. Would it not make sense for each individual to choose a location that was maximally congenial and that offered the mix of amenities that maximized his/her personal satisfaction and then link them all via advanced telecommunications? As technology advances inexorably, the advantages of disbursal and the disadvantages of crowding would both increase. However attractive this notion, it soon came under attack by other aspects of human interaction and by social scientists who analysed that interaction. Internet sales are, indeed, growing in importance but whether the purchase is a book or a computer, most consumers want to talk to a knowledgeable salesperson in a store. Often price is the result of a discussion and bargaining between buyer and seller. Some services, including analysis of financial documents and other 'back office' activities, can be done at a distant location using fax and e-mail, but large investors and deal-makers will always demand personal contact. Some have argued that what is most easily transmitted by telecommunication is information; transmission of knowledge is more of a two-way communication and remains best accomplished by face-to-face interaction.[4] Perhaps at some date in the future we will be able to ask

Scotty to 'beam me up' so that individuals themselves may be transmitted, but that will just be another means of accomplishing a face-to-face contact.

What is the relationship between advances in technology and face-to-face contact contacts? If the two proceed under their own individual logic then there may be no discernible impact of technological advance on the viability of large cities. The argument of Toffler is that the two are substitutes and that as the ease of use and cost advantage of the former increase, cities will be diminished in importance. However, if they are complementary, the two will grow in importance with large cities gaining an advantage over smaller towns and rural locations. In an examination of the issue of 'information technology and the future of cities,' Gaspar and Glaeser conclude that the two are indeed complementary and that 'improvements in telecommunications technology may increase the number of face-to-face interactions and the relevance of cities.' They find a clear connection between face-to-face interactions and telecommunications, and, using a Japanese study, that 'there is a strong positive relationship between telephone usage and urbanization.'[5] Drennan concurs in this and argues that 'the expanding information sector favors large places over small, and places with high levels of human capital rather than low levels,' and 'expansion of the information sector is accompanied by greater concentration of that sector in large metropolitan areas, despite the proliferation of distance-eliminating technologies.'[6]

A further interesting conclusion of Drennan is that counter to the notion that advances in technology do not have positive impacts on urban poor, 'the opposite appears to be the case, namely, city poverty rates are lower in metropolitan areas with higher share of earnings in financial and other producer services,' largely because these are the expanding sectors in the information technology economy and anything that pulls up the growth rate in an individual city will have positive impacts both on the employment and income picture for urban poor and for the housing and transportation infrastructures. Graham agrees that information technology has the potential to 'empower historically isolated individuals and groups and serve as a tool to enhance educational opportunities.'[7] Adequate access for low income marginalized individuals is, of course, the crucial question for public officials.

A second consideration is the demands highly educated and skilled workers have for non-job amenities of life. While some of these individuals are willing to live in rural areas with good skiing and fishing, many more look for museums, galleries, concert halls, premium dining, and the whole array of cultural and leisure time facilities that are to be found only in large cosmopolitan cities. Low wage steel and other manufacturing sector workers were not university graduates and often lived in ethnic neighborhoods that catered to their particular leisure time needs. As the work force increasingly becomes more technologically sophisticated, the assets of large cities will be increasingly attractive to these highly educated workers. Employers will seek out cities that are attractive to their high skill labor force, and cities will find they have to provide these amenities or be left behind as their competitor cities do and become centers of economic activities that are characterized by information technology, research and development, decision-making, advanced services and so forth. Research indicates that a city's cultural assets are a statistically significant determinant of urban competitiveness, both in overall competitiveness and in the ability of a city to attract and retain a highly educated and skilled work force.[8] Rogerson is correct to remind us that other things are of importance in one's perception of 'quality of life,' such as relationships with family and other people, spiritual life, health, job satisfaction and so forth, but it is other items such as cultural and other urban amenities that differentiate among cities, and that contribute significantly to their strong or weak relative competitiveness.[9] This is especially true in an economic environment that is so powerfully affected by technological advances and the application of those advances in production and distribution.

TECHNOLOGICAL ADVANCES AND THE ECONOMIES OF CITIES IN THE CONTEXT OF GLOBALIZATION

New technologies make it necessary for urban economies continually to restructure economic activities in light of their evolving comparative advantages. Giant steel complexes, such as those in Gary, Pittsburgh and Hamilton (Ontario) give way, in varying degrees, to mini-mills distributed throughout the nation in accordance with a new locational logic. Port cities lose much of their employment base as container logistics reduce the need for longshoremen and as intercontinental air cargo technologies allow flights to bypass the coasts and to land deeply in the interior of the country. New methods of organizing trucking have reduced the dominant positions of the last century's rail hubs. The recent history of such North American cities as Montreal, Vancouver, Baltimore, Chicago, St. Louis and Oakland are testament to the widespread importance of this phenomenon. Advances in information technology have made it possible for the individual activities of a firm to be located far from each other and far from the locus of central control – a production line can be monitored by a controller hundreds of miles away. Technological advance has also given rise to new products and to new industries for which the optimal location may no longer be based on factors such as a source of energy or raw material, or a transportation complex, or a market for the finished product, but rather on the existence of urban amenities that will attract a high-skill labor force, or proximity to a research university. In Chapter 2 the competitive situation of cities in this new environment was examined and in Chapter 7 we will discuss some of the ways in which cities can plan their responses most effectively. Certainly public officials do not have complete control over the events that have impacts on their city's economy, but they are with equal certainty not without any options in responding to these events.

At the most fundamental level of analysis, technological advances have dramatically reduced the need for labor in agriculture. A century ago over half of the labor force in industrialized countries was employed in agriculture; today that figure in most of them is under 5 per cent. One of the consequences has been a substantial and continuing migration from rural areas to cities. Today over 50 per cent of the Canadian population resides in its seven largest cities and two-thirds in its top 25 cities. In the USA, 58 per cent of the population lives in the 50 Consolidated Metropolitan Statistical Areas, defined as having a population of at least one million. This is up from 50 per cent of the population living in 39 CMSAs in 1990. Seventy-five per cent of Americans live in the 280 cities with populations in excess of 50 000. In the Canadian Prairies and the US Great Plains many small towns have lost so much of their population that they are on the verge of disappearing, or have already ceased to exist. Some labor is needed by large farming enterprises, but most of this work is seasonal and does not provide the basis for absorption of this immigrant labor. In North America and in Europe immigrations flows from the Third World and Central Europe are directed almost exclusively toward urban areas. Thus, the last decade or two of the 20th century have witnessed the most dramatic expansion of foreign-born urban residents since its first decade. This remarkable migration is made possible by advances in technology that have increased awareness of possible employment in industrialized economies for Third World emigrants, altered the structure and location of employment opportunities, and reduced the cost of making the trip.

Once in the city immigrants expand the labor pool, as they always have, but for the city that seeks to enhance its place in the urban hierarchy and its advantage in certain desirable areas of economic activity, this new labor force is often quite problematic. It is generally agreed by specialists in this area that immigrants have a positive net impact on the receiving country. City leaders often fix their attention on the immediate costs of new, low-skill residents – housing, schooling, health needs, increased pressure on the transportation infrastructure and so forth. The pressure for these concerns comes from workers who fear the loss of employment and lower wages and from taxpayers who are often not well informed about the actual, as opposed to the intuitive, consequences of migration.

If the immigrants have useful skills the net result is all the more positive. Immigration policies are invariably a combination of different objectives.

The USA has stressed family reunification in its approach with little requirement that the immigrant be skilled. By contrast, Canada has taken the approach of trying to enforce a policy of giving priority to immigrants with certain needed skills. Obviously this has had its impact on the qualities of the immigrant contribution to the work force in cities in both countries. While Canada has lost skilled workers to the USA for decades, it has also made up the gap this has created with skilled immigrants from Asia, Latin America and Central Europe. The gap has been filled in almost all areas of economic activity, with the exception of health care. Toronto and Vancouver have been the primary beneficiaries of these in-flows of skilled workers, largely due to their existing immigrant communities and the effect they have on the welcoming of new immigrants, as well as to their diversified economic bases. Montreal is less able to attract immigrants due to the French language requirement the government of the province of Quebec has imposed. In both Canada and the USA, excellent universities are a draw for young people from Third World countries and after their university education many of them find the job opportunities and working conditions are so attractive that they try to remain in that country. This is of obvious benefit to the cities in which they choose to reside and to work.

One of the primary elements of an innovative or a creative milieu is the ability of a city to attract a large number of individuals from other parts of its own country or from other countries. This is a common feature of creative cities as diverse as *fin-de-siècle* Vienna, pre-First World War Paris, Weimar Berlin, the Harlem Renaissance and post-Second World War New York. Each of these cities benefited enormously from migrants from the rest of the Hapsburg Empire, Europe, Central Europe, the American South and the Americas and Europe, respectively. We can see the same phenomenon with Silicon Valley and any other highly creative or innovative center in the global economy today. Thus national immigration policy, free flows of information, affordable travel and a welcoming environment are all important elements in a city's ability to enhance its competitive position and to create the economic futures to which its residents aspire.

A second impact of technological advance in the era of globalization is on the efficacy of policy response at different levels of government. Until the recent past, change in the global economy occurred relatively slowly and with ample time for national governments to comprehend the nature of the change and to design appropriate policy responses. Whether the sector was agriculture or manufacturing through the quarter-century following the Second World War, national governments adopted programs of subsidization, orderly marketing agreements and a wide variety of cleverly designed protectionist measures for favored national manufacturing firms or industries. Their actions were constrained only by the agreements, such as the GATT, to which they voluntarily subscribed and which imposed sanctions for non-compliant behavior. Other than the occasional armed conflict, the first real challenge to this world was the tripling of the price of petroleum by OPEC in 1973 and again in 1979. Here was a clear shock that had little forewarning and even less time for policy response. After OPEC's action substantial change occurred on a regular basis. Third World countries acted to realize the potential they had always been told they had for economic development and transformation by adopting a variety of policies that rapidly developed their capacity to produce intermediate and manufactured products and to assemble components for finished goods. This led to cries of anguish from negatively affected sectors, workers and regions of industrialized countries and to academic analysis of notions of global restructuring, deindustrialization, downsizing, and so forth. National governments were torn between their post-Second World War endorsement of freer trade and capital movements and the impact this was having on their own economies. While national government leaders understood the anguish, municipal and other subnational officials were the ones who were increasingly confronted with the necessity of formulating policy responses. National governments are always torn between rural and urban constituencies, between workers and corporate leaders, and between regions that are gaining from the experience and those that are losing. Metropolitan leaders in the public and private sector are faced with conflicting expectations of various groups in their political and economic region but never to the same degree that is true for national leaders. It is far easier to speak of what is best for the economic future of Denver or Philadelphia than it is for that of the United States, or even of Colorado or Pennsylvania.

But it is not just that national government decision-making processes are slow and cumbersome. Some writers, such as Ohmae, celebrated the end of the nation state and the arrival of the world 'without borders.'[10] The nation state was seen as the instigator of the many barriers to the free movement of people, goods, services and capital that generated inefficiency throughout the global economy. It can be argued that the executives of large companies and owners of capital used their clout to get national governments to reduce these barriers throughout the post-Second World War period for their benefit. But it is equally legitimate to argue that national governments were responding to the wishes of a variety of domestic constituencies or even to the power of the ideas of most economists. The result is the same: national governments have to a considerable degree imposed constraints on their capacity to come to the aid of their residents who are negatively affected by trade liberalization and technological change. Once again, we will examine more closely the process of urban economic strategic planning in Chapter 7.

At this stage of the argument, it will suffice to argue that cities have the capacity to respond quickly to the technological changes and challenges from other parts of the global economy that regularly buffets them. Chicago is an example of a city that has moved away from its traditional base in factory jobs in heavy and light manufacturing into financial and other services and some areas of technology-related and research-intense activities; Detroit is a city that has stayed with automobile production, for better or for worse. Mayor Rudy Giulani had a positive impact on New York City with his efforts to clean up the streets and to provide more safety and freedom from crime during his term in office. These urban amenity improvements had impacts on the city's attractiveness to visitors and businesses. Whether this can survive the negative consequences of the events of September 11 is yet to be determined, as will be discussed below. But it is clear that New York City was not helpless in a deteriorating situation, nor was Chicago. Pittsburgh has acted quickly in response to a deteriorating economy with expansion of technology-related activity west of the city, with its new cultural district and with plans for renewal of the downtown area. Sadly the economic base was not such that the latter succeeded, but the city did take quick action. Perhaps a more realistic assessment of the city's assets and challenges was needed.

A good test case of this assertion will be the cities in the US state of Ohio over the next few years. The US economy has lost 2.5 million jobs since 2000 and one-tenth of them have come from Ohio. The large cities of Cleveland and Cincinnati and several smaller cities have the responsibility of taking action that will turn around this loss of traditional manufacturing jobs.

TECHNOLOGY, BORDERS AND SECURITY POST-SEPTEMBER 11

The events of 11 September 2001, had as one of their least gripping, but still important, consequences the effect of raising the barriers to the international exchange of goods and services and to the free flow of workers, tourists and cross-border shoppers. The reality of contemporary production means that movement of manufacturing parts from Ontario or Tijuana is as inconvenient for a factory in St. Louis or Denver as it is for one in Buffalo or San Diego. It is not just border cities that have been affected; hence, the entirety of all national economies has an interest in re-establishing the degree of free movement that had been obtained prior to that date. Part of the response has to be one of policy, with national leaders coming to mutually satisfactory and beneficial agreements about control of their borders; the other part of the response is one that uses the most advanced technology to screen both individuals and cargoes. In North America, both the Canada–US and Mexico–US borders are receiving increased scrutiny, with the USA understandably being the keenest to establish tighter controls. But it is not just trucks and automobiles that can transport a threat to the nation; airplanes and container ships pose threats that are in many ways more challenging and potentially more cata-strophic in their impacts.

Beyond these inherently speculative concerns about the consequences of threats to national security, there are others that are more amenable to eco-nomic analysis; it is these that will be the focus of this section. These impacts will follow from a few basic notions. Cities are high density concentrations of individuals and activities that usually make optimal use of scarce ground space by stacking things vertically in buildings that may exceed 80 or more floors. Furthermore, it is efficient to cluster many of these tall buildings together so as to achieve economies in transportation, communication, a variety of services and business contact. All of these factors combine to make city centers theoretically prime targets for threats to security, whether they take the form of hijacked aircraft, as was the case on September 11, or the use of saran gas in the Tokyo subway, or explosives in the Moscow theater and subway. Currently, very serious concerns relate to nuclear, biological, chemi-cal and explosive attacks that could be made against any large city. London has long been a prime target for attacks on buildings, such as Lloyds; Jeru-salem has had an even more dramatic history of explosions in buses and buildings; most recently Madrid has joined the list of cities that have been subject to a horrific act of violence. Attacks in rural areas are far less likely due to the lower concentration of people and activities in these locations. Nonetheless, individuals and firms continue to locate in London, Jerusalem, Tokyo, Madrid and New York. In spite of the occasional horrific event, the probability that one will be a victim of this violence is sufficiently low that normal life seems to continue with only a short-run dislocation.

In some sense, while these acts of mass violence are horrific the question remains as to the impact they will have on urban economic life. A counterpart can be found in the negative impacts on the perceptions people have had of urban life that have been exercised by reports of the familiar array of urban pathologies: high crime, traffic congestion, social alienation and isolation, noise, pollution and so forth.[11] A sufficient number of individuals finds the excitement of cultural life, employment opportunities, the chance to explore various lifestyles, and the professional and social face-to-face contact with a wide variety of people to more than offset the negative aspects of urban life to maintain the population of even our largest cities. There has certainly been a movement of some activities out to suburban or edge city locations, but this took place during most of the 20th century. The city centers of vibrant cities such as New York, Boston, Chicago and San Francisco, among others, have not deteriorated as some observers anticipated they would, while some others have definitely suffered. There has been a sorting out of what activity will take place among the centers of large cities, peripheral sites within the urban space and smaller cities at a considerable distance from the large cities. So the question remains: what will be the consequence of violent attacks on national security on the vitality of our largest cities?

The first impact that can be anticipated is on the spatial location of economic activity. Glaeser and Shapiro identify four factors of significance with regard to this issue: (1) cities have always provided large numbers and safe harbor to those fleeing marauders in the country-side, (2) the low cost of transportation has always made clustering together in cities an attractive option, (3) large aggregations of people have also served as rich targets for bandits and (4) once buildings have been destroyed the question must be raised as to whether they ought to be rebuilt or simply abandoned, whether for safety or for cost considerations.[12] Cities survive violent attacks because the strength of the first two factors are positive enough to cause the fourth to be decided in the positive. Most of these cities more or less continuously blend into their peripheral areas and relocation of activities within the metro area has consequences that are less than calamitous. The most significant action in the USA was, however, the September 11 attack on New York – the action against the Pentagon in Washington and the aborted crash in rural Pennsylvania were not of the same magnitude either in human or structural impacts. New York is distinctive in the USA in that the business center has historically been an island, Manhattan, and spill-over or flight has escaped the New York area into neighboring boroughs or states, New Jersey and Connecticut. It should be noted that San Francisco is another US city that has some of this same geographical, though not its political, situation. Hence, one concern that has been raised is whether firms would abandon Manhattan and New York City in an effort to seek a location in another political entity that is less likely to be attacked. This would further weaken New York with regard to its vitality, its fiscal viability and its image as a global city. A second concern is whether the World Trade Center and its downtown neighborhood would be abandoned for office space in midtown Manhattan. Glaeser and Shapiro suggest the latter is likely for a couple of reasons. First, while downtown had been a historic location of the financial industry it had been on the decline for many years until government subsidies caused the World Trade Center to be built as the anchor of a revitalization effort. Glaeser and Shapiro conclude that in the absence of further government subsidies 'downtown New York will continue its slide.'[13] It now appears that much of this necessary subsidization will be forthcoming, but this may not be sufficient to overcome the current advantages of sites other than lower Manhattan. Second, midtown has many advantages in terms of hotels, cultural life, restaurants, and access to suburban areas. Many firms have already shifted activity northward from downtown to midtown and at some moment in time this move will have become significant enough for the 'intellectual spillovers' that have long been associated with downtown to have been duplicated elsewhere in Manhattan. The crucial question remains that of the willingness of city, state and federal governments to continue to divert sufficient revenues from other pressing needs to subsidies for financial firms, many of which seem to be doing quite well financially, to locate in one part of Manhattan rather than another, that is, to remain in Manhattan rather than somewhere else in the New York Consolidated Metropolitan Statistical Area. The case for downtown over these other areas is not apparent to dispassionate observers.

The viability of tall buildings is a second impact of the events of September 11. Edwin Mills focuses on issues such as the insurability of tall buildings, the willingness of tenants to rent space on the top floors of buildings 80 or more stories high, and the consequences of these acts of violence on transportation and residential preferences. If insurance companies are not willing to underwrite the risks attaching to tall buildings, the notion of a business center in the heart of an urban area may be decreasingly viable. Market forces will simply respond to relative prices and risks, and economic activities may be disbursed throughout a metropolitan area, with increased risks of central location being financially and safety-wise more than offsetting increased costs of contact and transportation from dispersion. Concentrations of tall buildings require workers to use subways, buses and trains to get from home to work. These are the forms of transportation that have been most subject to attack by explosives and chemical weapons since they offer concentrations of victims in one coach. Increased perception of high risk to this commuting would make automobile use more attractive since individuals are likely to be more concerned about the unknown probability of attack on mass transportation systems than the known likelihood of death or injury through automobile accident. While mass transport systems go from periphery to center in fixed paths, auto travel is done on networks of expressways that now link periphery to periphery as well as periphery to center. This could further reduce the viability of urban area central business districts in relation to suburban or edge city locations.

The third impact of September 11 we will examine is that on local finances. In both of the above aspects, the action of government is crucial to the viability of central business districts with their concentrations of high-rise buildings. And it is unlikely that local and state governments will act in the absence of substantial participation by the federal level of government in Washington. Unfortunately, the Republican administration that was in office during and after September 11 did not appear to be friendly to urban interests or issues. It is symptomatic that while the Republican Party chose to have its 2004 Presidential Convention in New York, at first House Majority Leader Tom Delay wanted to house delegates and have convention activities take place on a large ship anchored off Manhattan, thus limiting the financial benefits to the 'evil' city of the convention while also limiting the impacts of the 'evil' convention city on Republican delegates. This was changed, of course, but it does suggest the unsympathetic and negative view that some senior Party officials have for large urban centers. Admirers of city life have always argued that the post-Second World War subsidization of mass commuter transportation and mortgage deductibility were largely designed to convert urban apartment dwellers who voted Democratic into suburban home-owning Republicans. Seen in this light the recent enmity between the Bush administration and urban issues should not be at all surprising. What it does suggest is that until there is a change of government in Washington there is not likely to be the sort of support for subsidies either for cities in general or for New York in particular. One could anticipate the move from center to periphery of urban regions and to smaller cities to continue. And, of course, if one city, such as New York, should try to force the issue to stop intra-metro region relocation, both firms and individuals should be expected simply to move to another large city that would offer many of the advantages offered by the city in question.

In addition to the decisions of elected officials at all levels of government with regard to policies and funding priorities, the net result of September 11 on urban central business districts may well be decided by a battle of competing technologies. Science has made it much easier for those who wish to attack large numbers of individuals, infrastructure and structures to do so. But science is also increasing the ability of societies to discover and to neutralize these measures. Sadly, it is in the nature of this sort of interaction that societies will always be playing technological catch-up to new methods of destruction or slaughter. Since this is such a rapidly changing situation, in this chapter we will only examine a couple of the recent efforts in this regard.

Subject to acceptable levels of security, the primary issue here is the smooth and swift movement of goods across national borders. Container ships pose a potentially enormous challenge to border security forces. These containers arrive at the port of origination from thousands of plants and distribution centers in over 100 countries. Each has the possibility of being a carrier of a nuclear, chemical, explosive or biological agent or device which can be activated once in the destination port or country. To inspect each of them would be a task of such expense and time that commerce would be significantly and unacceptably curtailed. General Electric produces light bulbs under the name Osram in Slovakia. The problem facing GE is to get them into the USA in a timely and cost-effective manner. Working with the US government, through the Container Security Initiative, GE has placed an individual in the Osram plant who is certified by the US government to inspect and seal each container. Then an electronic signaling device is attached to the container so its progress can continually be monitored. When the container reaches a US port, it can quickly be determined if the seal has been tampered with, and if it has not and if the monitored progress of the container is satisfactory it can be moved from ship to truck without further inspection. A similar procedure has been introduced for truck traffic between Canada and the USA – the Free and Secure Trade (FAST) program. In this case plants are certified on a regular and continuing basis to send trucks from a plant in Canada to one in the USA with virtually no delay at the border. This is of obvious benefit for automobile companies shipping parts fabricated in one country to a production facility in the other in a just-in-time inventory system. The NEXUS program allows similar clearance for individuals who cross the border frequently and qualify for an identity-access card containing biometric data.

The Canadian, Mexican and US governments have implemented Smart Border agreements as well as a variety of other measures for, among others, pharmaceutical trade and sanitary and phytosanitary risks linked to agricultural trade. Understandably some of these measures are adopted with the interests of both security and the industry in mind. The Smart Border agreement between the USA and Mexico refers to plans to develop planning, infrastructure needs, passenger information, facilitation of travelers, exchange of information and similar things. But the document issued by the White House is rather skimpy on actual initiatives put in place. The US–Canada document, in contrast, contains 30 specific actions that have been, or will soon be, taken. These range from issuing identity cards to airport in-transit preclearance, joint (high risk) passenger analysis, harmonizing commercial processing of low-risk shipments, introducing an intelligent transportation system using GPS technology for monitoring ships and joint crime-enforcement initiatives.

Most of these initiatives to ensure secure intra-NAFTA borders could not be adopted, or even considered, without advances in technology. Hence, it is clear that the consequences of the attacks on September 11 on national economic life and on that of our largest metropolitan economies, specifically the smooth continued flow of goods and people, have been made significantly less burdensome by a wide array of applications of advanced technology.

WHO HAS THE POWER OR CONTROL IN THIS NEW ENVIRONMENT?

One of the commonly observed phenomena of the past decade is the gathering of anti-globalization protesters at meetings of such organizations as the World Trade Organization, NAFTA and the World Bank as well as meetings of officials to discuss initiatives such as the Free Trade Agreement for the

Americas. While the articulate response may be focused on the implications of these deliberations on environmental or labor policy of national governments or on their implications for workers and the ecology in general, there is a less articulate protest from individuals in all sectors of society and in all countries against a perceived loss of the ability of people to have at least some minimal control over the general context in which they live and work. As national governments have constrained themselves in their capacity to come to the aid of individuals, firms and regions that have been negatively affected by free trade and capital movements, by plant closures and by migrations of workers who are perceived to be a threat to existing jobs and incomes, individuals feel themselves to be vulnerable to monstrous forces over which they have no control. Workers with 25-dollar-per-hour jobs with good benefits lose those jobs and are hired as managers of fast food restaurants at half the income and with greatly reduced benefits. The dreams of home ownership, children in university, annual vacations and so forth disappear and there is little hope that they will be regained. Who is behind this? Where are the social agencies and political forces that were assumed to provide some protection against just this? With real incomes in the USA stagnant for the past two decades, what economic life can their children anticipate? How did it all go so wrong? Firms that have been viable for decades and have provided residents with good economic lives, now see themselves in decline, and ask the same question with the same feeling of powerlessness and frustration. Naturally, there is a visceral reaction against a system that would generate this result, in spite of what economists, out of government, may say about trade adjustment assistance, worker re-training and all the sadly under-funded policy responses to these dramatic changes.

The same can be said about metropolitan and state economies that find themselves adapting poorly to the challenges and threats to existing economic activities that emanate from competing regional economies thousands of miles away. In Chapter 2 we discussed the concept and impact of international economic competitiveness; in Chapter 7 we will examine the strategic planning options that are available to urban economies. But the fact remains that many local government leaders find themselves to be seemingly as impotent in the face of these forces of change as do individuals and firms.

This flies in the face of assertions and assurances offered by many observers that technological advance would liberate us all, including citizens of Third World countries, middle class workers in mind-numbing jobs and poor people in industrial countries, from exploitation, oppression, boredom and self-serving corporate power and corruption. Prices of goods and services would be lowered, new products would enrich our lives and workers and consumers would gain power to control the courses of their lives. Sadly, as has been the case with centuries of magical elixirs and patent medicines, for many if not most people the curative power of what was offered has proved to be far less than was promised. Jobs remain unsatisfying, only some people in only some Third World countries have seen their situation improved, urban and rural poor in industrial countries remain poor and marginalized, and recent examples from all continents show that corporate power and greed remain to be controlled. Those who are concerned with this failure to transform societies are led to examine the issue of the control of technology, of the pace of technological advance, of the application of new technology, and the relationship between those who control technological advance and the political process. Rather than being a class-neutral force for betterment, technological advance, and the in-dustries that are related to it, are designed to improve the economic and political situation of some privileged sectors or actors in society at the disregard or disadvantage of others.

Traditional economic theory has from its beginning been concerned with the question of the distribution of the gains from liberalized economic activ-ity in a society. Heckscher and Ohlin told us that the abundant factor of production would gain with free trade. In the analysis of Marx the owners of the means of production exploit those who own only their labor power. Economic geographers inform us that the center usually gains in relation to the periphery. Micro-economics tells us that those who can develop a posi-tion of market power can gain with regard to those who do not. Veblen examined the power of advertising and psychological manipulation to give sellers dominance over consumers. While efficiency in the allocation of re-sources has always been the central focus of economists, equity in the distribution of income, wealth and power has not been far behind.

Starting with the most general examination of this question, Borja and Castells argue that fundamental to the 'new techno-economic mode' is the fact that 'the deepest social exclusion processes manifest themselves in an intra-metropolitan duality, particularly in the large cities of nearly every country.'[14] Specifically, they find four processes are generating this duality: (1) the housing and urban-services crisis, (2) the persistent and growing social inequality in large cities, (3) the urban poverty affecting a good deal of the population, and (4) social-exclusion phenomena themselves. Sassen noted the development of a technologically based duality in the labor market in her seminal book *The Global City*, as had several contributors to the book *Dual City*, edited by Mollenkopf and Castells.[15] Borja and Castells conclude that this urban dualization 'reflects an urban social structure that is based on interaction between opposite and equally dynamic poles of the new informa-tional economy, whose developmental logic polarizes society, segments social groups, isolates cultures and segregates the uses of a metropolitan space that is shared by differing functions, classes and ethnic groups.'[16] To be sure, social exclusion, urban social pathologies, and dual labor markets have been with us for centuries and have been commented upon and analysed with regularity since the Industrial Revolution in England exacerbated those phenomena; what interests us here is the ways in which these most recent causal factors, rapid technological advance and the emergence of a new industrial structure, have exercised their impacts on urban economies today.

It is in this context that Borja and Castells refer to the notion Castells introduced in his *The Informational City* of a virtual economy of a 'space of flows' replacing the traditional one of a 'space of places.'[17] This new 'flow society' is one 'in which the material basis for all processes is made up of flows, and in which power and wealth are organized in global networks carrying information flows ... (consisting of) financial flows, technological flows, image creation flows, information flows.'[18] In this new global economy, its 'spatial logic is characterized by domination of the space of the flows, structured in electronic circuits that link together, globally, strategic nodes of production and management.'[19] They suggest that flows of manufactures are more important than manufacturing zones.[20] Urban hierarchies are being replaced by networks of cities. The largest of our cities will retain their importance because they have four necessary attributes; they are: (1) centers of economic, technological and business dynamism, (2) centers of cultural innovation, symbol creation, and scientific research, (3) centers of political power and (4) the connection points for the world communication system.[21] Among cities of all sizes there is a need to base the development of their economic activity on these functions and on the information flows rather than on notions of factor endowment, location, tax and subsidy policy and other traditionally important characteristics of a specific territorially-based local economy. Failure to do so will bring the dreaded economic marginalization and stagnation.

One of the consequences of advanced technology and the development of the 'space of flows' economy is the enhanced capacity of government to monitor the behavior of its citizens. Improved surveillance of movement, contact, and communication by use of mini-cameras, scrutiny of e-mail and Internet communication and access to the paper trail left after purchases of goods and services of food, airline tickets and books, and of an extensive array of things such as library activity and political participation and contributions transform the Orwellian nightmare into a reality. New technologies combined with aggressive merger and acquisition activity among large corporations in the entertainment, broadcasting, and newspaper sectors is feared to lead to a narrowing of the range of political thought, cultural values and discussion in our media. The content of this narrowed range of thought will, of course, be determined largely by those who have the material wealth to attain control over the few, large entities that will survive the consolidation process. One scholar who has examined the question of 'whether information and communication technologies, in their current forms and trends of development, are plausible democratic vectors in relations of both production and reproduction,' is François Fortier.[22] The promise of advances in technology is that in some positive or objectively desired way society will be transformed; that shortcomings of the existing society will be overcome; that individuals will gain some control over their actions in the social space, they will have higher standards of living, and better access to information and to each other. Fortier finds that little of this has been realized and that, in reality, just the opposite has happened.

Fortier focuses on the impacts of 'information and communication technologies (ICT),' which he states are 'tools and processes that permit us to produce, manipulate, and communicate information,' and include 'computer hardware, input and output peripherals, storage media, software, and digital communication systems.'[23] The primary question he raises is whether ICT enhances or diminishes the democratic process. In a globalized economy 'production is delocalized, trade and investment are liberalized, and labor is fragmented.' The result is that capital is able to shift its geographic location so as to avoid political confrontation with the state and with disaffected categories of individuals, so as to diminish the power of any individual state over it.[24] The advance of ICT is robbed of its revolutionary potential and merely enhances the logic of capitalism but does not transform it.[25] Relations among workers, managers, capitalists, men, women and so forth are not essentially changed but ICT mainly serves 'the intensification of exploitative and oppressive relations between (sic) these social sectors.'

In the 1930s, University of Chicago free-market economist Henry Simons asked whether a market economy could function without having the development of aggregations of market power lead to political power *vis-à-vis* the peoples' elected representatives and to a diminution of the democratic process. This was written in the time of Hitler, Mussolini, Salazar, Primo de Rivera, Stalin and Tojo – the totalitarian threat to democracy was impossible to avoid. Simons argued that the power of the state had to be used to stop the rot at its root through the breaking up of large corporations and unions, and imposition of a steeply progressive income tax and a confiscatory inheritance tax.[26] Almost 70 years after Simons wrote, Fortier made his assertions that: 'It is not the sovereignty of the state that is reduced so much as the sovereignty of citizens over the state.'[27] Fortier's conclusion is quite harsh as a comment on contemporary political economy and the impact on it of ICT: 'In fact, ICTs serve capitalist accumulation, its globalization, the subjugation of labor, the manipulation of consumers, the hegemonization of discourse, the surveillance of citizens and the repression of dissent rather well. They therefore contribute little to equity and democracy.'[28]

NEW THOUGHTS ON CLUSTERS, AGGLOMERATION, AND OTHER CONSTANTS

Since Alfred Marshall first examined the concept of the industrial district, economists have given considerable attention to the notions of clusters and of economies of agglomeration. The literature is filled with recent studies of the success of Silicon Valley, Cambridge, the Third Italy and so forth. One of the advantages of having firms locate in close proximity to one another is the ease of gaining skilled labor from a relatively large shared pool of workers. Another advantage is the ease of sharing information and knowledge with regard to production in that industry. What impact will advances in technology have on access to knowledge and the advantages of large cities? Will technological advances diminish the attractiveness of agglomeration and clustering? It is appropriate that this chapter should end with a discussion of some new thoughts on these traditional concepts and understandings since the previous sections have raised several considerations that bring into question some of these long-held notions. These can be summarized under the following eight potential consequences of changes in technology for structural and behavioral aspects of the economies of large cities:

1.　The importance of face-to-face contact may be reduced, thereby making large cities less valued, or it may restructure interaction in ways that make large cities valued for some sorts of activities but less valued for others.
2.　As the labor force is increasingly characterized by high skill and technology-intensive workers, urban amenities, such as cultural assets, cosmopolitan dining and shopping and high density housing will make city life more attractive.
3.　Technological advance will generate new products and new economic activities for which proximity to raw materials or transportation complexes or markets will be less important than proximity to educational and research infrastructures and a high skill labor force, and these latter assets are primarily big city attributes.
4.　Technological advance takes place in a creative milieu and this requires the mix of innovative individuals from many places, cultures and ways of thinking – large cities have always attracted these migrants.
5.　Rapid changes in the economic context require agility in implementation of a wide variety of policies and, while government does not have a history of policy agility, city governments are closer than national or regional governments to the actors who require and articulate the need for these initiatives and they have fewer competing interests, such as agricultural and rural constituencies, to challenge this policy change.

6. Post-September 11 security concerns will undoubtedly make buildings that soar above others that surround them and mass transportation, such as subways and commuter rail, strike many corporate decision-makers as obvious potential targets that should be avoided, if this is at all possible.
7. If superior levels of government are dominated by elected officials who have an anti-urban bias, city governments will be confronted with an unwillingness to continue subsidies for urban housing, infrastructure, conference centers and so forth, in deference to subsidies for rural development and agricultural producers.
8. With flows of manufactures becoming more important than manufacturing zones and with the service sector gaining in importance every year, city governments that recognize their strengths in this New Economy and that can participate in networks of cities will continue to be vital and will expand both in activity and in function; those that cannot or do not will be marginalized.

Obviously, these consequences work both in favor of cities and against them, and the net effect will be a combination of how they are seen in the eyes of the beholder and of some operational fundamentals and exigencies. We can represent these eight factors in the following utterly unscientific equation:

The importance of large cities = f (importance of face-to-face + number of high skill workers + importance of education and research + inflow of migrants + need for policy agility – security concerns – anti-urban bias of national and regional officials + importance of flows and networks).

While all but two factors favor large cities, it must be admitted that either of the two negative factors has the potential of being large enough to trump the others. A reasonably objective, but still speculative, examination of the potential impacts of an anti-urban bias in state or national government would have to recognize the potential danger, but also the negative political consequences for a government that chooses to implement aggressively policy based on this bias. It is true that city voters tend to be liberal and suburban to be conservative, but the economy of the suburbs is to a significant degree dependent upon the vitality of the city. Any extended anti-urban policy posture could in the end turn suburban voters toward the party that supported investment in the city. With regard to the security concerns, as was suggested above, this is going to be an individual appraisal of the advantages of a city location and the possibility of future terrorist attacks. On the other side of this consideration, however, must be placed the probability that other sites in rural areas or smaller cities will be subject to, among other things, natural disasters such as tornados, hurricanes, forest fires and earthquakes. What will be the net effect? Office space in a cluster of tall buildings of roughly equal height and a commute in a personal automobile may in this context appear to be relatively safe. Drennan sums this up by stating that: 'The economic gains achieved by information sector firms from clustering together in large cities are simply too great to be sacrificed in an emotional search for safety.'[29]

As a consequence, most economists and economic geographers tend to argue for the continued importance and centrality of large cities. Several writers have examined the face-to-face aspect. Howells concludes there is a 'distinct distance-decay effect in "knowledge" transfer.'[30] This is especially significant in the case of tacit rather than codified knowledge. The latter can be written down and transmitted over any distance, but tacit knowledge must be passed on from individual to individual so that in many situations 'the knowledge spillovers process remains localized and that this holds true, at least initially, for codified knowledge.' Similarly, Wood states that: 'Successful consultancy, however, requires sustained interaction with clients and is contingent on specific forms of tacit relationship ... (and) the potential available for this type of encounter to succeed is probably often much greater in core cities than in other types of region.'[31] As noted above, Gaspar and Glaeser conclude that face-to-face contact is vital and that 'we should expect cities and spatial proximity to gain importance as information technology improves.'[32] Finally, Gertler studied the importance of proximity for manufacturing firms and draws somewhat more nuanced conclusions than the others referred to here. He finds that for manufacturers 'lack of "closeness" appears to be especially onerous for smaller enterprises and for domestically owned single-plant establishments,' but he does not argue that large cities are crucial to this closeness; he also concluded that '"closeness" is to be understood in an organizational and cultural sense, as well as in the more traditional physical sense of the term.'[33] We are left with a general understanding that the need for proximity and face-to-face contact will privilege large cities, but that this advantage will not extend to all economic activities.

Few would dispute the growing importance of skilled labor, education, and research in what is often referred to as the New Economy. What is at issue is how this will affect the economic vitality of large cities. Glaeser finds that cities that have taken advantage of their supremacy in these assets have been the most successful cities during recent decades, cities such as Boston, Berlin, Minneapolis, Edinburgh and Columbus (Ohio).[34] One dissenting view is offered by Shachar and Felsenstein who find that evidence does not support the assertion of a direct and positive relationship between universities/science parks and high technology companies, even those in close proximity to them.[35] However, it must be noted that this skepticism is based on studies in small countries, Belgium, Netherlands and Israel, in which international con-

nections may be important to a degree that does not obtain for larger countries, and that the results for Israel appear to be the consequence of intervention
at the national level in a way that has failed to develop the supporting local
context for the firm. In a study of US cities, Kresl and Singh demonstrate that
the eight statistically significant determinants of urban competitiveness include the percentage of the population with university degrees, the city's
ranking according to its cultural assets (taken as a proxy for urban amenities),
and the share of the labor force in high skill categories.[36] Furthermore, the
determinants of the high skill component of the labor force include the
increase in the percentage of the population with university degrees, the
number of research centers divided by manufacturing value added and the
absolute number of cultural institutions. Lambooy corroborates this by stating that: '(T)he place-related qualities can be very important in the attraction
of knowledge-workers. In general, it can be contended that, now that distance
is less important, place-related qualities are becoming more decisive for the
development of a knowledge-based city.'[37] Clark and Hunter give more
specificity to this notion in a study that indicates that 'amenities are consistently found to influence middle-aged and older males,' with labor market
opportunities being attractive to younger workers who, in their study, are the
most attracted to central city counties; high taxes are seen as a negative factor
primarily by workers 55 or more years old.[38] For a final word on this we have
the conclusion of Daniels and Bryson:

> A focus on knowledge as the key factor of production brings us back to the
> importance of cities as pools, or potential pools, of educated workers as well as
> providing environments that are conducive to interaction between companies.
> Urban resources such as universities and science parks are becoming more clearly
> incorporated into the production system. Such environments need to be nurtured
> in order, first, to continue to attract educated workers and, secondly, to provide
> places for the interaction that leads to new products and new innovations.[39]

Advances in technology, the continued growth of the service sector, and
the rise of information technology, both as an industry itself and as a production factor in a wide range of other industries, have had and will continue to
have profound impacts on the economic viability and vitality of all large
cities. Even for many smaller cities relative obscurity and traditional isolation
will decreasingly provide a protective buffer from these contextual changes.
What, then, can be said about the prospects of large cities at this stage in the
development of the global economy? The previous sections of this chapter
summarized the most important of these factors and concluded that large
cities will continue to play an important role. The more important question is
how that role will be changed and what individual cities can do to ensure
their continued vitality. For manufacturing firms, Capello has summarized

the changes that are related to new information-communication technologies: flexible technologies of production, just-in-time production, diffused responsibility, function integration, customized production and decentralized production.[40] As a first response, she argues that firms will try to relocate the activities of the firm within its existing geographic structure – they will find new ways in which this territory will be utilized without abandoning existing sites for new ones. This entails a shuffling of tasks and a centralization of strategic functions combined with a decentralization of operations. The second response will entail the spatial relocation of firms. Central locations, such as existing headquarters, will retain decision-making and strategic functions, marketing and finance will find new locations, and production will be in peripheral locations. The same point is made for the individual urban economic space by Anas, Arnott and Small in their survey of the literature on urban spatial structure: 'the forces that are ascendant throughout the world are producing decentralization and dispersion at a citywide scale, and agglomeration at a local scale.'[41] This suggests that large cities will continue to maintain their place in the urban hierarchy, but that the range of their activities will be narrowed and strategic functions will expand.

The analysis offered by Borja and Castells that was presented earlier in this chapter also gave strong support to the continued importance of large cities because of their advantages with regard to centrality in communication, innovation and research, economic and technological dynamism, and political power. As a conclusion to his study of public and private sector networks, Malecki posits that: 'All the issues that have risen to the top of the research agenda over the past 30 years are relevant – indeed essential – for urban competitiveness. These include high-tech, agglomerations and clusters, entrepreneurship, amenities, education, knowledge ... the list goes on. Having only some of these conditions in good order is not enough; moreover, assembling them all demands public–private cooperation.'[42] A general consensus position is offered by van Geenhuizen and Nijkamp who assert that 'the city is a privileged spatial-economic actors as a result of scale and urbanization advantages.'[43]

A final issue to be raised in this chapter is whether cities that specialize will perform better than those that are more diversified in their economic activity. Research results on this question are divided in their results, as the following studies make clear. Feldman and Audretsch examined 19 US consolidated metropolitan statistical areas and innovation in 15 distinct industries. They found that 'diversity across complementary economic activities sharing a common science base is more conducive to innovation than is specialization ... (and) that the degree of local competition for new ideas within a city is more conducive to innovative activity than is a local monopoly.'[44] Drennan takes a different approach to the question by asking whether diversity or specialization has a more positive impact on a set of seven aspects of urban economic activity. His study includes 25 large US cities and 21 smaller cities. His two general conclusions are that specialization improves the level of income, and the positive relationship between per capita income and human capital has increased over time (1969 and 1996).[45] Beyond that the impact depends on the sector being studied. Specialization has a relatively positive impact on incomes and population growth in the service sector, but negative impacts in manufacturing and distribution. Thus from these two studies the conclusion seems to be that specialization is another phenomenon that is nuanced in its effects.

FINAL COMMENTS

In this chapter we have examined the effects that advances in technology are likely to have on the economic activity and even the economic vitality of large cities. Public and private sector leaders in urban economies should be aware of a few potential problems with which they will be obligated to deal if their cities are to avoid economic marginalization and stagnation. Clearly security concerns and any anti-urban bias at the state or national level are potentially powerful negative factors. However, we have suggested there are reasons to believe that neither is certain to be an important factor in the future of our major cities. Other factors are clearly in favor of the future importance of large cities. We have identified several aspects of new technologies of information-communication, production and distribution that should enhance the role of large cities in the urban hierarchy. Furthermore, as research and education grow in importance, the institutions and infrastructures that support these activities will similarly grow, and both research and education have strong presences in large cities. The work force that is required by these sectors is an educated and high income one, and is one that demands the cultural, leisure time, dining and retail, housing and transportation assets that are found almost exclusively in large cities. Certainly smaller cities with large university communities will do well, but many of the cities that have been strong in the traditional manufacturing economy and that fail to make the necessary transition are facing, and will continue to face, major challenges.

NOTES

1. Drennan, 2002, p. xi.
2. Drolet and Morissette, 2002, p. 3.1.
3. Toffler, 1980.
4. Howells, 2002, pp. 872–3.

5. Gaspar and Glaeser, 1998, p. 138.
6. Drennan, 2002, pp. 8 and 133.
7. Graham, 2001.
8. Kresl and Singh, 1999.
9. Rogerson, 1999.
10. Ohmae, 1990.
11. Bartlett, 1998.
12. Glaeser and Shapiro, 2002, pp. 205–24.
13 Glaeser and Shapiro, 2002, p. 221
14. Borja and Castells, 1997, p. 38.
15. Sassen, 1991, and Mollenkopf and Castells, 1991.
16. Borja and Castells, 1997, p. 42.
17. Castells, 1989.
18. Borja and Castells, 1997, pp. 12–13.
19. Borja and Castells, 1997, p. 44.
20. Borja and Castells, 1997, p. 27.
21. Borja and Castells, 1997, p. 31.
22. Fortier, 2001, p. 3.
23. Fortier, 2001, p. 7.
24. Fortier, 2001, p. 102.
25. Fortier, 2001, p. 5.
26. Simons, 1948, pp. 40–77.
27. Fortier, 2001, p. 103.
28. Fortier, 2001, p. 102.
29. Drennan, 2002, p. xiv.
30. Howells, 2002, p. 880.
31. Wood, 2002, p. 1001.
32. Gaspar and Glaeser, 1998, p. 137.
33. Gertler, 1995.
34. Interviewed by Wessel, 2000.
35. Shachar and Felsenstein, 1992, p. 843.
36. Kresl and Singh, 1999, pp. 336–9.
37. Lambooy, 2002, p. 1033.
38. Clark and Hunter, 1992, p. 363.
39. Daniels and Bryson, 2002, p. 989.
40. Capello, 1994, p. 203.
41. Anas *et al.*, 1998, p. 1460.
42. Malecki, 2002, p. 941.
43. van Geenhuizen and Nijkamp, unpublished paper, Delft University of Technology, October 1998, p. 2.
44. Feldman and Audretsch, 1999, p. 427.
45. Drennan, 2002, pp. 110–111.

5. Urban governance in the era of globalization

Economic globalization is a fact of life. Naturally, much attention has been paid both to globalization and the ICT revolution, but relatively little to a key third leg of the 21st century tripod, urbanization. Globalization is intensifying, and the rapidity of technological change is without precedent. Distance, time and place have become less important in the knowledge economy, and this may call into question the future of cities, or at least of central cities, in spite of the trend toward growing urbanization. Dreier, Mollenkopf and Swanstrom suggest that at first glance globalization and a world of 'virtual communication could render obsolete the traditional reasons why people gathered together in cities: to be close to jobs, culture and education, and shopping.'[1] Peter Drucker goes even further and presents one of the more radical perspectives on the future of central cities:

> Today's city was created by the great breakthrough of the nineteenth century: the ability to move people to work by means of train and streetcar, bicycle and automobile. It will be transformed by the great twentieth-century breakthrough: the ability to move work to people by moving ideas and information. In fact, the city central Tokyo, central New York, central Los Angeles, central London, central Paris, central Bombay has already outlived its usefulness. We no longer can move people into and out of it, as witness the two-hour trips in packed railroad carriages to reach the Tokyo or New York office buildings, the chaos in London's Piccadilly Circus, or the two-hour traffic jams on the Los Angeles freeways every morning and evening. We are already beginning to move the information to where the people are outside the cities in such work as the handling of credit cards, of engineering designs, of insurance policies and insurance claims, or of medical records. Increasingly people will work in their homes or, as many more are likely to do, in small 'office satellites' outside the crowded central city. The facsimile machine, the telephone, the two-way video screen, the telex, the teleconference are taking over from railroad, automobile, and from airplane as well. The real-estate boom in all the big cities in the seventies and eighties, and the attendant skyscraper explosion, are not signs of health. They signal the beginning of the end of the central city. The decline may be slow; but we no longer need that great achievement, the central city, at least not in its present form.[2]

Drucker wrote this passage near the end of the 1980s and the ICT revolution has continued unabated, with the wireless Internet, cell phones and other innovations seemingly fortifying his argumentation. In spite of this, people continue to flock to municipalities at a rapid rate, and the 21st century will be known as the first 'urban century' with over half of humanity congregated in municipalities by the end of the first decade of the century and perhaps two-thirds by as early as the third decade.[3] In addition, urbanization will transform just about every corner of the world, with 76 per cent of the population of the North and 41 per cent in developing countries already urbanized. Moreover, the urban population of Latin America, Asia and Africa will explode, doubling in just the short period between 2000 and 2025.[4] At the end of 2003, the United Nations published new estimates of global population growth, with 2.6 billion people expected to be added by 2050, the vast majority of whom will be concentrated in urban centers of the developing world. The development of large cities will also continue, and by 2015 there will likely be 27 cities with more than 10 million inhabitants and 516 with more than one million, with the total urban population globally surpassing 4 billion.[5] In addition, the agglomeration of vast metro populations is also occurring, with only small distances separating populations of 20 to 30 million people in such areas as the Pearl River Delta between Hong Kong and Guangzhou, the Jakarta–Surabaya corridor, and Japan's Tokaido region which includes Tokyo, Nagoya and Osaka.

Without any doubt, in an era of globalization, the governance of small, medium, and large municipalities is more challenging than ever before. Jeffrey Sellers refers to a new age of 'global urban dualization' which is leading to a profound urban transformation, adding that 'newly localized governance inhabits a world of nations-states, multilevel policies, transnational information flows, global firms and international regimes.'[6] At a minimum, will the public sector at the municipal level be able to keep pace with unprecedented change in the civil society it represents? The former chief administrative officer of a mid-sized Canadian city opines that 'all municipalities are coming to realize that it is not enough simply to do well in relation to last year or their neighboring municipality. Economic regions, often more than provinces or countries, are competing with one another in the global economy.' He adds that 'municipal governments must project an approach that says they understand the need to be competitive and to be accountable for that competitive position in a way that satisfies any objective observer, critic, or investor.'[7]

So much is expected of those who govern modern cities. UN-Habitat defines good urban governance in the following manner:

> Urban governance is inextricably linked to the welfare of the citizenry. Good urban governance must enable women and men to access the benefits of urban citizenship. Good urban governance, based on the principle of urban citizenship, affirms that no man, woman or child can be denied access to the necessities of urban life, including adequate shelter, security of tenure, safe water, sanitation, a

clean environment, health, education and nutrition, employment and public safety and mobility. Through good urban governance, citizens are provided with the platform which will allow them to use their talents to the full to improve their social and economic conditions.[8]

In order to achieve good governance, UN-Habitat insists that there should be (a) legitimacy and accountability of government, (b) freedom of association and participation, (c) empowerment of women as a key poverty eradication strategy, (d) fairer and legal frameworks for a predictable and secure living environment for citizens, (e) availability and validity of information, (f) efficient public sector management and (g) formal mechanisms for taking into account the needs of children in the decision-making process.[9] It adds that vital component parts of good governance should include sustainability, subsidiarity, equity, efficiency, transparency and accountability, civic engagement and citizenship, and security.[10]

Ideally, municipal officials will deliver 'urban amenity, efficiency, sustainability, environmental quality, increased livability, urban competitiveness, reduced development costs, minimal housing and infrastructure backlogs,' and that is just the beginning of the list.[11] All of these goals are apparently to be accomplished regardless of global conditions, unprecedented technological change and accelerated creative destruction, the actions of regional and national governments, and the performance of the local private sector. To govern urban regions effectively in the 21st century is a monumental task, and the success or failure in achieving efficient and equitable governance at the local level will significantly affect overall global prosperity and vitality in the decades ahead. Peter Hall adds that cities in Europe, North America, Asia, and Australasia currently 'compete for primacy in transport and communication hubs, market places, finance centers, regional centers, entertainment and major event centers and centers for major projects, company headquarters, producer services, and high tech firms.'[12]

This chapter will examine the major challenges now being faced by municipal leaders and then offer an initial blueprint for successful municipal governance.

THE SETTING

From a global perspective, Peter Hall and Ulrich Pfeiffer divide major cities in the world into three distinct categories. The first category is designated as *hypergrowth cities* which are primarily found in Sub-Saharan Africa, the Indian subcontinent, the Middle East and some poorer areas in Latin America. They are rushing to keep up with explosive growth, much occurring because of the influx of people from the countryside. They must deal with urgent issues such an infant mortality and other severe health and nutrition problems, and still cope with developing an infrastructure which will help to create new jobs on a timely basis. The second category consists of *dynamic growth cities* which are at the stage of developing a significant middle-income group of residents. These cities are found in much of Eastern Europe, Latin America and certain parts of the Middle East. They are growing at a very rapid rate and are hoping to push forward with economic development so that they can provide the quality-of-life amenities which middle-income residents increasingly expect. The third category consists of *mature cities* which are found in the North and encompass North America, Europe, Japan, parts of East Asia and Australasia. These cities are characterized by 'stable or declining population, the challenge of aging and of household fissioning, slow economic growth and adaptation, and social polarization.'[13] In all three categories, urbanization is considered as the 'precondition' for successful development, and 'cities are engines of growth. They make people more productive.'[14] To be more precise, 'cities are quintessentially places that offer opportunities and risks, obscene inequalities and extraordinary opportunities.'[15]

Although this chapter will deal almost exclusively with metropolitan areas in the North, much of the discussion should be germane for municipal leaders in the South. However, one must freely admit that even within the countries of the North, municipal governance can differ rather dramatically. First of all, most of the countries have unitary systems which concentrate the preponderance of governmental authority at the central level. A few, including the three major nations of North America, have federal systems which divide authority between national and regional governments. Intergovernmental relations which can be so crucial to the overall development of municipalities can be quite different in unitary as opposed to federal systems. Moreover, even within unitary or federal systems, municipal governance and intergovernmental linkages can differ dramatically, such as the major differences between the United States and Canada. Secondly, many consider municipal governance in Europe to be guided by a different set of priorities than similar governance within the United States. For the members of the European Union, 'Europeanization offers cities a relative capacity to escape the constraints and hierarchies of the national political system,' or at least some of the constraints.[16] If a European model exists, it may well exemplify an emphasis on strong social citizenship and relative equality, whereas the US model often relies on finance-driven capitalism and is more tolerant of inequality.[17]

CHALLENGES FACING THOSE WHO GOVERN MODERN METROPOLITAN AREAS

With the lion's share of export activity, foreign direct and portfolio investment, business creation and destruction, and the settlement of immigrants occurring within large urban centers in the North, much of the impact of globalization is being felt by residents of municipalities. It would be nice to have the ability to develop a special template that could be used by all city leaders to improve municipal governance in an era of globalization. Or it would be nice to compile a list of 'best practices' from cities around the world and anticipate they could be easily adapted globally. Unfortunately, such easy solutions do not exist. This section will discuss some of the major challenges to governance facing cities located primarily in the United States and Canada.

The United States has both a large number of government units and a huge population base. At the end of July 2002, 3034 county governments, 19 429 municipal governments, 16 504 town or township governments, 13 504 school districts and 35 052 special districts with functions as diverse as mandating limits on pollution to the eradication of mosquitoes, were operational in the United States.[18] The USA has also experienced explosive population growth over the past century, with the population base of 74 million in 1900 increasing to 157 million in 1950 and then to 294 million in 2004. During the 1990s, the US population grew by 33 million, and the number of people residing in the United States is expected to increase to at least 500 million by the end of the century, or by an average of more than 20 million each decade.[19]

Almost all of the growth during the 1990s occurred within metro areas, but relatively little in the central cities of the metropolitan region. Indeed, 83 per cent of the population growth in the top 50 metro areas was attributable to suburban growth, with the central cities in 43 of these areas actually having a smaller percentage of their metro area's total population in 2000 compared with 1990.[20] Approximately 72 per cent of the total metropolitan population in the United States is now suburban, and this is expected to increase to 76.5 per cent by 2020. Is it possible to govern urban areas rationally and efficiently in view of the huge number of separate government entities and the disparate fortunes being experienced by central and suburban cities within the same metropolitan area?

The following provides a laundry list of challenges facing mainly US cities, but urban leaders around the world will be able to identify with many of them.

Challenge of Place

Revolutionary changes in transportation, communications, and technology in general especially the growing influence of cyberspace, have given added impetus to 'space' and diminished emphasis to 'place.' It took humankind only 66 years from the first manned flight on earth at Kitty Hawk to land a craft on the moon. In the very near future, small regional jets and a new generation of compact commuter planes, capable of carrying a handful of people, should allow residents of even modest-sized communities situated in relatively remote places to be within easy reach of major metro airports, from where they can travel to cities around the world within the same day. Basic innovations such as central heating have made cold places much more bearable, including northern tier cities in the United States and almost all major cities in Canada, Russia and Scandinavia, as well as extreme southern tier cities in South America, Africa and Australasia. Air conditioning has done the same for cities in the tropics and very warm desert areas. Daniel Solomon reaches the following conclusion about technological change and human settlements: 'The technology of the last century – the automobile, the air conditioner, television, and the computer – have each in different ways transformed human settlements, habitation, and work.'[21]

Nevertheless, place still matters. There are often major advantages to being situated next to oceans or in areas with mild climates and abundant sunshine. During the 1990s in the United States, 'warm, dry places grew. Cold, wet places declined.'[22] Indeed, regional location and climate were the most important factors for growth during that decade, with the human-capital base ranking second.[23] Over the past several decades, there has been a significant population movement away from the US Northeast and the so-called 'rust belt' of the Midwest to the South and the West. This drift southward and westward is best exemplified by the 85 per cent growth in the population of Las Vegas during the 1990s, whereas Hartford, Connecticut suffered a 15 per cent decline during the same decade.[24] Cities with harsh climates or in rugged terrains face special challenges in maintaining their population and economic bases in an era when human mobility both domestically and internationally is at record levels. It is often said facetiously that the four seasons in Los Angeles consist of earthquakes, fire, mudslides and drought. Although these conditions can indeed cause significant damage, many local leaders around the world would be ecstatic to have the abundant sunshine, moderate temperatures, beautiful beaches, modern seaports, and close proximity to large and affluent consumer markets enjoyed by the urban residents of coastal southern California.

Creative Destruction

This phenomenon discussed briefly in Chapter 1 is occurring in a variety of areas. In the field of immigration, almost all new arrivals to the United States are settling in urban areas, but in some of these cities native-born Americans are leaving both inner cities and the near suburbs, leading to major changes in the ethnic and linguistic composition of the urban region. Large cities such as Detroit, which was once the world's role model for economic development during the Fordist era, have been decimated by the loss of manufacturing jobs, many of which have been transferred overseas to lower-wage metro areas. Smaller retail establishments, especially those in inner cities, have been unable to compete effectively against the large suburban malls. Many have also succumbed to the 'Wal-Martization' of the North American economy. As Robert B. Reich points out, 'Wal-Mart is the logical end and the future of the economy in a society whose pre-eminent value is getting the best deal.'[25] Wal-Mart has emerged as the largest corporation in the United States in terms of revenues and is also the largest private employer in Mexico.[26] It is the USA's largest grocer, toy seller and furniture retailer, operating nearly 3000 stores in the United States and planning to add another 1000 over the next five years. It accounts for 20 per cent of the total sales of the 100 largest retailers in the United States and locates almost all of its stores in suburbs.[27] Many small retailers simply cannot compete against Wal-Mart and this has had a devastating effect on urban retail establishments and retail workers, especially those hoping to survive in downtown locations.

With merger and acquisition activity reaching record highs in the period up to September 2001, the business composition of some cities has been altered substantially, and along with that the civic contributions made by corporations have changed dramatically. For example, Los Angeles was once world headquarters for the *Los Angeles Times*, Atlantic Richfield, and a number of other companies which over the past few years have been absorbed by other corporate entities with headquarters far away from Los Angeles. In general, corporate giving and corporate sponsorship for civic projects traditionally provided by these targeted companies have waned. Seattle has also felt the impact of Boeing moving its corporate headquarters to Chicago, where it sought out a 'more globalized' city. Idec Pharmaceuticals of San Diego is one of the world's largest companies in its field of specialty and was a significant contributor to local community projects. In 2003, it was purchased by its rival Biogen for 6.8 billion dollars and its headquarters have now been moved to Cambridge, Massachusetts.[28] Such losses often portend not only less involvement in civic projects, but also a diminution in important service-related jobs such as legal and accounting staffs which are associated so closely with corporate headquarters.

Creative destruction has also gravely affected the local work force. With so many cities losing relatively high-paying manufacturing jobs, workers have either moved elsewhere, found employment in lower-paying service-related jobs, or collected unemployment and welfare checks until such time as they could find some sort of employment. In the United States today, over 30 million jobs are lost annually, many in the manufacturing sphere and many concentrated in urban areas. Fortunately, usually over 30 million jobs are also created each and every year, but the distribution of job creation differs significantly from industry to industry and city to city (in 2002, 32.2 million jobs out of roughly 114 million in the private sector were lost, while 31.7 million were created).[29] One job loss at General Motors does not correspond equally with one job created at Wal-Mart, because wages and fringe benefits at General Motors might equal roughly 25 dollars per hour versus wages and fringe benefits at Wal-Mart at less than half that level. With cities so dependent on property and retail sales taxes for their revenue base, these rapid shifts in business and job prospects can wreak havoc on municipal budgets from one year to the next.

Political Fragmentation

The 15 largest metropolitan areas in the United States each have on average 520 distinct governmental units, and many reflect a great deal of regional polarization and balkanization.[30] Los Angeles is the 'quintessential fragmented metropolis' with its five-county region home to 16 million people in a land area almost the size of Ohio and with a production base equal to the twelfth largest national economy in the world.[31] Within the greater Los Angeles region are to be found more than 200 separate cities, of which 33 have over 100 000 residents. Hundreds of special districts are also scattered around the region. Its overall population grew by 25 per cent during the 1980s and 13 per cent during the 1990s.[32] In order to enhance its overall economic competitiveness, the metro region was in dire need of improving its capacity to move goods to and from the ports of Los Angeles and Long Beach, the busiest ports by far in North America. The lack of metro-wide coordination had resulted in major bottlenecks in getting containers off ships and on to trucks and trains which would transport them throughout the region and many parts of the continent. It took many years to convince the various government units to band together in order to build a new transportation grid known as the Alameda Corridor, a 20-mile rail connector, with half below the surface level, running from the seaports to the main rail and truck transfer facilities.[33] Even though it was very clear that the metro region would benefit enormously from the corridor project, various governments worried about how the new transportation routes would affect their own local populations, resorting to the not-in-my-backyard (NIMBY) posture. Eventually the project was completed, but not without some delays and questionable compromises.

The United States also suffers from some of the most egregious central city-suburban city cleavages in the entire world, and is infamous for its urban sprawl. According to a Brookings Institution study, the developed areas of cities increased by 47 per cent between 1982 and 1997, compared with a population growth in the affected areas of only 17 per cent.[34] In most major urban areas, population density continues to decline, with the notable exception of municipalities hemmed in by water, mountains or federal and state government-owned land. Urban sprawl is largely attributable to population pressures, racial and ethnic disharmony, transportation infrastructures, land speculation, school-financing systems, the shifting of jobs from core areas to suburban enclaves, competition among municipalities for tax revenues and a proclivity among Americans for detached homes with yards.[35] This sprawl phenomenon helps to weaken older communities within central cities and the older tier of suburbs immediately adjacent to the central city, as emphasized by Bruce Katz, Director of the Brookings Center on Urban and Metropolitan Policy.[36] When core cities and their near suburbs begin to lose population, the first reaction of local officials is generally to raise property taxes in order to compensate for the loss of taxpayers, a short-term fix which may eventually accelerate the exodus of residents to the outer rings of the metro region where property taxes are relatively low.[37] This cycle thus exacerbates the difficult conditions already facing inner cities and may also threaten older suburbs, with Myron Orfield, Executive Director of the Metropolitan Area Research Corporation in Minneapolis, estimating that 40 per cent of the population in the 25 largest US metro areas now lives in 'at risk suburbs.'[38] Peter Hall believes that Chicago, Detroit and Atlanta are among the US cities which confront deteriorating conditions in the inner rings, stating that they face 'an isolated island of mega-development, separated from the rest of the city and suburbs by a wide belt of decay and dereliction.'[39]

Jurisdictional competition and rivalries are also legendary with cities in the same metro area often pitted against one another to provide investment incentive packages to corporations in order to entice them to locate to their particular area of jurisdiction or to convince them not to leave. New York City, for example, has provided billions of dollars in incentives to some of the largest corporations in the United States in order to keep their facilities within the five boroughs instead of moving them a few miles to nearby suburbs in New Jersey or Connecticut.[40]

International and Internal Migration

As mentioned earlier, the US population growth during the 1990s was the largest ever experienced. Fifty-nine per cent of this growth was attributable to immigrants and births to immigrants who arrived during the 1990s, with more than one-half of these immigrants coming from Latin America, mainly Mexico. Ninety-five per cent of immigrants settled in urban areas, and almost one-half of the total foreign-born population of 32.5 million in 2002 lived in the Los Angeles, New York City, San Francisco, Miami and Chicago metro regions.[41] In Canada, 78 per cent of new immigrants settled in Toronto, Vancouver, Montreal, Calgary, and Ottawa.[42] In New York City, the foreign-born population increased by 975 000 or 38 per cent during the 1990s, constituting 36 per cent of the population of the five boroughs.[43] Just shy of one-half of the total metro population over the age of five in New York City spoke a language other than English at home in 2000 compared with 41 per cent in 1990, and approximately 14 per cent of families included at least one undocumented immigrant.[44] Some studies indicate that the average first-generation immigrant imposes about a 25 000 dollar cost on state and local governments during his or her lifetime, whereas second and third-generation immigrants become net financial contributors to these levels of government.[45] Consequently, the inflow of immigrants, especially those with limited educational backgrounds and skills, into major metro areas can have an immediate deleterious effect on local government finances.

Residential Segregation and Concentration of Poverty

Among the nations of the North, the United States has the dubious honor of having the most profound segregation of ethnic and racial groups in the urban landscape, plus the highest concentration of poverty within inner cities. Dreier, Mollenkopf and Swanstrom conclude that 'no other country has urbanized areas that are so sprawled out and economically segregated.'[46] Marcuse and van Kempen stress these characteristics and describe what they consider to be the 'undesired US model of urban spatial form and social content, including (a) increased segregation, (b) shrinkage of public amenities, (c) commercialization of civic life, (d) the decline of central cities and (e) social polarization.[47]

In 1990, the median US household income in central cities was less than 75 per cent of the median income in the suburbs, the unemployment rate was 70 per cent higher, and the poverty rate in central-city households was over twice as high.[48] One should add that the plight of many residents in central cities in the United States is shared by some residents in other cities around the world, such as in some of the *banlieues* surrounding Paris and various larger cities in the United Kingdom, or in Canada where aboriginal groups living in urban settings suffer from a 55 per cent poverty rate.[49]

In 1950, almost 70 per cent of the population in the 168 largest metro areas in the United States lived in central cities; by 1990, over 60 per cent of the population in the 320 largest metro areas resided in suburbs and a majority of the jobs was also found in suburban locales.[50] Among the dozen largest central cities in the United States in 1950, ten hit their highest population levels during that decade, even though almost all metropolitan areas continued to grow over subsequent decades.[51] To illustrate the dwindling population base of some major central cities, the number of residents in Detroit declined from 1.85 million in 1950 to 925 000 in 2002, and the number of Cleveland's residents from 915 000 in 1950 to 468 000 in 2002.[52] During 2003, the mayor of Pittsburgh asked the governor of Pennsylvania to put into effect Act 47, an action tantamount to a declaration of municipal bankruptcy. Pittsburgh's credit rating was slashed by Standard and Poor's to below investment grade, the lowest of any major city in the United States. If Act 47 were ever implemented, it would place Pittsburgh under direct state government control in a last-ditch effort to manage its onerous debt problems. In 1950, the City of Pittsburgh had 677 000 residents. This number had dwindled to 328 000 by 2002, but the municipal government continued in its efforts to maintain and modernize the city's infrastructure and provide expensive public safety services to a population which had gradually been halved over the previous five decades. Mayor Tom Murphy blamed Pittsburgh's predicament in part on the lack of support from its suburban governments and even alleged that racist views harbored by some suburban government representatives were impeding metro-wide cooperation.[53]

During the 1990s, four of every five new additions to the US population were 'persons of color'or what the Canadian government refers to as 'visible minorities,' and many of these new residents wound up in segregated urban neighborhoods.[54] This influx resulted in a majority of central US cities becoming 'majority "minority"' for the first time in American history.'[55] In effect, the 100 largest cities continued the transformation of becoming 'truly multiracial, multicultural centers.'[56] The non-Hispanic white share of the population of these 100 largest cities fell from 52 per cent in 1990 to 44 per cent in 2000, with about two million whites exiting these metropolitan areas. In contrast, the Hispanic population grew in 97 of the 100 cities and the Asian population grew in 95, whereas the black population fell slightly from 24.7 per cent of total residents in 1990 to 24.1 per cent a decade later.[57]

Ethnic and racial groups in the large US metro areas are still living apart from one another. More than three-quarters of blacks in the Washington, DC metro area live in neighborhoods which are at least 80 per cent black.[58] No racial or ethnic group constitutes a majority in the Los Angeles metro area, but 71 per cent of students enrolled in the Los Angeles Unified School District is Hispanic.[59] Urban residential segregation remains very high in the United States, although the 2000 Census did reveal that segregation between blacks and non-blacks actually declined in 272 metro areas between 1990 and 2000, whereas it increased in only 19 areas.[60] However, urban segregation on the basis of ethnicity, race, or linguistic community still remains very high, and John Logan predicts that 'rather than disappearing, residential segregation is extending beyond the city limits and adding new colors, and it promises to persist as an American dilemma well into the 21st century.'[61]

In 1990, almost 85 per cent of high-poverty census tracts in the United States was situated in urban areas, with 'underclass ghetto poverty' defined as residential areas where over 40 per cent of the people live below the official poverty line.[62] In 2000, the federal government classified one in eight central cities as 'doubly burdened,' defined as having at least two of the following three conditions: (a) an unemployment rate at least 50 per cent higher than the national average; (b) a poverty rate at least 20 per cent higher than the national average; or (c) a loss of population of at least 5 per cent since 1980.[63] Among the list of doubly-burdened cities were New York City, Los Angeles, Dayton, Ohio and Flint, Michigan, and central city residents in general continue to lag behind suburban residents in income and jobs, with the median-income differential between cities and their suburbs widening over the past two decades.[64] An alarmingly high percentage of residents in inner cities receives welfare payments and has access to very limited funds, and they often pay more for goods and services than their richer counterparts in the suburbs. For example, many of the large grocery chain or department stores, which usually offer the most competitive prices through high-volume purchasing, refuse to locate in areas of concentrated poverty, leaving the local business to small street-corner merchants who invariably charge higher prices and offer a much more limited selection of items. Dreier, Mollenkopf and Swanstrom emphasize that the poor in central cities allocate about 30 per cent of their income for food versus a national average of less than 13 per cent. They add that the poor are much more likely to rely on pawnbrokers and check-cashing services because of the relative absence of full-service banks in their neighborhoods.[65] Because of high crime rates, insurance for modest homes or apartments and for automobiles in the inner cities also tends to be much higher than in the surrounding suburbs.

Myron Orfield refers to modern US 'metropolitics' as often resulting in concentrated poverty, urban sprawl and inequitable distribution of resources.[66] He points out that students in segregated minority schools are 11 times more likely to be in schools with concentrated poverty, whereas 92 per cent of predominantly white schools does not face a similar problem. Both residential segregation and inequity in the distribution of property taxes help explain this differential, and school segregation actually rose during the 1990s in US urban areas.[67]

There is not only a big disconnect between urban and suburban schooling opportunities, but also between where jobs are located and where potential job seekers live. In the United States, two-thirds of new jobs are located in the suburbs, whereas three-quarters of welfare recipients who desperately need work opportunities are located in central cities or rural areas.[68] Inadequate, affordable mass transit from the inner-city neighborhoods to the work sites in the suburbs has impeded many welfare recipients from securing meaningful employment opportunities.

Fortunately, residential segregation and the concentration of poverty in urban areas are not being replicated by most cities in other countries in the North. In Europe, for example, place of residence seems to have little effect on social mobility, and 'the poor are much more integrated with the lives of the working and lower-middle classes than are the poor in American cities.'[69] This, of course, was not always the case, especially in the great industrial cities of Great Britain during the 19th century where widespread poverty, pollution, sewerage problems, absence of potable water, infectious diseases and the lack of nutritious foods provided ample fodder for criticisms lodged by Charles Dickens, Karl Marx, Friedrich Engels and others.[70] An additional important contemporary contrast between the United States and Europe is that in the latter education is funded nationally and good schools are less dependent on the prosperity of local neighborhoods.[71]

Another great irony of the American experience is that many well-to-do urban dwellers practice their own self-imposed version of residential segregation. Roughly one in six Americans lives in communities governed by a homeowners' association ranging from co-op buildings to suburban subdivisions, and these people represent among the most affluent elements of urban society. These associations often determine the rules of the game for what goes on within the residential boundaries, and an increasing number are walled off from the surrounding metro area through locked and guarded main doors or gated residential entrances.[72] In effect, by virtue of having abundant financial resources, many of these people perceive that they are able to enjoy the positive features of urban existence while barricading themselves away from what they consider to be the unsavory elements of city life. This conscious effort of self-isolation and exclusion, which often also results in sending their children to private schools, means that adults with the resources and acumen to help solve major urban problems deliberately remove themselves from the required regenerative process.

Limited Intergovernmental Cooperation

Whether in unitary or federal systems, cities are generally treated as 'creations' of higher levels of government and subject to their tutelage and control. The Canadian constitution clearly places provincial governments in control of municipalities within their jurisdiction, empowering provincial leaders to create, disband or otherwise alter governments and boundaries at the local level. This has resulted in Canadian cities being treated at the 'political margins' by Ottawa and the ten provincial governments.[73] State governments in the United States exercise similar authority over their local governments, and federal government policies have often been biased in favor of municipal fragmentation and suburbanization over the past five decades.[74] In most unitary systems, the national government is provided with ultimate jurisdiction over local governance.

In too many ways, cities are treated as marginal actors in intergovernmental relations and relegated to a very low position on the food chain when it comes to governance issues. They also suffer the consequences of misguided decisions made at higher levels of government. National, state and provincial governments in the United States and Canada often saddle cities with 'unfunded mandates,' requiring municipal leaders to carry out certain functions without providing adequate funds to pay for these new responsibilities.[75] This has certainly been the case in the United States after September 11 where municipalities have been expected to assume more anti-terrorism duties and improve first-response emergency services with very limited funding provided by Washington, DC or the state capitals. Washington's insistence on much more stringent visa standards for foreigners to visit the United States has also sharply curtailed tourism earnings for many cities. In 2000, foreigners visiting the United States spent over 100 billion dollars, including passenger fares, and accounted for almost one million local jobs. In 2002, foreign visitations were 20 per cent below 2000 levels. In contrast, world tourism returned to record levels in 2002 after the disquieting events of September 2001, with 703 million international visits and spending by these visitors totaling 474 billion dollars.[76] Unfortunately, international visits to the United States fell from 50.9 million in 2000 to 44.9 million in 2001 and then to 41.9 million in 2002. Revenues generated by these visitors, including passenger fares, plummeted from 103 billion dollars in 2000 to 83.6 billion dollars in 2002, and the number of international visitors is not expected to return to 2000 levels until late in the current decade.[77] In large part, this drastic decline in visits from abroad is attributable to new federal government policies and the projection of an image abroad that Washington is not very interested in having foreigners come to the United States, in spite of the key revenue generator and job creator international tourism represents for New York City, Miami, Orlando, Los Angeles, Las Vegas and scores of other US cities.

The dialogue between national, regional and local leaders is very sporadic in most countries, and especially so in the United States where little interaction occurs between federal and local officials. From the 1950s onward, federal policy consistently supported urban sprawl and suburbanization as massive funding was provided for new highways leading to near and distant suburbs, but relatively little was allocated for urban renewal and local mass transit. Federal and state tax laws also often favor suburban developers at the expense of new development or restoration in central cities. Even though most Americans are urbanized, intergovernmental cooperation devoted to improving urban life, especially in inner cities, leaves much to be desired. The US government's Department of Housing and Urban Development has played a very modest role in shaping overall urban policy, and this, unfortunately, has been mirrored in neighboring Canada where a federal Ministry of State for Urban Affairs was finally created in 1971, over a century after Canada became a sovereign country, only to disbanded eight years later.

Inadequate Revenue-generation Flexibility and Urban Public Investment

Many cities around the world are faced with limited flexibility in generating sufficient local revenue to carry out needed reforms which will assist the urban population to compete effectively in an era of economic globalization. As a consequence, many remain very dependent on transfers from higher levels of government, with the amount of payments predicated on the particular priorities of officials who are far removed from the local operations of government. In the United States, transfers from Washington and the states are diminishing as a percentage of total local government revenues, and relatively few funds are available for major public investment projects such as infrastructure modernization. In 2002, general fund revenue for the municipal sector consisted of 26 per cent being derived from property taxes, 13 per cent from sales taxes, 7 per cent from local income taxes, 14 per cent from other types of taxes, 10 per cent from special fees and charges, 13 per cent from state aid, 2 per cent from federal aid, and 15 per cent from other revenues.[78] In the period 1998–2002 in Canada, federal revenues increased over 33 per cent, provincial revenues 26 per cent, but local government revenues only 7.7 per cent, in part because of the onerous restrictions placed on local officials in raising funds.[79] Federal and provincial government transfer payments in Canada in 2000 represented only 18.7 per cent of total municipal revenues, compared with 27 per cent for cities in the United States and 31 per cent for cities in the European Union.[80] US cities often have more flexibility to impose taxes and user fees than their Canadian counterparts, but even here it differs from state to state. California's Proposition 13, which was overwhelmingly approved by voters in 1978, severely limits the ability of local governments to generate revenues from property taxes. As a result, these governments rely more extensively on sales tax revenue and often attempt to attract retail establishments in order to garner new taxes, thereby distorting the overall needs of the community in terms of a balanced mixture of manufacturing, commercial and residential properties.

The economic downturn in 2001 and 2002, rapidly escalating health-care and pension costs, additional unfunded mandates handed down by the federal and state governments, and diminished transfer payments from the higher levels have left US cities to face a severe fiscal crisis. When asked the question in a National League of Cities' survey on whether they were less able to meet financial needs this year than in the previous year, the negative responses were the highest ever recorded since the survey was first administered in 1990. Eighty-one per cent of municipal representatives responded negatively for 2003, and 83 per cent perceived that 2004 would be worse than 2003.[81] The inability of cities to raise sufficient revenues locally, when combined with a proportional drop in intergovernmental transfers, has left some US cities in dire financial straits. Moreover, even when the economy improves, there is a big question about how many new jobs will be created in the central cities, and how much more financial burden will be shouldered by municipal governments in a nation with a rapidly ageing population base.

Limited or Misguided Infrastructure Modernization

Silicon Valley has been viewed by many around the world as the ideal model for economic development, but even this region has been heavily burdened with astronomically high housing costs and perpetually clogged freeways. Cities have limited funds to develop world-class infrastructures with transfers from higher levels of government for such investments usually being quite sparse. Several cities have also engaged in rather ill-conceived projects to develop huge convention space in order to attract business conferences, and sports stadia in an effort to entice people from the suburbs downtown to witness professional football, soccer, baseball, basketball or other athletic events. The ability to attract and maintain professional sports teams is frequently considered as the ultimate badge of approval conferring 'big city' status nationally or even internationally. In the case of Montreal and the 1976 Summer Olympics, city and provincial residents are still paying for the costs of the Olympic Stadium which is already beginning to crumble. The Canadian Football League team in Montreal no longer plays its games in the stadium, and the professional baseball team will soon be departing to a location south of Canada's border. Other city leaders also seem to forget that professional teams are owned by private individuals or corporations and that these private entities should take the responsibility for building and maintaining their own facilities from revenues generated through gate receipts, media contracts, and the hawking of merchandise. With money so scarce for infrastructure projects which will improve economic competitiveness, provide more affordable housing, modernize mass transit, improve recreational and cultural opportunities, reverse environmental degradation and promote an overall improvement in the quality-of-life for local residents, subsidizing private-sector activities such as sports franchises is almost always a major mistake.

Public Education Deficit

US students in general have fared poorly on international standardized tests dealing with mathematics, science and reading comprehension. Moreover, high school students are ranked lower internationally than are eighth graders, and eighth graders do more poorly than fourth graders, meaning that as students progress through their kindergarten to the twelfth grade school curriculum, they tend to fall further behind their counterparts in most advanced industrial societies and even in some of the developing nations. In general, US students rank in the bottom half and sometimes the bottom third in many of these tests administered in selected nations around the world.[82]

The worst performances nationwide are registered by public-school systems in major central cities. Under the administration of George W. Bush, the 'No Child Left Behind Act' administered by the US Department of Education labeled 8652 public schools as 'failing' in 2002, many of them concentrated in inner cities. The National Assessment of Education Progress (NAEP) test administered in 2000 found only 32 per cent of fourth graders to be proficient in reading, 26 per cent in mathematics, 29 per cent in science, and 18 per cent in history. Over half of all low-income children enrolled in public schools lack basic reading and mathematics skills.[83] Nearly two-thirds of students enrolled in central city public schools are from minority groups compared with 40 per cent nationally, and 61 per cent of inner city students is eligible for free or reduced-price lunches, compared with 43 per cent nationally.[84] The close linkage between poverty, ethnicity, residential segregation in central cities, and 'miseducation' is illustrated in the following, which also starkly warns of the terrible national consequences:

> The seven million in urban poverty, disproportionately represented by children of color, attend school in the 120 largest school districts. Every one of these districts is a failing school system in which greater size correlates positively with greater

failure. Every miseducated child represents a personal tragedy. Each will have a lifelong struggle to ever have a job that pays enough to live in a safe neighborhood, have adequate health insurance, send their own children to better schools than they went to, or have a decent retirement. In most cases their lives are limited to dead end jobs, or wasted away in street violence or prison. Living in the midst of the most prosperous nation on earth, the miseducated will live shorter lives characterized by greater stress and limited life options. Miseducation is, in effect, a sentence of death carried out daily over a lifetime. It is the most powerful example I know of cruel and unusual punishment and it is exacted on children innocent of any crime. Most Americans avoid the personal tragedy aspect of this massive miseducation by not sending their own children to school in these failing urban districts. This includes a majority of the teachers who work in them! In effect, those with options cope with miseducation as a personal tragedy by fleeing the major urban districts in order to protect their loved ones from the contamination of miseducation. While flight can appear to be a successful strategy for coping with miseducation as a personal tragedy, it does not address the question of how miseducating other people's children on this massive scale affects the survival of the total society. Every three years the number of dropouts and pushouts adds up to a city bigger than Chicago. For how long can a society continue to create cities the size of Chicago every three years filled with 'no hopers' and still survive as either a free or prosperous nation?[85]

With many white parents fleeing to the suburbs or enrolling their children in private schools, central city public schools cater more and more to minority students, many of whom are first or second-generation immigrants. In Illinois, 179 of the 232 schools on the federal government's 'failing list' in 2002 were in Chicago, and 178 of these 179 schools had predominantly black or Hispanic enrollments and were concentrated on the south and west sides of the city.[86] In New York City, 40 per cent of the public schools, including most middle schools, does not meet new federal standards.[87] In Washington, DC, only 4 per cent of fourth graders and 3 per cent of eighth graders are white. In the 2002 national assessment test, 69 per cent of fourth graders in the Washington, DC public schools scored below basic proficiency in reading, as did 52 per cent of eighth graders. In writing skills, 27 per cent of fourth graders and 34 per cent of eighth graders fell below the level of proficiency, meaning that they risked being functionally illiterate as adults.[88] These low levels of proficiency among students are found in many central cities in the United States and call into question the capacity of these cities to compete effectively in a globalized economy which places a growing emphasis on brainpower and advanced skills, and a diminishing emphasis on relatively low-skilled manufacturing or services' employment. Even in Silicon Valley, the reputed world leader in innovation and high technology, only 55 per cent of Hispanic students graduate from high school, a very negative indicator for the future.[89]

Marginal Attention by Leaders to Globalization and the ICT Revolution

The vast majority of US municipal leaders has little knowledge about the opportunities and challenges to be faced in an era of globalization and rapid technological change. As mentioned in Chapter 3, John Kincaid discovered in his extensive survey for the National League of Cities that most city leaders continue to focus almost exclusively on local and regional markets, and are only in the beginning stages of comprehending the ramifications for their local constituents of what is transpiring internationally.[90] In this regard, they are far behind their counterparts in other countries. Officials in Canadian municipalities are generally quite aware of what is occurring in at least North America, in part because of the creation of NAFTA and in part because almost 40 per cent of their nation's GDP is linked to exports to the United States, US direct investment in Canada and visits by American tourists and conventioneers to Canada. Municipal leaders in Europe are even more internationally oriented than Canadian leaders, in large part because a high percentage of their nations' GDP is also linked to export activity, and as a result of the growing international linkages within the European Union and among nations which are hoping to join the EU. Japanese prefectures have also had international programs for several decades, and many local leaders participate in international trade missions and Sister-City exchanges.

The pressures of globalization are manifested in myriad ways at the local level. As Andrew, Graham and Philips point out:

> Canadian cities are now developing in an internationalized environment, part of an internationalized economy that is characterized by increasingly footloose financial and human capital. The fact that this economy is increasingly knowledge and service based, rather than dependent on natural resources and manufacturing, has social implications for our cities. Knowledge workers in Toronto or Montreal may have more in common with their counterparts in Berlin or Atlanta than they do with fellow residents who are not participating in the new economy. This bifurcation of the population is characterized not just by income differences but also by differences in mobility and commitment to place.[91]

A group working to improve engagement and cooperation between San Diego and neighboring Baja California in Mexico emphasizes that 'our companies are frequently being asked to compete on a global playing field. The wages we pay our workers are compared not just with those of Akron or Austin, but also with those of Frankfurt, Shanghai, and Sao Paulo.'[92] The group adds in reference to San Diego and its cross-border neighbors in Tijuana and northern Baja: 'in many ways we can be offered as a poster child for globalization: an increasingly integrated economic region that spans an international border and joins the developed and developing world.'[93]

Few US municipal leaders can as yet identify with the Japanese expression *dochakuka*, which means 'global localization' or 'glocalization.'[94] David Rusk argues that 'the global economy sets the rules, but local areas can decide how to play the game.'[95] Rusk may be too optimistic concerning the policy latitude available to local leaders to play by the global rules of the game, but there is certainly the potential to do much more than US mayors and other city officials are currently doing, whether it be effective participation in Sister-City programs, involvement in the international activities sponsored by the National League of Cities and US Conference of Mayors, active engagement in trade and investment missions arranged by their state governments, or the creation of effective multilingual websites to spur on local economic development through the promotion of international trade, investment, and tourism activity.

A BLUEPRINT FOR GOVERNANCE

As is by now quite evident, modern urban areas face a plethora of deeply entrenched challenges. In spite of their facing formidable obstacles, the following laundry list should help metropolitan leaders to govern more effectively and be much better prepared to take advantage of the opportunities found in a globalizing world.

Democracy, Transparency, Accountability and Institutional Reform

Mayors, elected members of city councils, professional personnel such as city managers, and all other local governmental employees will require a great deal of intelligence, savvy and adaptability in order to navigate the formidable shoals of urban governance in the 21st century. Challenges emanating from the regional, national and international realms will come quickly and at times ferociously. Local governments in Silicon Valley might have been riding high and dry in early 2001 with an envious 1 per cent unemployment rate, robust business expansion in the high-technology sector, and rapidly rising local and state tax revenues. Within months, this bullish picture would deteriorate drastically, with unemployment skyrocketing, business closures escalating and revenues plummeting. New York City was already beginning to see some business contraction prior to September 11, but the tragic events of that day would help plunge the economy into a morass, with a net loss of 235 000 private-sector jobs between the end of January 2001 and the summer of 2003, and the gross city product declining for ten consecutive quarters.[96]

Any successful municipal government in the 21st century must be anchored in democracy, transparency in the decision-formulation and decision-implementation processes, and consistent accountability to the people whom government officials represent, with ultimate respect for and adherence to the rule of law. Democracy is the cornerstone, and more people than ever before are living in political systems where democracy is a political reality. At the end of 2003, Freedom House estimated that out of 192 'sovereign' countries, 88 were 'free,' representing 44 per cent of the world's population. Another 55 countries were 'partly free,' accounting for 21 per cent of the global population, and 49 were 'not free,' constituting 35 per cent of the population. In the 31 years Freedom House has conducted its surveys, this is the largest percentage of people ever to live in free systems, and 44 countries have actually become 'free' in just the past 15 years.[97]

All stakeholders must have an opportunity to participate and express themselves, including elected officials, civil servants, business and educational leaders, labor union officers, representatives of non-governmental organizations and residents in general. Local governments should utilize the latest innovations to deliver better services to their constituents in a timely fashion, including more in the way of e-governance. Civil servants should be paid well, but the services they provide should be able to compete favorably against the best available in the private sector, and any government monopolies in the delivery of public services must remain under constant scrutiny. Stephen Goldsmith, the former mayor of Indianapolis, argues that privatization of government services will lead both to better services and lower costs, although other observers would consider across-the-board privatization as precipitating uneven public services and a general lowering in local wages.[98]

The local tax base must be sufficient to provide a high level of government services, but not so high as to chase businesses and residents away to other areas of jurisdiction. This does not mean that services must be kept at a minimum. Business leaders and their employees desire a high quality of life and understand that money must be spent to provide a world-class infrastructure and cultural and recreational opportunities. They also understand that a first-class public education system providing well-educated and highly skilled young people will be the key to the future success of their businesses in particular and the local economy in general. On the other hand, government officials must also remain sensitive to the demands of their local business community, because these businesses will provide the jobs for local residents and much of the tax base needed to permit effective local governance.

In the pages that follow, recommendations will be made which will be onerous for elected officials to carry out and for local residents to support. Much more in the way of regional cooperation will be needed to help urban areas to keep pace with rapid changes transpiring nationally and internationally. The amalgamation of local governments, including many special districts, would represent a major departure from the status quo in US municipalities.

Suburbs should be expected to help central cities to catch up, assuming some
of the burden in ending residential segregation and the plight of inner-city
schools. Not only will municipal leaders need to think globally and act
locally, but they will also have to expand their horizons and accept the notion
of 'urban regions' aimed at curtailing political fragmentation and the inter-
jurisdictional rivalries which currently exist. In the process, urban sprawl
may be arrested and even reversed, ethnic and racial tensions dissipated,
public education improved dramatically, intergovernmental and international
networking accelerated and the overall quality of life for the local citizenry
enhanced significantly.

Amalgamation or Extensive Intermunicipal Coordination

Over the past decade, many of Canada's major metro areas, including Toronto, Montreal, Ottawa, Winnipeg and Halifax have begun the process of the
amalgamation of local governments. Several Japanese cities have been moving in a similar direction over the past few decades. In contrast, little has been
done in the United States, with a few exceptions such as some governmental
consolidation in Portland, Oregon, in the Twin Cities in Minnesota, and the
recent amalgamation of the City of Louisville and Jefferson County in Ken-
tucky. Historically, the most notable amalgamation in the United States
occurred in 1898 when the five boroughs in and around Manhattan joined
together to form greater New York City. Instead of replicating the New York
City model, most urban areas from that time on adopted a strategy of allowing suburban communities to form their own local governments which would
become quite distinct and separate from their central-city nucleus.

Amalgamation of all local jurisdictions within counties, leading to the creation of one governmental unit for the entire county, would be the best strategy
for US urban areas to pursue. In the special case of large metro regions such as
Los Angeles which encompasses five counties, one multi-county government
should be created. John Friedmann proposes an emphasis on 'city-regions
which would extend out 50 to 100 kilometers from the core, with the governmental structure giving priority to investment in human capital, social capital,
cultural capital, intellectual capital, environmental capital, natural capital, and
urban capital.'[99] School districts and all special districts should also be consolidated and placed under the direct control of the duly elected urban regional
government. Most members of the new and expanded metro council would be
elected on a district-by-district basis and a few would be elected on an at-large
basis (representing the entire region). These amalgamated governments would
become the new basic unit of the American governmental system, and would
represent the laboratories of democracy and innovation largely determining US
competitiveness through the remainder of the 21st century.

Because so little has been accomplished in the way of formal amalgamation in the United States, it might be more politically feasible to begin the process by encouraging the various city and county governments within the same urban region to agree voluntary to work across jurisdictional lines and coordinate their policies in a number of important areas. Above all, they would work together to establish a common mass transit system catering to the needs of the great bulk of their regions' residents. For example, Portland, Oregon, Salt Lake City, the San Francisco Bay Area and Washington, DC are among the regions which have developed extensive region-wide light rail, subway and bus corridors. Secondly, they should coordinate and consolidate their housing, zoning and land use policies so that all new developments have a mixture of low, middle and high-cost single-family occupant and high-density structures. These metro-wide rules of the game should also be biased in favor of higher-density habitation within the region, leading toward greater urban 'compactness' and away from perpetual suburban sprawl and the persistent development of strip malls. Thirdly, they should establish uniform policies for schools and insure that high-risk schools receive the greatest attention and financial resources until such time as the inner-city schools are performing as well as those in the nicest suburbs. Fourthly, governments within the urban region should agree on a formula for dispersing property taxes in an equitable manner. Because most school districts rely on property taxes for their revenues, and the differential between rich and poor areas can vary so dramatically, such as a 28 to one disparity in the tax base among some of the school districts in Chicago, this equalization scheme would go a long way toward providing critically needed funds for the inner-city schools.[100] Fifthly, they should put together a master plan for economic development and infrastructure modernization, and agree not to engage in jurisdictional wars in which costly incentives are provided to the existing business community or to attract new businesses to the region. Any support to new or existing businesses should be limited to general infrastructure improvements which can benefit most residents, and training at high schools and community colleges for the development of special skills or foreign languages. Any incentives beyond this basic package should require the approval of the voters at the next regularly scheduled election.

Whether done formally or informally, municipal officials must begin to think on a regional basis and understand that central cities and their suburbs are interdependent parts of a shared regional economy.[101] As William Hudnut III, another former mayor of Indianapolis has asserted: 'It is worth a try to get out of the 19th century and into the 21st as far as governmental jurisdictions are concerned.'[102] Local officials can then move toward the creation of a 'city without suburbs,' and begin the process of breaking 'the link between place, income, and quality-of-life outcomes.'[103] Moreover, regional officials can learn from real-world examples, whether they be the modest programs in place in Portland and the Twin Cities, or more formal and ambitious programs in Toronto, Winnipeg or Halifax. Such region-wide planning and coordination will be critical in the quest to create or perpetuate globally competitive urban regions in the United States and around the world.

Multi-level Government Cooperation

Governmental cooperation within city regions must also be accompanied by much better planning and coordination on an intergovernmental basis. The economic fortunes of urban regions cannot be divorced from what transpires at the national and regional governmental levels. For example, several major urban areas in the United States are highly dependent on domestic and international tourism as a revenue generator, but unless the US national government loosens its new restrictive policies on the issuance of visas to foreign visitors, these cities face severe financial hardships. Documented and undocumented immigration is also a federal responsibility in the United States, but little is done by Washington to help ease the financial burden on local governments which are the recipients of the lion's share of these immigrants. Washington also controls the criteria for determining legal entry of immigrants into the United States, and puts much more emphasis on extended family reunification than on educational background and targeted skills which would make it much easier for these new arrivals to secure employment opportunities which pay a living wage.

In Canada, municipalities are very restricted in terms of the types of taxes that they can levy. The provincial governments could ease this burden through legislation, and Ottawa could insure that more transfer payments are made from the national to the local levels. In December 2003, the Council of Federations was created in Canada by the ten provincial and three territorial governments.[104] This organization is intended to improve the dialogue among the regional premiers and provide a forum for direct discussions with the federal government. It should add as one of its foremost goals a formal mechanism for regular discussions with leaders from Canada's major urban regions. Prime Minister Paul Martin has also created a new post of parliamentary secretary responsible for cities and has pledged to transfer some additional tax revenue directly to municipal governments.[105] This is a major step in the right direction, but Urban Affairs should become a permanent agency in Ottawa and the transfer of revenues should be codified so that it will continue at guaranteed levels for an indefinite period of time. Provincial governments must also do more to insure that the recent bold experiments in urban amalgamation in Canada have adequate resources to succeed and that urban leaders are provided a priority status in meetings with provincial cabinets and members of the provincial legislatures. The Quebec and Alberta governments' pledges to provide high-speed Internet lines throughout their provinces, and Quebec's promise to provide computers and computer training to low-income households, are also innovative policies which will help to enhance the economic futures of their local communities.

Once again, the United States is far behind Canada in moving toward more productive and regularized intergovernmental consultations and collaboration. The periodic renewal of the massive Transportation Equity Act (ISTEA) for the 21st century by Congress should emphasize the development of new or modernized mass transit systems within urban areas and place much less emphasis on constructing new urban freeways. Moreover, city leaders cannot fight poverty on their own. As Dreier, Mollenkopf and Swanstrom suggest, federal policies should be geared to (a) leveling the metropolitan playing field, (b) limiting bidding wars among subnational governmental jurisdictions, (c) implementing federal programs on a metropolitan-wide basis, (d) promoting metropolitan cooperation and governance, (e) linking community development to the overall regional economy, (f) strengthening public schools, (g) making work pay through expanding earned income tax credits, raising the minimum wage above the poverty line, expanding health insurance and child-care benefit, and deconcentrating urban poverty and (h) mobilizing civic engagement through strict enforcement of the Voting Rights Act and reforming labor laws to facilitate the formation and expansion of unions.[106]

David Rusk claims that the federal government has had a 'suburban policy' since the end of the Second World War, and must now shift gears and pursue a truly 'urban' policy which would help diminish racial and economic segregation through promotion of (a) 'fair share' policies that encourage the construction of low and middle-income housing in all local jurisdictions, (b) fair employment policies to ensure full access by minorities to metro-wide jobs, (c) housing assistance programs to disperse low-income families to small-unit scattered-site housing projects and (d) tax-sharing arrangements that would offset tax-base disparities between central cities and their suburbs.[107] As for state governments, Rusk urges that they improve annexation laws to permit more consolidation between central cities and their suburbs, enact laws encouraging city-county consolidation and the reorganization of local governments, require local governments to have affordable housing laws, establish county-wide tax-sharing arrangements, and enact strong state-wide growth management laws in order to curb urban sprawl.[108]

Whether in unitary or federal political systems, effective and continual intergovernmental cooperation and coordination will be needed in order for urban governance to be efficacious in a period of unprecedented global interdependence and rapid technological change. Even the best and most visionary local governments will not be able to succeed if they are burdened with indifferent and apathetic regional and national governments. Governance at the local level where most people now live cannot be divorced from governance at these higher levels, and intergovernmental cooperation must be enhanced and given much greater credence in all nation states around the world.

Fiscal Reform

To enhance the overall attractiveness and competitiveness of urban regions, local governments must be provided by their national and regional governments with the ability to levy a wide variety of taxes and to begin to move away from regressive property and sales taxes, especially the deplorable sales tax on basic food items purchased at grocery stores. This flexibility is more important in Canadian urban areas than those in the United States, because property taxes have recently constituted just under 50 per cent of all municipal revenues in Canada versus 21 per cent in the United States.[109] However, both nations must institute significant reforms at the local level. The national and regional governments should also make transfer payments to the local level as predictable as possible, end the practice of unfunded mandates and offer added financial support to local governments for the implementation of programs under direct federal, state, or provincial jurisdiction, programs such as the settlement of immigrants and enhanced homeland security.

In addition, local governments must be very careful about their own expenditures and not place an undue burden on their taxpayers. These governments should cease providing investment incentives and subsidies to individual companies. Their role must consist of providing a world-class infrastructure and educational system, plus a reasonable regulatory and taxation regime. Beyond this, companies should be expected to compete on their own and not anticipate receiving financial handouts from any level of government. Moreover, municipal governments around the world tend to be heavily unionized. This is not necessarily a problem, but the services provided by public unions should be as high quality and cost effective as any comparable services found in the private sector. Unions must also be adaptable and willing to adjust to the rapid economic and technological changes occurring nationally and internationally.

Achieving fiscal soundness is easier said than done, as major metropolitan governments have to adjust to the steady inflow of immigrants and the rising medical and social costs associated with an ageing population base in most nations of the North. The problem is especially acute in the United States which is the only developed country in the world without universal health insurance, and where the number of physicians per capita has not increased in low-income inner-city neighborhoods.[110] A healthy and viable business sector and adequate intergovernmental financial transfers will be necessary in order for local governments to cope with rising costs, and elected officials should be mindful of the high-quality public services that must be delivered in order for local businesses and their workforces to compete favorably against their counterparts in the developed and developing nations alike.

Best Practices

The exchange of information in the world today has never been greater or easier to obtain, but many local officials are unaware of practices in other urban areas around the world which might help them to increase the competitiveness and quality of life in their own jurisdictions. In the United States, the US Conference of Mayors and the National League of Cities compile best practices within the national context, and at times even within the international context. Similar municipal associations in Canada, Europe and Asia are also in the process of highlighting best practices of local governments in their regions. As an illustration, state and local governments in Wisconsin have been working together to lower the costs of overall governance. A new website has been created which allows local governments to purchase equipment at the state government's bulk prices, providing an opportunity to save a great deal of money.[111] Various US local governments would also like to work with their counterparts in Canada to procure pharmaceuticals from Canada for their employees and their families at prices well below what is currently available in the United States.

International organizations such as United Cities and Local Government can serve as clearinghouses for the gathering of best practices from cities around the world. Sister-city relationships can also contribute to this needed exchange of information, and local governments should foster exchanges of officials so that they can gain a firsthand knowledge of how cities operate in other parts of the world. A variety of comparative studies are also available to local officials, and academics have been compiling lists of what they consider to be best practices.[112] No one should be resting on his or her laurels thinking that they have found the very best way to govern their municipalities. In particular, US local leaders have much to learn from their counterparts around the globe, because American cities face some of the worst conditions and most formidable challenges to be found anywhere in the developed world.

International Networking

Saskia Sassen has observed that:

> Over the centuries cities have been at the crossroads of major, often worldwide processes. What is different today is the intensity, complexity, and global span of these networks, the extent to which significant portions of economies are now dematerialized and digitized, hence the extent to which they can travel at great speeds through some of these networks, and the number of cities that are part of cross-border networks operating at vast geographic scales.[113]

Going hand in hand with awareness of best practices among municipal governments is the opportunity to actually network with local governments around the world, an opportunity which is easier to achieve than at any other time in history. One dimension of this network is in the transnational realm where local businesses may already be internationally connected, especially those engaged in accounting, law, advertising, finance or the mass media. A way for municipal government officials to gauge the degree of international involvement by local firms is to apply what Sassen calls the 'transnationality index,' which is simply the average based on the ratios of foreign sales, assets, and employment to the enterprise's total activity in each category.[114] In 1998, this index among companies in the European Union was 56.7 per cent, compared with 38.5 per cent in the United States and 79.2 per cent in Canada.[115] The higher the index rating, the more dependent the local company is on international markets, and the overseas experience of local business representatives is a valuable resource which can often be tapped by municipal officials in the establishment of international networks.

Furthermore, the National League of Cities, the US Conference of Mayors, the Federation of Canadian Municipalities and the various European and Japanese regional groups discussed in Chapter 3, plus Sister-Cities International, are among the organizations which facilitate the international networking of local governments, including those which represent relatively modest population bases. A plethora of academic literature is also available on top-tier, second-tier, third-tier and other types of global cities and how they have morphed into global cities. Sassen's edited book on *Global Networks* examines Mexico City, Beirut and Sao Paulo as 'cross-border regions,' and Hong Kong, Shanghai, Buenos Aires and Amsterdam as 'network nodes.'[116] Yue-Man Yeung focuses on Tokyo, Seoul, Taipei, Hong Kong, Manila, Bangkok, Kuala Lumpur, Singapore, Jakarta, Osaka and Nagoya. His thesis is that 'the world cities in Pacific Asia are networked in a functional system built around transportation, telecommunications, finance, production services, and so on,' adding that these municipalities qualify as world cities by fulfilling at least four roles for the global economy: personal services, goods and commodity transactions, information flows and financial services.[117] John Friedmann analyses the overall 'world city hypothesis' and offers seven theses concerning world cities, which he considers are the 'organizing nodes' of the global economic system: (a) the form and extent of a city's integration with the world economy, and the function assigned to the city in the new spatial division of labor, will play a decisive role in future structural changes occurring within the city; (b) key cities throughout the world are used by global capital as basing points in the spatial organization and articulation of production and markets; (c) the global functions of world cities are directly reflected in the structures and dynamics of their production sectors and employment situation; (d) world cities are major sites for the concentration and accumulation of international capital; (e) world cities are destinations for large numbers of both domestic and international migrants; (f) world city formation brings into focus the major contradictions of industrial capitalism, including spatial and class polarization; and (g) world city growth generates social costs at rates that may exceed the fiscal capacity of the local community.[118]

Some of Friedmann's theses are somewhat controversial and may cause local leaders, especially those in smaller or medium-sized urban regions, to question the wisdom of being engaged internationally. However, they really have little choice. The global is descending on the local at a rapid pace, and municipal governance requires that leaders maximize what international benefits might be available for local constituents while attempting to minimize the costs. Moreover, with Internet and telephone access being so rapid and so inexpensive, it is easier and more cost-effective than ever before to be involved in a variety of international networks tailor-made to the specific interests of the urban region (tourism, ports, higher education, medical equipment, software, hardware, agribusiness, media services, manufacturing and so forth).

Immigrants and Ethnic Groups as Municipal and 'International' Assets

Without any doubt, first-generation immigrants who possess few skills and have modest educational backgrounds can place onerous short-term strains on a local government's health, education, and social welfare service networks.[119] On the other hand, highly skilled immigrants have been playing crucial roles in the development of Silicon Valley and other globally competitive technological centers around the planet. Throughout the history of the United States and in some other developed countries, immigrants have also been the bulwark of industrial and technological development, ranging in the USA from Andrew Carnegie in the steel industry to, much more recently, Andy Grove in semiconductors.[120] They have also been major contributors to the regeneration of some inner cities, especially in downtown Los Angeles.

An *ad hoc* downtown Los Angeles reconstruction agency decided several years ago to target small businesses instead of larger conglomerates in an effort to revitalize a deteriorating and moribund downtown area. There are now over 15 000 companies in downtown Los Angeles, employing more than 300 000 workers. Many of these companies, ranging from the production of tortillas to bicycling outfits, are run by immigrants and they are generating more than 54 billion dollars in annual sales and have brought new life and vigor to the downtown corridor.[121] The positive effects of immigration in Los Angeles have prompted other cities such as Pittsburgh and Albuquerque to begin the recruitment of selected immigrants with the intent of transforming their own inner-city areas.[122]

Many of these immigrant groups can also play a pivotal role in the development of international networks for urban regions. AnnaLee Saxenian emphasizes that 'foreign-born entrepreneurs are becoming agents of globalization by investing in their native countries, and their growing mobility is in turn fueling the emergence of entrepreneurial networks in distant locations.'[123] In particular, she points to the 'extensive evidence of brain circulation, or two-way flows of highly skilled professionals, between California and fast-growing regions in India and Greater China.'[124] She then discusses how local governments can take advantage of unprecedented immigration flows: 'Local and state governments are the most appropriate scale for building cross-national relationships that parallel the bottom-up transnational networks that immigrants are building between the United States and their native countries.'[125] In addition,

> Economic activity, particularly information-technology-related entrepreneurship, is highly localized everywhere in the world. Regional governments in such places as India and China are closest to, and most aggressive in promoting technology-related entrepreneurship and growth. This fact suggests that coordination between these lower levels of government in different countries (rather than at the national level) may be an effective way to both facilitate and monitor many of the transnational activities of immigrant professionals and their communities.[126]

As ethnic groups grow in numbers and local influence, they are creating their own associations and often assist their fellow immigrants to secure loans for businesses and housing.[127] These associations can serve as the facilitators for the creation of sister-city relations and provide much of the manpower and energy needed to insure the continuity and success in these international linkages. They can also help spawn cross-border joint ventures, joint licensing arrangements, and other types of business collaboration which will assist local communities to become more internationally competitive and thereby generate more and better-paying jobs for local residents.

Physical Infrastructure and Education

Urban regions are largely responsible for developing the physical infrastructure which will assist the local business community to attain and then maintain global competitiveness. World-class transportation and communication networks are key component parts of this infrastructure, and development of the information highway is imperative. Up until significant cutbacks in US municipal budgets in the period 2002–4, there had been significant spending, at least in nominal terms, on urban mega-projects such as the building or modernization of highways, mass transit, airports, sports facilities and convention centers. Some of these projects were desperately needed for the future competitiveness of the urban region, such as the Alameda Corridor project in Los Angeles. Other projects were and continue to be quite questionable, such as mass public financing for the aforementioned professional sports facilities. Altshuler and Luberoff recommend that widely accepted criteria be used for evaluating the efficacy of major public investment projects. These criteria should include the following: (a) major public investments should generally provide net benefits for society as a whole; (b) in cases where there are specific beneficiaries, particularly corporations, they should bear a proportionate share of the project's costs and risks; (c) projects should not significantly harm individuals, communities or the natural environment; (d) decisions to proceed should be arrived at democratically and with utmost transparency; and (e) access to the courts for review of significant issues of statutory interpretation and compliance should be relatively liberal, but the judicial process should not be used simply as a delaying tactic by project critics. The authors do believe that critics should have the right to initiate a referendum on whether or not mega-projects should proceed, but that local elected representatives should maintain the right to reaffirm their original decision even if the anti-project referendum passes. To do so on the part of elected officials, of course, could greatly imperil their own individual chances of reelection.[128]

Perhaps more important than any other part of infrastructure improvement is the provision of world-class primary, secondary, and post-secondary public educational facilities and instructors. Both businesses and workers will suffer unless young people receive superior educations and develop marketable skills. Richard Florida estimates that about 30 per cent of current employees in the United States constitutes the 'creative class' and this group is providing much of the competitive edge which some American cities currently enjoy.[129] Unless the vast majority of the other 70 per cent improves its skills in the near future, it is difficult to see how the United States will maintain its global leadership position, even though the inward migration of skilled workers from around the world has helped to bridge some of the gap caused by an inferior K-12 public education system in many central cities.

More resources for public education must be provided by all levels of government, and teachers must be compensated more generously, but in return their own training both before and after entering the profession must be upgraded significantly. The allocation of educational resources must also be shifted dramatically from administrative and support services to the classroom. Students must be expected to master the basic component parts of education, but they should also be actively engaged in learning about topics most germane in a period of globalization, including computer training, foreign languages, mathematics and statistics, geography, civics, international relations and overall problem-solving and analytic skills. Some argue that learning a foreign language is no longer necessary because most of the world's residents will soon speak English as their first or second language. This argument is specious because knowing another language increases awareness and empathy for people in distant lands, and as many young people enter the workforce, they will begin to comprehend that the most important language in the world is the language spoken by current or prospective customers. Students should also be provided with the best technology in the world to assist them in the learning process, and businesses must be prepared to contribute material and human resources whenever it is feasible, because they will be directly contributing to the education of their future employees.

Strategic Planning

Municipalities within an urban region should join together to create a strategic plan detailing specifically how they will move their metropolitan area forward in the era of economic globalization. The plan should ideally take into account what David Rusk has termed the 'total community package,' including (a) an available labor force, reasonably prepared and trainable, motivated with minimal racial and class antagonisms, (b) a decent metro-wide public school system whose operations are financed by a combination of local, state and perhaps some federal money, (c) respectable state university and community college facilities, including an emphasis on technical training in the latter institutions, (d) available and reasonably priced land, industrial bond financing, a good transportation network and reliable and affordable energy supplies, (e) highly competent local government and a moderate but adequate tax base, with at least 90 per cent of all commercial and industrial property being located within the metro area and (f) a satisfactory and improving quality of life for the vast majority of local residents.[130]

The development of a strategic plan will be discussed in much greater detail in Chapter 7, but it definitely should include an inventory of each urban region's apparent strengths and weaknesses as it confronts a globalizing economy. This checklist should indicate the quality of the 'global' infrastructure within the metro area, the number and types of international companies, the international transportation capability, international organizations with headquarters or branches situated locally, the international media presence, civic organizations with international ties, major research-and-development facilities, higher education institutions, ethnic group associations, tourism attractions and convention and exhibition facilities capable of hosting international conferences. John Logan and Harvey Molotch suggest that metro areas might concentrate on developing one or more areas of emphasis, including becoming headquarter cities (New York, Los Angeles, Chicago), innovation centers (Silicon Valley, Austin, Boston, the Research Triangle in North Carolina), module-production places (Baltimore, Omaha, Houston), developing world 'entrepôts' (Miami, San Antonio, San Diego), or retirement centers (Tampa, St. Petersburg, Tucson).[131] Tourism centers, 'consumption spaces' (casinos, malls, sports stadia, convention facilities), and agribusiness centers would be additional categories, and metro areas can also engage in developing clusters in a broad range of manufacturing and technological fields.[132]

The strategic plan must be brutally honest in assessing the region's shortcomings and how these weak spots will be ameliorated over time. Weaknesses should not result in a major gnashing of the teeth, because most can be eventually overcome. Singapore, Hong Kong and Taipei are among the cities devoid of most natural resources but they have still excelled over the past several decades under very difficult geopolitical and economic conditions. Indeed, such a renowned urban expert as Peter Hall has proclaimed that Singapore is 'perhaps the most extraordinary case of economic development in the history of the world.'[133]

The strategic plan itself must include input from all segments of local society and indicate how the civic infrastructure will be improved along with the physical infrastructure, and how public-private sector consultation and collaboration will be optimized. Sections of the plan should also deal with reinvigorating downtown corridors and enticing new permanent residents such as empty nesters and young professionals who tend to enjoy the historical, cultural, recreational, and other amenities available in vibrant central cities.[134] Entrepreneurship, both in civic and business terms, must also be highlighted in the plan, with pertinent lessons learned from Silicon Valley and other clearly entrepreneurial cities or regions.[135] Finally, elected officials should give careful consideration to creating international cabinets or protocol offices which would focus on the global dimensions of the urban region's plan.

Thinking Globally and Acting Locally: a Case Study from the Salt Lake City Urban Region[136]

Thinking globally and acting locally has become somewhat of a truism. It must be adapted on a case-by-case basis depending on the exigencies of globalization and specific local conditions. The following provides a case study of the adaptation to globalization found in the Salt Lake City urban region, also known locally as the Wasatch Front.

Many people perceive that the US Intermountain West consists of wide open spaces and panoramic vistas. This image is accurate, but the day of the cowboy and small rural settlements has long since passed. Indeed, the West has become increasingly urbanized, with 74 per cent of the population residing in metropolitan areas in 2000 compared with only 50 per cent a half century earlier. Although representing one of America's smaller metropolitan areas, Utah's Wasatch Front seems to be in relatively good shape to confront the challenges of globalization and the New Economy, even though the urban region has a small population base, is totally landlocked, isolated in a mountainous and relatively remote part of the United States, subject to cold winter and very hot summer temperature extremes and surrounded by vast expanses of land predominantly owned by the federal government.

The region has fewer than two million people, but it has been growing rapidly, with the Provo-Orem area ranking 10th and Salt Lake City-Ogden 39th in the country for the rate of population growth during the 1990s. Utah and its neighboring states of Nevada, Arizona and Colorado were also the four fastest growing states during the past decade, measured by the percentage increase in population.

The Wasatch Front is clearly the leading region in the state of Utah, with its overall importance to the state eclipsing that of most other metro-state relationships in the other 49 states. Indeed, the Wasatch Front is a 'city-state' economy which dominates Utah in so many dimensions.[137] Over 76 per cent of the entire population of the state lives along the Wasatch Front from Provo in the south to Ogden in the north, with Salt Lake City representing the heart of the region and also serving as the state's capital. Economically, the region's importance is even more pronounced, with 83 per cent of the state's personal income and almost 86 per cent of payroll wages concentrated along the Front. The state has also benefited from having one of the lowest poverty rates and the highest employment rates in the nation.

Demographically, the Wasatch Front is the youngest in the nation and has the largest-sized nuclear families. It also has the youngest work force nationally, a work force which is growing at twice the national rate and is expected to expand by 60 per cent over the next two decades. The participation rate within the work force is also well above the national average. About 6 per cent of the

Front's population was foreign born in 2000, little more than half of the nationwide percentage of 10.3 per cent, and at the beginning of the 1990s 120 000 residents spoke a language other then English at home. The Hispanic population in Utah more than doubled during the 1990s and it now accounts for about 7 per cent of Utah's population (compared with 13 per cent nationally), with African Americans accounting for 1 per cent (12.3 per cent nationally), American Indians and Alaska Natives 1.4 per cent (1 per cent nationally), and Asians and Pacific Islanders 2.6 per cent (3.6 per cent nationally).[138] Although Utah's residents are still mostly Caucasian, there has been a rapid acceleration in the diversity of the Wasatch Front's overall population, and more than 44 per cent of the children currently enrolled in the Salt Lake City school district is a member of various ethnic minority communities.[139]

The Wasatch Front also stands out because of the dominance of one religious group, the Church of Jesus Christ of Latter-day Saints, colloquially referred to as the Mormon Church. In 1990, 64 per cent of all the residents of Salt Lake and Weber counties identified themselves as Mormons, as did 74 per cent of the residents in Davis county and 90 per cent in Utah county. The only other US state that approaches the one-religion domination in Utah is Rhode Island, with 64 per cent of the residents identifying themselves as Catholic.[140] Salt Lake City is also the world headquarters for the church, and in the late 1940s a majority of the one million members of the church actually resided in Utah. In contrast, a majority of the 11 million members of the church today lives outside the United States.

The church has always stressed the importance of education, which helps explain why the region ranks near the top of the nation in literacy and educational attainment rates, in spite of having the largest class sizes from kindergarten through high school. One-quarter of all adults in Utah possesses at least a BA or BS degree, and the region ranks near the top of the nation in the percentage of households with computers, with more than two-thirds having desktops or laptops.[141] In 2000, approximately 80 per cent of Wasatch Front households also had access to high-speed Internet services, far higher than the 55 per cent for the state as a whole.

Many Utahns may harbor second thoughts about the ability of local companies to compete internationally, especially against large US-based and foreign-based corporations. With a gross state product of over 70 billion dollars in 2001, Utah would have ranked as the 43rd largest 'national' economy in the world, with a production base larger than Chile's. Thus, out of approximately 200 nation states in the world today, Utah alone could be placed in the top quarter of all national economies, and the greater Salt Lake City metropolitan area, with almost 60 billion dollars in annual production of goods and services, would have ranked in 2001 as the 44th largest 'national' economy, just ahead of Pakistan.

In Utah, the major municipal and county governments have small business development offices and many maintain sister-city programs with selected municipalities around the world. The Utah Valley Economic Development Association (UVEDA) is actively involved on a county-wide basis in the southern part of the Wasatch Front, and the privately run Economic Development Corporation of Utah considers the entire Wasatch Front to be its priority area. Some regional governmental groups such as the Wasatch Front Regional Council and the Mountainland Association of Governments also look at special issues such as transportation and environmental quality, with transportation planning being by far the most successful on a region-wide basis. Nonetheless, the Wasatch Front is not in the same league with the Silicon Valley Partnership or the Greater Seattle Trade Alliance in terms of effective regional planning and public–private partnerships.

By default, the state government of Utah, which is headquartered in Salt Lake City, has been leading the way in promoting international competency and competitiveness along the Wasatch Front, and has actually been quite energetic in a state considered to be very conservative politically and socially. Utah's governor usually leads one to two international missions annually. Recent governors have also hosted many foreign delegations and consider it a priority to make Utah better known abroad and to encourage Utah's residents to have a better awareness of the nature of international competitiveness. The International Business Development Office (IBDO), which is part of the Utah Department of Community and Economic Development, has placed on retainer local hires in Beijing, Brussels, Dortmund, London, Mexico City, San Paulo, Santiago, Seoul, Singapore, Stockholm and Tokyo who work part-time for Utah. These representatives are paid on a project-by-project basis with each project intended to generate business opportunities for Utah-based companies or attract foreign direct investment and tourists into the state. This network of representatives is among the largest of any state in the United States and is thought to be superior to the much more expensive bricks-and-mortar strategy of states such as California which have traditionally operated their own facilities overseas, often staffed them with state government employees, or at times even made quasi-patronage appointments of friends of the governor or other political leaders. The risk for Utah, of course, is that some of these foreign-based representatives will perform poorly, and that the very best will be hired away by bigger states or even private companies willing to provide better incentive packages. Indeed, some states have already hired away a few of Utah's most productive overseas representatives. The Salt Lake City-based IBDO continues to rank in the top half of the US states in terms of the number of employees, with seven specialists covering Europe, Asia, the Americas, and the Middle East. On the other hand, its budget has been stagnant over the past several years and some specialists have actually been seconded from Japanese and South Korean agencies through the Government Executive Exchange Program involving Utah and these two countries.

The IBDO sponsors 'how-to-export' seminars for local companies on a regular basis and facilitates participation by local companies in trade shows and trade missions which span the globe. More than 1500 Utah companies have participated in IBDO export seminars and 150 in international trade shows. The IBDO also produced and notarized in 2000 alone over 5000 Certificates of Free Sale for foreign governments on behalf of Utah companies, certificates which are required by many countries before US companies can export products to them. These certificates have been especially important for Utah's growing health-supplement industry in its efforts to increase export sales. The IBDO also hosted nearly 60 foreign trade delegations during 2001 and participates annually in about 25 international trade shows. Moreover, it has been an active player in inviting and hosting almost 100 ambassadors from foreign embassies in Washington, DC.[142] The intent of this latter program is to give these ambassadors first-hand knowledge about the Wasatch Front, and the itinerary of these ambassadors usually includes visits with state and local government officials, university, church and ethnic group leaders, and representatives of local chambers of commerce and individual companies. The IBDO also maintains a website with over 4000 pages of text. At one time, the website included an automatic translator which would take text in English and transform it into six different languages. The site is now totally in English, based in part on the fact that the automatic translator had various flaws, and in part on what might be a faulty premise that the language of business around the world is increasingly English, especially for foreign companies seeking joint venture partners or to engage in other types of commercial activities within the United States.

About 1200 companies in Utah exported 3.6 billion dollars in merchandise goods in 1999, ranking Utah as the 35th largest exporter among states, about in line with its ranking of 34th population-wise and 35th in gross domestic product.[143] Over 91 per cent of all Utah merchandise exports originated in companies located along the Wasatch Front and the state's only Foreign Trade Zone is situated next to the Salt Lake City International Airport. The US Department of Commerce estimates that 61 400 Utah manufacturing jobs were dependent on exports in 1997, but this figure may only be half the true level. Manufacturing exports exclude business services such as software and other service products, an area of particular strength for Wasatch Front companies. In addition, various goods and services from the Salt Lake City urban region are shipped to Pacific and Atlantic Coast airports and seaports, and then sent overseas. These shipments are never credited as Utah's exports. Moreover, component parts made in Utah and then placed in finished products elsewhere in the United States, before being exported abroad, are never counted.

Despite this significant underestimation of its export activity, the Wasatch Front still ranks among the top 20 per cent of merchandise exporters in metropolitan areas, being listed in 1999 as 49th among 253 metro areas and just ahead of New Orleans.[144] In spite of Utah's strong emphasis on being a leader in the New Economy, almost one-third of its merchandise exports consists of copper and steel, and exports in this sector have been stagnant since the mid-1990s. In particular, the state has been hurt by the slow growth in demand in many Asian economies, and its overall growth in exports over the past eight years has ranked only 42nd among the 50 states.[145] During the 1993–99 period, the percentage increase in exports from Salt Lake City–Ogden ranked 64th among 253 metro areas, and the increase in Provo-Orem only 145th.[146] Transportation equipment (15 per cent), electronic equipment (11.5 per cent), instruments (7 per cent), chemicals (5 per cent), processed food (4.5 per cent) and coal are also very significant exports for Utah, with the value-added products being overwhelmingly fabricated by companies along the Wasatch Front.

With Salt Lake City being by far the largest city along the Wasatch Front and serving as the state's capital, coordination between city and state leaders is fairly good, much as is the case with Denver and the state government of Colorado and various other states where the largest municipality also serves as the state's capital city. Municipal officials and private sector representatives in Salt Lake City were the primary actors in attracting the financially successful 2002 Winter Olympics to the region, but state government support was critical once the bid was accepted by the International Olympic Committee. Officials at both the local and state government levels are now engaged in using the successful Olympics' experience and the international recognition which was gleaned by the Wasatch Front as a springboard for attracting new businesses, conventions, and tourists to the Salt Lake City urban region.

In conclusion, some of the experiences of Salt Lake City should be replicable in many other moderate-sized municipalities around the world. Successful efforts will include the development of modern metro-wide infrastructures, effective intergovernmental and public-private sector cooperation and collaboration, and a bold strategic plan leading to active municipal participation in an increasingly globalized economy.

NOTES

1. Dreier *et al.*, 2001, p. 2.
2. Drucker, 1989, pp. 258–9.
3. Hall and Pfeiffer, 2000, p. 5, and Brantley Liddle and Fred Moanvenzadeh, 'Introduction,' in Moavenzadeh *et al.*, 2002, p. 2.

4. Hall and Pfeiffer, 2000, p. 3.
5. Ibid., pp. 3–4.
6. Sellers, 2002, pp. 10 and 377.
7. Fenn, 2003, p. 302.
8. UN-Habitat, 'The global campaign on urban governance,' at www.unhabitat.org.
9. Ibid.
10. Ibid.
11. Hall, 1999, p. 401.
12. Ibid., p. 394.
13. Hall and Pfeiffer, 2000, pp. 318–20.
14. Ibid., pp. 319–20.
15. Ibid., p. 15.
16. Le Galès, 2002, p. 110.
17. Ibid., p. 275.
18. US Bureau of the Census, data for 2002.
19. Estimate by the United Nations released in December 2003.
20. Taylor and Carroll, 2002, p. 3.
21. Solomon, 2003, p. xi.
22. Glaeser and Shapiro, 2003, p. 31.
23. Ibid.
24. Bruce Katz and Robert E. Lang, 'Introduction,' in Katz and Lang, 2003, p. 6.
25. *New York Times*, 7 December 2003.
26. Ibid.
27. Ibid.
28. *San Diego Union-Tribune*, 24 June 2003, p. A1.
29. US Bureau of Labor Statistics, data for 2002.
30. Dreier *et al.*, 2001, p. 44, and Orfield 1997, p. 2.
31. Dreier *et al.*, 2001, p. 187.
32. Ibid.
33. Erie, 2004 and Altshuler and Luberoff, 2003, p. 278.
34. *Wall Street Journal*, 9 July 2001, pp. A2 and A17.
35. Ibid.
36. Ibid.
37. Ibid.
38. Ibid.
39. Peter Hall, 1998b, p. 985.
40. Fry, 1998, p. 118.
41. Katz and Lang, 2003, p. 9, and Taylor and Carroll, 2002, p. 12.
42. Bradford, 2002, p. 4.
43. *New York Times*, 30 May 2001, pp. A1 and A7.
44. Ibid., 22 July 2003.
45. Taylor and Carroll, 2002, p. 13.
46. Dreier *et al.*, 2001, p. 53 and Peter Marcuse and Ronald van Kempen, 'Conclusion: A changed spatial order,' in Marcuse and van Kempen, 2002, pp. 257, 260, 261.
47. Marcuse and Kempen, 2002, p. 3.
48. Alan Altshuler, William Morrill, Harold Wolman and Faith Mitchell, 'Executive summary,' in Altshuler *et al.*, 1999, p. 4.
49. Bradford, 2002, p. 37.
50. Rusk, 1995, p. 5.
51. Ibid., p. 7.
52. Ibid., p. 14 and the US Census Bureau, 2002 data.
53. *Pittsburgh Post-Gazette*, 4 December 2003.
54. Katz and Lang, 2003, p. 8.
55. Ibid.
56. Ibid., p. 9.
57. Ibid.

58. Alan Berube, 'Racial and ethnic change in the nation's largest cities,' in Katz and Lang, 2003, p. 153.
59. Ibid.
60. Edward L. Glaeser and Jacob L. Vigdor, 'Racial segregation,' in Katz and Lang, 2003, pp. 219 and 225.
61. John R. Logan, 'Ethnic diversity grows, neighborhood integration lags,' in Katz and Lang, 2003, p. 255.
62. Dreier *et al.*, 2001, pp. 47–8.
63. Ibid., p. 16.
64. Pastor *et al.*, 2000, p. 3.
65. Dreier *et al.*, 2001, p. 77.
66. Orfield, 2002, p. 10.
67. Ibid., pp. 16 and 49.
68. Dreier *et al.*, 2001, p. 58.
69. Ibid., p. 55.
70. Thorns, 2002, pp. 16–17.
71. Dreier *et al.*, 2001, p. 58.
72. *New York Times*, 27 July 2003, I, pp. 1 and 20.
73. Bradford, 2002, p. 27.
74. Pastor *et al.*, 2000, p. 176.
75. Caroline Andrew, Katherine A. Graham and Susan D. Philips, 'Introduction,' in Andrew *et al.*, 2003, p. 10.
76. World Tourism Organization, 2003.
77. Office of Travel and Tourism Industries, International Trade Administration, US Department of Commerce.
78. Pagano, 2003, p. 2.
79. Bradford, 2002, p. 11.
80. Federation of Canadian Municipalities, 2001.
81. Pagano, 2003, p. 1.
82. Websites of the US National Center for Education Statistics, the International Mathematics and Science Study (TIMSS), and the Program for International Student Assessment (PISA).
83. *USA Today*, 17 December 2002.
84. *Washington Post*, 23 July 2003. Data are derived from the 2002 National Assessment of Educational Progress report issued by the US Department of Education.
85. Haberman, 2003.
86. *Chicago Tribune*, 21 July 2002.
87. *New York Times*, 11 November 2003.
88. Ibid.
89. Piller, 1999, pp. C1 and C7.
90. Kincaid, 1997, pp. 55–84.
91. Andrew, Graham and Philips, 'Introduction,' in Andrew *et al.*, 2003, pp. 7–8.
92. San Diego Dialogue, 2000, p. 1.
93. Ibid.
94. Czarniawska, 2002, p. 12.
95. Rusk, 1995, p. 38.
96. *New York Times*, 11 November 2003.
97. Freedom House, 2003.
98. Goldsmith, 1997, p. 19.
99. Friedmann, 2002, pp. 3 and 28.
100. Orfield, 2002, p. 163.
101. Pastor *et al.*, 2000, p. 3.
102. *Pittsburgh Post-Gazette*, 4 December 2003.
103. Rusk, 1995, p. 9, Altshuler and Luberoff, 2003, p. 12, and Soja, 2000, p. 415.
104. *Globe and Mail*, 4 December 2003.
105. *Toronto Star*, 13 December 2003.

106. Dreier *et al.*, pp. 209–28.
107. Rusk, 1995, pp. 129–30.
108. Ibid., p. 130.
109. Bradford, 2002, p. 11.
110. Dreier *et al.*, 2001, p. 68.
111. *Milwaukee Journal Sentinel*, 11 December 2003.
112. Van den Berg *et al.*, 2001; the Sellers' text which compares the performance of mid-sized cities in Germany, France, and the United States; the Kemp text which looks at some of the resurgent inner cities in the United States; and Bourne, 2000, pp. 45–6.
113. Sassen, 'Introduction,' in Sassen, 2002, p. 25.
114. Ibid., p. 12.
115. Ibid.
116. Ibid., various chapters.
117. Yeung, 2000, p. 30.
118. Friedmann, 1995, pp. 317–31.
119. Borjas, 1999.
120. Florida, 2002, p. 253.
121. von Hoffman, 2003, p. A23, and Scott, 2002.
122. *New York Times*, 30 May 2001, pp. A1 and A17.
123. Saxenian, 2002, p. 1.
124. Ibid., p. 51.
125. Ibid., p. 55.
126. Ibid.
127. Light *et al.*, 2002, pp. 151–67.
128. Altshuler and Luberoff, 2003, p. 289.
129. Florida, 2002, p. 8.
130. Rusk, 1995, p. 67.
131. Logan and Molotch are quoted in Peirce, 1993, p. 293.
132. Thorns, 2002, p. 6.
133. Hall, 1998b, p. 982.
134. Rebecca R. Sohmer and Robert E. Lang, 'Downtown rebound,' in Katz and Lang, 2003, p. 71.
135. Lee *et al.*, 2000.
136. This last section is adapted from Fry and McCarlie, 2002, which was part of a larger project sponsored by the Los Angeles-based Pacific Council on International Policy that looked at the effects of globalization on Los Angeles, San Francisco, San Diego, Seattle and the Salt Lake City area. Written permission for this adaptation was kindly provided by the Pacific Council on International Policy.
137. Ohmae, 1995, p. 143.
138. US census, 2000 data.
139. Ross C. 'Rocky' Anderson, Mayor of Salt Lake City, 'State of the City' address, 9 January 2001.
140. *Encyclopedia Americana*, 2000 edition.
141. *Deseret News*, 17 October 2000, with information derived from a US Department of Commerce survey.
142. Interview with Dan Mabey, Director of Utah's International Business Development Office, 27 April 2001.
143. International Trade Administration, US Department of Commerce, and Utah Division of Business and Economic Development.
144. International Trade Administration and Exporter Location Series, US Census Bureau.
145. International Trade Administration, US Department of Commerce.
146. International Trade Administration, 'Export sales of US metropolitan areas, 1993–1999,' at http://www.ita.doc.gov/TSFrameset.html.

6. Inter-city relations and structures

City to city relationships have not been looked upon favorably by many of those who are interested in urban economic development. This is because the standard sort of relationship that was instituted by many cities, and that got the most publicity, is of the 'sister-city' type. While sister-city relationships have their value, they have little to do with the economy of either city. An ethnic community in one city, typically North American, urges its mayor to establish a relationship with a major city in the nation that was the homeland of that community. New York City and San Juan or Chicago and Warsaw would be examples with the large Puerto Rican and Polish populations. The consequence of this tends to be limited to exchanges of cultural events, high school choir trips, and so forth. Rarely do they go beyond this to reach into economic institutions or economic development planning community of the rest of the North American city.

In Europe most cities, of even the smallest population, have established one or more sister-city relationships with similar cities elsewhere in Europe. In addition to putting a symbolic end to a long history of conflict and war, these linkages are one effort toward the goal of creating a European identity or a sense of European-ness in the sensibilities of the residents of the cities that are involved. Recently the governments of Germany and France made explicit their interest in this initiative by establishing mandates in each country to increase instruction in the language of the other, to develop linkages between and among subnational entities in the two countries and, in the terms of the French minister for European affairs, to insert France in the minds of Germans and Germany in the minds of the French.[1] In this chapter we will argue that the sister-city relationship need not be the only type of inter-city relationship and that these relationships can be valuable components in the city's effort to strengthen or to transform its economic base. In the course of making this argument we will examine the various initiatives cities have actually taken in recognition of the value of inter-city interaction.

INTER-CITY COOPERATION AND COMPETITION AND THEIR IMPACTS ON THE POSSIBILITY OF INTERACTION

It is clear that in the contemporary global environment internationally en-gaged cities cannot escape the consequences of the actions of other cities, near or far. In the 19th century when the railroad augmented the stage coach or the canal as a means of moving goods, producers in every city became instantly vulnerable to competition from goods produced hundreds of miles distant. Today this impact is transmitted by container shipping, air freight and trucking linked through inter-modal transportation systems, increased cus-tomer mobility and Internet shopping. Hence, when one city does something to enhance its position in some sector of economic activity, other cities are bound to be negatively affected, or at least subjected to a challenge to their existing economic structure. All of these cities seek to induce multinational companies to locate production, research, distribution or headquarters facili-ties in their urban economic region, they strive to be the site of major international events such as the Olympic Games, and they all try to advance their position in the international urban hierarchy in numerous ways. Thus, intense competition is one major aspect of the relationship among these cities. However, it is not the only one as there is much each of these cities can learn from the experience of other cities and there are many things they can do together for their mutual benefit. In other words, cooperation is another major aspect of their relationship. It is this latter relational aspect that we examine in this chapter.

The underlying relationship of competition understandably makes city leaders reluctant to share the details of their successes with their counter-parts elsewhere and reinforces their first instinct to see their city as being in a unique situation which can best be dealt with exclusively through their own actions, with the aid of a consultant or two. For many, inter-city interaction is seen as a zero-sum game in which the gain of one city is equaled by the loss of another. In some areas, such as competition for some major event or the headquarters of a major company, this is certainly true. But for many other areas there are positive externalities from which all cities can gain. For example, if one city is successful in developing its cultural institutions and arts scene, when its newly arts-interested residents travel to other cities they will be more likely to include arts activities during their visit. As a consequence, cultural tourism is rapidly becoming a bul-wark of the downtown economy of an increasing number of cities. Thus, there are areas in which each city will want to be wary of cooperation with certain other cities and other areas in which such cooperation is beneficial. Finally, there are issues such as fiscal transfers, transportation expenditures, and macro-economic policy that make it necessary for all cities to work together to influence the national level of government and other issues that favor joint action with national and regional associations of state governors and provincial premiers.

The question of inter-city cooperation is then one that is more nuanced than it would appear to be at first glance, and city leaders must carefully consider the nature of these interactions and design an approach to the issue that will bring maximum net benefits to their local economy.

STRUCTURES OF INTER-CITY COOPERATION

Once we are open to the notion of beneficial inter-city cooperation, we must understand that there are several distinct versions of this cooperation that can be both observed and imagined. The experiences of cities in Europe and in North America are quite distinct and we will want to examine what has been accomplished on each continent for a variety of reasons, not least of which is the possibility that cities on each continent could learn something from their counterparts on the other. The concentration on European and North American cities is done in recognition of the experiences and knowledge of the authors, rather than a suggestion that this is where the interesting activities are to be found. In this section of the chapter we will examine, first, structures of relationships that are to be found at the city level in both North America and Europe. What has been attempted, what has succeeded and what has failed are predominantly reflections of the cultures, traditions, institutions, and aspirations of people on each of the continents. Clearly this will pose constraints on the extent to which each set of cities will be able to apply what has worked for the other. Second, we will examine some examples of cross-border urban agglomerations that have been thrown into prominence by regional and global structures, and others that are continental and global in scope. Cities on the edge of a national economic space have their reach truncated by the barriers to economic activity that are posed by the national border. When the economic consequences of that border are removed, economic agents in the city can complete their reach into the other national economic space. When two cities are in close proximity on opposite sides of the border the result can range from creation of a cross-border urban agglomeration to new opportunities for interaction. Finally, city leaders have established several institutions that link cities on a continental or global basis so that large internationally engaged cities everywhere have the opportunity to share their concerns, successes and failures to mutual benefit.

As a result of these initiatives on various levels, there exists today a rich texture of inter-city interaction. No city leader should find him/herself in the position of having to 'reinvent the wheel.' An impressive mass of knowledge and information are available which is made accessible by these structures of interaction, and it is to them that we now turn our attention.

National Inter-city Interaction in North America

For a variety of cultural, structural and political reasons the interaction among cities in the United States and Canada is less developed than is the case in Europe, as will become clear in the course of the next few pages. It is nonetheless true that, as is often the case, Canadians find themselves to be positioned somewhere on the continuum between the individualistic and market-oriented USA and the more structure-oriented Europe. Therefore it will be most appropriate if we begin with the situation of cities in the USA and then take up Canadian cities, before turning to the European experience in the next section. Cities in the USA are relatively isolated and do not have assured access to higher levels of government. One reason is the competing interests of cities in the same state. This is the case for cities in California, Texas, Florida, Ohio, Pennsylvania, New York, Tennessee and Missouri. Each of these states contains two or more major cities, with each city having a distinct role, orientation or economic structure. Hence each city will try to exert its own demands for resources, infrastructure and policies in competition with the other large city or cities in that state. This becomes clear when we think, for example, of the needs and roles of Dallas-Fort Worth, San Antonio and Houston; or Miami, Orlando and Jacksonville; or Philadelphia and Pittsburgh. In each situation, while the cities may be able to present a united front on some issues, such as state support for urban renewal or a particular aspect of the tax code, on many issues the cities will have interests that are not congruent. In this situation the voice of the cities will be discordant and weak.

In other situations the primary city in the state is in a battle for the attention of the state government with rural and agricultural interests. One thinks immediately of Chicago and down-state Illinois or New York City and up-state New York, but this situation is found in almost every state in the union. Rural economic development competes with inner-city renewal; airport expansion competes with highway construction; development of cultural institutions in the large city compete with small town amenities that are needed to keep young people living in rural areas; and many items in the state tax code generate urban–rural conflict. It is generally the case that state political districting favors rural areas so urban people feel underrepresented in the state legislature. While all of this is frustrating urban leaders and urban dwellers, city leaders have long argued that the large city is the economic driver of the economy of the entire state economy and in cases such as Chicago or New York the driver of a multi-state regional economy. Without a vibrant large city economy, it is argued, the entire state or multi-state region suffers. This may be true for smaller cities in the urban region but farmers see this argument as self-serving and as having little or no relevance for their sales of agricultural products. So the conflict is not subject to resolution.

In Canada, only Ontario, Quebec and Alberta have two large cities, although Saskatchewan and New Brunswick have two smaller cities that compete for the attention of the provincial government and in British Columbia Vancouver must contend with the attention that is paid to Victoria, the provincial capital. In provinces with large internationally-engaged cities, British Columbia, Ontario, Quebec and Nova Scotia, the conflict between rural and urban interests is present. In the other provinces the largest city is typically the capital and both it and other cities are linked positively to the strength of the agricultural, fishing, mining and timber sectors of the provincial economy.

In the United States the federal government has had an explicit interest in urban affairs since the Housing Act of 1937, however, it was not until 1965 that the Department of Housing and Urban Development (HUD) was established. The mission of HUD is 'to increase homeownership, support community development and increase access to affordable housing free from discrimination.'[2] The latter was added in the aftermath of the urban riots and destruction that followed the assassination of Dr Martin Luther King in 1968. This mission is fully in line with previous federal government policies, such as home mortgage deductibility and subsidies to automobiles/highways and commuter rail service, which encouraged not only home ownership but also the massive movement of families from large cities to suburbs. As a consequence, much of the federal government's urban policy has worked to the detriment to the social and economic interest and strength of the nation's cities. The rise of homelessness in the nation's large cities, the loss of manufacturing jobs and the flight of companies to low-wage, non-union locations in the US South and Third World countries have made it necessary for Washington to develop new programs for homelessness and brownfield site development. As this chapter is being written there is a Republican administration in power in Washington and neither it nor President Bush has much affection for large cities. The flight to the suburbs has always been promoted most enthusiastically by the Republicans, on the understanding that property owners are more likely to vote for them than are city apartment renters. President Bush has always promoted the image of himself as a small town, rural kind of guy. Only when the economic and social situations in cities demand attention are they likely to get it.

Canada has not had a minister for urban affairs, but during the past several months, as the government of Jean Chrétien has made way for that of his Liberal Party successor Paul Martin, mayors of cities of all sizes have joined the clamor for Mr Martin's attention. Just one month prior to his taking over, he reiterated a commitment made some time ago to work out a new deal or new relationship for the cities.[3] He recognizes that 80 per cent of Canadians now live in cities and that most of the nation's economic activity is undertaken in them; they are also host to most of the country's social problems. In addition to the usual needs for infrastructure, housing, and public transportation, large cities are also bearing the brunt of the consequences, both positive and negative, of inflows of immigrants. Mayors argue that this is an example of a national policy issue that is being dealt with primarily by a small number of large cities. While it is true that only time will tell whether Mr Martin will in fact take a new look at the needs of cities, it has been a long time since so much attention has been given to them by a prime minister.

Given this reality of frustration when cities look to superior levels of government for assistance, it is quite natural for them to create structures within which their concerns and issues will be the sole driving force. In North America, city leaders have established many such organizations and in this section of the chapter we will examine three of them: the National League of Cities, the US Conference of Mayors and the Federation of Canadian Municipalities. Clearly the three tend to the needs of cities in the USA and in Canada, but beyond that we can note differences in their functioning and mandates.

The National League of Cities

The National League of Cities (NLC) was founded in 1924 and is the largest of the US city associations, with over 1700 cities as members plus 18 000 cities that participate in the 49 state municipal leagues that are members. Originally it was established by ten state municipal associations, or leagues, for the purposes of research, information sharing, and advocacy in the halls of federal and state governments. The specific interests of the NLC can be understood from the categories into which its research publications are classified: children and families, diversity, economy/economic development, elected officials, finance, housing/human services, public safety and technology/telecommunications. While most of these topics have some relevance to the economic competitiveness of the urban economy, most of the research reports listed in the NLC website, even in relevant topic areas, have little to do with the economy. As would be imagined, the material on economic development is most directly to the point. Here the coverage ranges from downtown redevelopment, to tourism, poverty, real estate and tax structures. Most relevant are reports on the positioning of cities in the global economy and their region. In its 2003 Strategic Plan, the NLC emphasized six foci: membership, advocacy, stature and credibility of the organization, and three topical areas: early childhood, hometown security and relationships with corporate America. The accomplishments listed for the year 2002 include:

youth and families, race equality and making smaller communities 'e-cities.' In all of this, the specific interests of the city that is trying to focus on its competitiveness do not appear to receive much attention.

The United States Conference of Mayors
The USCM was founded eight years after the NLC as a response to federal assistance being given directly to cities for the first time in recognition of their needs as the Great Depression deepened. This was initiated by the administration of President Hoover, and the USCM was chartered on the eve of President Roosevelt's inauguration. Presently the organization has 1183 members who are mayors of cities in excess of 30 000 inhabitants. It articulates its primary roles to be: development of a national urban/suburban policy, federal-city relationships, improving the leadership and management of mayors and providing a forum for mayors to share ideas and information. The USCM lists about 30 key programs. Many respond to basic city maintenance requirements such as: after-school, cancer awareness, livability, clean air, AIDS, waste management and affordable housing. Almost none of the initiatives of the organization are directly related to urban economic development or competitiveness. Of the dozens of resolutions adopted at the 2003 annual meeting in Denver, most of those on urban economic development treat debt refinancing, fiscal relief, the federal sugar subsidy and the federal initiatives 'America saves' and 'Equity for reservist act.' Only one, 'US metro areas as engines of the American economy,' has anything to do with economic development.

The USCM has three subgroups for Democratic Party and Republican Party mayors and for women mayors. This is a clear indication of the many fissures that divide the nation's mayors. In addition to party and gender, mayors are separated by city size, city role in the urban hierarchy, city international engagement, city economic base and so forth. While city mayors may come together for very general lobbying in Washington or in state capitals, and while they share many concerns about brownfield development, poverty or tax structures, the specific problems that concern large internationally engaged cities have not gained center ring in the USCM, in spite of it hosting an international conference of mayors in conjunction with its 2003 annual meeting.

The Federation of Canadian Municipalities
The FCM originated with the first meeting of Canadian mayors in 1901, the Union of Canadian Municipalities. It was formed primarily to gain for municipalities some control over utility companies. In 1935 the Dominion Conference of Mayors was formed and the two organizations merged in 1937 to form the Canadian Federation of Mayors and Municipalities two years later. The effects of the Great Depression prompted the mayors to unite and

their first action was to lobby the federal government to undertake the support of payments for unemployment relief and they also urged the federal government to pay taxes on Crown-owned properties. The former was accepted by Ottawa in 1941 and the latter in 1945. This was in part the consequence of the support for both positions that was given by the Rowell-Sirois Royal Commission on Dominion-Provincial Relations of 1939. The FCM has grown to include over 990 municipalities in all ten provinces and three territories, plus the provincial and territorial municipal associations. Their subsequent activities have been clustered in the same activities that have occupied the two US associations; crime environment, finance, infrastructure and transportation. In addition, the FCM has committees on northern issues, rural issues and municipal aboriginal relations. The rural issues sub-committee deals with rural health issues and the farm crisis; that on northern issues deals with health; and the aboriginal relations group has sub-committees on municipal aboriginal relations and cooperation among communities.

One aspect of the FCM that differentiates it from the USCM and the NLC is its 'Big City Mayors' Caucus.' This is composed of 22 mayors of Canada's cities from Toronto and Montreal down to Gatineau, Quebec, which has fewer than 100 000 inhabitants. In the past couple of years the Caucus has pressed the federal and provincial governments for policy initiatives that are of particular importance to the big cities, such as diversion of some of the federal fuel tax to city governments to be used for improvements of their transportation infrastructures, and increased autonomy and access to more flexible revenue streams. Most importantly they asked federal ministers to work with them to develop a new Canadian national urban strategy. As we shall see shortly, this explicit structure for large cities puts the Canadian approach somewhere between that of the US and the European Union.

The North American approach

What is distinctive about the three North American city organizations is the fact that they are open to cities of virtually all sizes, from world class cities such as New York and Toronto to cities of a few thousand inhabitants, and the fact that each is headed by a mayor of a rather small city. The current head of the NLC is the mayor of Minnetonka, Minnesota, the USCM is led by the mayor of Hempstead, New York, and the president of the FCM is the mayor of Gatineau, Quebec. In each, the focus of the organization is comprehensive and while this encourages the participation of the largest number of cities, it does diminish the importance of it to any collection of large and internationally engaged cities. The services provided and the research done is probably quite important to smaller cities but far less so to the largest. While all cities feel pressure and experience opportunities that come from outside their historic economic space, large internationally engaged cities have specific concerns and needs that these organizations cannot possibly meet. The model for these latter cities in the US is for them to seek to ensure their economic futures individually rather than in concert with cities in similar situations; the FCM has a structure that gives explicit recognition to the specific concerns of large cities and provides them a voice as well. The approaches of inter-city organizations in the USA and Canada are quite different than the experience of their counterparts in Europe.

Inter-city Interaction in Europe

There are many international structures in which European cities participate: Metropoles, Winter Cities, Port Cities and Northern Cities, to name a few. As can be imagined from their names, these structures are global in their participation. There is one, however, that has membership of only European cities – Eurocities, and it is this one that will be discussed as it is the structure that is most relevant here. Eurocities issued its 'Manifesto' in 1989. The Manifesto was an effort to put before leaders in other levels of government in national capitals and in Brussels the role of cities in shaping the EU economic space and in dealing with the primary problems that were confronting Europe. The text began with a cry to action: 'Europe is today undergoing a rapid process of political, economic and cultural integration. While the States have logically been the protagonists of European construction, the regions have progressively received from the community organization the recognition and economic attention they deserve. Now it is the turn of the cities.'[4] The Manifesto was signed by the mayors of 14 cities; by the mid-1990s the number of Eurocities members had risen to over 50 and today it is composed of over 75 of Europe's large and internationally-engaged cities.

A major document was issued by the Eurocities Policy Advisory Group in 1994 in which the authors sought more clearly to define the roles of the EU agencies, the regions, and Europe's major cities.[5] From this date to the present, Eurocities has insisted on the pairing of two policy objectives that are shared by all levels of government: economic competitiveness and social exclusion. Social exclusion refers to the homeless, unemployed, economically and socially marginalized, and those who experience social and ethnic or racial discrimination. In addition to skin color, language and religion are causal factors. While these problems are not confined to large cities, the reality is that a large and increasing percentage of those who suffer from social exclusion are resident in large cities. Immigrants in all societies seem to gravitate to large cities as do those who are unable to find employment in rural areas. Given the free mobility of labor, whether employed or not, among EU member countries, as well as the porous borders the EU has with Central and Eastern Europe, Africa and the Middle East, cities are increasingly faced with the need to find housing, jobs, language instruction, health care, education and so forth for these migrants. Failure to meet these needs is not only a moral issue; it becomes a threat to EU political stability. Thus the EU problem becomes a city problem and vice versa.

The 1994 policy document also differentiates between the EU's explicit and implicit urban policies. The explicit policies are those expenditures of structural (regional development) funds that have benefits for the cities. But many of the Directorates of the EU Commission have powerful impacts on the economic and social welfare of cities: specifically industrial, competition, environmental, transport, energy, R&D, and agricultural policy.[6] If these complex problems are to be dealt with effectively, the established principle of 'subsidiarity' (that each initiative should be undertaken by the level of government closest to the people that can accomplish it) mandates that city governments be explicitly and effectively brought into the policy-making and implementing processes.

The final suggestion of the 1994 document is something that all those who have done research on European cities will appreciate. The policy advisory group stated that: 'We need a better urban data base at the European level to identify the range of urban opportunities and problems that an expanded policy would address.'[7] Entities such as Eurostat and the Urban Observatory (an initiative of the UN-Habitat program) do their part, but much still needs to be done and Eurocities is the natural agent to undertake this initiative. A search of the Eurocities' website suggests that much remains to be done in this area.

The current (2003–4) effort, under the chairmanship of France's Valéry Giscard d'Estaing, to write a new constitution for the European Union has given Eurocities an opportunity to press its case for an enhanced role in policy for the EU's cities. In addition to the role of cities in the twin policy objectives of economic competitiveness and social cohesion, Eurocities continue to stress the 'democratic challenge' and argues that

> the European institutions must be brought closer to the citizens, who are calling for a clear, open, effective, democratically controlled approach towards the governance of the European Union. We are convinced that the local and regional governments of Europe, which are responsible for implementing a majority of European policies and legislation, have an important and positive contribution to make towards the future of the European Union.[8]

Eurocities argues that it and its members must be an integral component to any effort to deal with Europe's major social and economic problems and seeks to insinuate itself into the policy processes of the various Directorates General and agencies such as the Committee of the Regions.

Eurocities differs from intercity interaction in North America in at least two important ways. First, it is not an inclusive organization. While it notes that there are 250 'larger' cities in the EU, less than one-third of them are members. There are some smaller cities that are members of Eurocities, such as Oulu (Finland) and Aarhus (Denmark), but the agenda is dominated by the interests and concerns of cities with large populations: Lyon, Birmingham, Turin, Barcelona and the Randstad, for example, have been active from the beginning. As was noted above, the Canadian and American organizations are open to smaller cities, although the Federation of Canadian Municipalities does have its 'Big City Mayor's Caucus,' and it would be hard to argue that large cities control their agendas. Second, while the North American organizations tend to focus on housing, infrastructure and other essentially local concerns, Eurocities has focused on bigger questions such as the competitiveness of EU producers, social exclusion, competition policy, agriculture and culture. Europe's large cities argue their necessary involvement in solving the major problems that confront the EU as a multinational economic and social space. They assert the notion that Europe is a network of cities, as a complement to Europe as a network of regions.

Cross-border Urban Structures

In addition to inter-city structures that are established on a continental or national basis, both the EU and North America offer several examples of entities that link cities in close proximity to each other that have been kept apart by the barriers to interaction that are posed by national borders. These range from cross-border urban agglomerations, such as Seattle–Vancouver and Öresundia, to more loosely integrated urban clusters such as Regio Tri Rhena. Once again, we will find that cooperation across national borders is done more effectively in Europe than it is in North America. The greater region of Seattle and Vancouver has been seen as one of the most promising in North America and has had more development of structural interaction than has been attempted elsewhere on the continent. We will begin with this and some other efforts to develop cross-border relationships of cities along the Canada–US and Mexico–US borders, and will then examine counterpart structures in Europe.

North America

The US borders with Canada and Mexico have only one pairing of cities of similar size and international engagement: Seattle and Vancouver. Montreal, Winnipeg and Calgary have no cross-border urban partner which would serve as the basis of a significant urban interaction. This is also the case with Cleveland in the USA, and with Tucson on the Mexican border. Another possible pairing, San Antonio and Monterrey, involves a distance of over 300 miles. Only two US cities, San Diego and El Paso, have cross-border partner cities, and they as well as the pairing of Detroit and Windsor on the Canada–US border will be discussed shortly. Toronto and Buffalo tried to make something of their proximity (of about 100 miles) on the 'horseshoe,' the eastern end of Lake Ontario, but the size differential, lack of complementarities of the two urban economies, and the weakness and stagnation of Buffalo soon made evident the futility of this initiative.

One would have thought that the enormous flows of goods, and services needed to facilitate these flows, and the sometimes staggering numbers of individuals crossing these two US borders, would have generated major cross-border pairings of cities. But, of course, the cities in the three countries were established long before these flows and for reasons that had little if anything to do with proximity to the border. Indeed some of them, such as El Paso and Detroit, were settlements and trading bases long before there was a border. Good, well-functioning partnerships of the sort that are being discussed here require not only proximity, but also adequate infrastructure to support interaction, complementary economic structures, reasonable similarity in size, and political structures that value that interaction and a true cooperation in economic initiatives and activities. The four above mentioned candidates for North American cross-border urban interaction, which will now be discussed, will serve to show how difficult it is to nurture and to maintain such a structure.

Seattle–Vancouver   Seattle, Washington and Vancouver, British Columbia, present a tantalizing prospect for a powerfully integrated cross-border urban agglomeration. On the map it seems to be a natural development. The two cities are situated on the same large inlet on the Pacific Ocean, cut off from the rest of the continent by a forbidding chain of mountains, and just 140 miles from each other. Isolation and proximity have seemed to many observers to constitute a powerful inducement to cooperation and to forging a common identity and role in the North American economic space. Furthermore, they are both large and internationally-engaged cities – the population of the Seattle MSA is 5.5 million and that of the Vancouver CMA is 2 million. These two cities are also the central feature of several other cross-border structures, some based on ecology and others on economics. The most inclusive is the Pacific Northwest Economic Region, established in 1991, which encompasses British Columbia, the Yukon and Alberta in Canada and, on the US side, Washington, Oregon, Alaska, Idaho and Montana. This entity is explicit recognition of the cross-border regional basis for the economic concerns of the constituent political units. In 1988 there was an oil spill at Gray's Harbor in Washington that made clear the fact that pollution on one segment of the Pacific Coast was a concern of all segments. While the two national governments objected, a task force was established at the subnational level that included British Columbia and all US states from Alaska to California.

Environmentally sound economic development and urban management are the focus of the Cascade Corridor Commission, set up in the early 1990s by British Columbia, Washington and Oregon. The High Speed Transportation Committee has pressed for a TGV line from Vancouver to Eugene, Oregon, and the I-5 Corridor is the focus of efforts to improve the road/interstate transportation among the cities between Vancouver and Eugene. Finally, there is the Georgia Basin–Puget Sound Initiative, a project to create an ecological region that consists of the Pacific inlet that includes Vancouver, Victoria, Seattle, all the towns and cities between them, the Queen Charlotte Islands, the Strait of Juan de Fuca and the islands of Puget Sound. There have been many cooperative and joint projects introduced that have as their focus the sustainable development of the entire eco-region.

These several geographic conceptualizations are in addition to the Seattle–Vancouver urban agglomeration, Sea-Van. While Sea-Van appears from the map to be a natural for such cross-border urban interaction, in reality this interaction is faced with several formidable difficulties. First, the multiple notions of the region blur the definition of Sea-Van itself from a tight urban region to one that fades into looser and more inclusive regions. Second, the Pacific Northwest region is fraught with conflict at the subnational level. Washington and British Columbia have been marked by the conflict that attaches to states and provinces that have as important bases of their econ-omies undifferentiated primary products that are sold in the same markets. Salmon and timber disputes have induced Washington and British Columbia to work with their respective national governments on opposing sides in bitterly contested NAFTA and WTO dispute procedures. This subnational conflict makes it difficult for the cities to get the subnational governments to give them the assistance and policies they both need at the urban level. Third, the two cities have had their own conflict as competing transportation nodes, whether for container shipping and inter-modal logistics with rail networks, or as cruise ship ports, air hubs, and 'gateways' for trans-Pacific travel.

In spite of these obstacles, the two cities have made several efforts over the years to create an integrated cross-border urban agglomeration. Some of the proposed projects have come to naught, for example the efforts a decade ago to establish joint cultural institutions such as a symphony or an opera com-pany. Neither city has been capable of supporting these cultural assets on its own, so it was thought that together they might succeed. In addition to the complexities of operating in two countries, financial support was weak for institutions in which neither patronage community has a strong sense of ownership. One academic observer has given three areas in which the two urban regions have mutual interests in close cooperation: sustainability, transportation, and trade, tourism and economic development.[9] Sustainability and transportation initiatives have just been mentioned. What cannot be ignored is the fact that the two cities are separated by a national border that impedes the free flow of people and goods in both directions. This is the context for the trade and tourism initiatives that have been pursued.

The border crossings at Point Roberts, Blaine, Lyndon and Sumas in Washington are the busiest in the USA along the Canada–US border. Depending on the exchange rate between the two currencies, there are always shoppers looking for bargains, as well as commuters driving to work, and individuals and families going to recreational homes and facilities on the other side of the border. The two cities have engaged the assistance of Washington and British Columbia in lobbying with their two national capitals for additional lanes and personnel, and new technology to facilitate these flows. These efforts met with some success, additional lanes and the staff to support them. The post-September 11 climate put the policy of increasingly open borders on hold and the USA initially imposed increased scrutiny on all of its border entry points. Ultimately the pressure of business groups, such as the (Canadian) Coalition for Secure and Trade-Efficient Borders and various other groups and large companies in both countries, for procedures that would accomplish the twin objectives of border security and ease of commerce in a day of just-in-time inventory management led to the Smart Border Declaration of 2002.[10] While this was not a Seattle–Vancouver joint initiative, it does represent what can be gained if it benefits entities on both sides of the border, US–Canada as well as US–Mexico, when joint efforts are directed at the relevant national capitals.

The experience of Seattle and Vancouver suggests to us the difficulty in forging an effective and dynamic cross-border urban interaction. In spite of some apparent advantages for such a structure, it is difficult to overcome long-lasting differences in culture and aspiration, as well as powerful tendencies to focus on local advantage rather than to seek gains from a broader regional economic space.

Detroit–Windsor   The situation with these two cities is quite different. The population of Detroit is over 4 million and of its MSA 5.5 million, while that of Windsor, across the river in Ontario, is just 400 000 – smaller than two other cities in the Detroit MSA, Ann Arbor and Flint. So Windsor in some sense is little more than a suburb of Detroit. The dominant feature of the interaction between these two cities is, of course, the auto industry. Since the Canada–US Auto Pact of 1965, the industry has become fully integrated across the national border. Parts, components and finished vehicles are routinely transferred among production, assembly and sales entities with little regard for the border. This intra-industry trade has required that at least in this segment of the border that border be as seamless as is possible. It has meant that the principal concern, once the sectoral trade agreement was in place, is efficient bridge and tunnel connections. Currently 10 million vehicles and 15 million individuals cross the one bridge and one tunnel linking Detroit and Windsor per year. At present there is discussion of a second bridge connecting the US Interstate 75 and the Trans-Canadian Highway, the 401, south of the other connections.

Beyond automotive industry-driven activities, the interaction of the two cities is surprisingly limited. The casino in Windsor and some topless bars seem to have been the primary attraction for Detroiters, but establishment of the MGM Grand Detroit Casino in Detroit in 1998 has made this less of a draw. This experience is illustrative of the need for cross-border coordination of activities and the difficulties that one partner city has when anything it does to give itself an edge can be duplicated by the other. Economists instinctively think of specialization and exchange, but there is no assurance in a dynamic, evolving environment that any such specialization can be maintained with any assurance in the long run. The intra-industry cooperation and specialization that is found in the automotive industry may be difficult if not impossible to replicate in other sectors of the economy.

Neither city takes the other into account in its economic planning, but sees itself as part of its own state or provincial urban/county economic region. Detroit has a Master Plan, the most recent apparently dated 1992, in which there is only one reference to Windsor, in the Intergovernmental Relations Policies section in which the Free Trade Agreement is discussed. The text states that the city should encourage 'joint development opportunities with Windsor, working together to establish the region as a new international marketplace,' and market 'the region as a hub of international trade, since the Detroit/ Windsor region is the largest international trade region in North America.'[11] Detroit appears to have directed its attention almost exclusively to its own urban problems, such as unemployment and housing, and to implementation of several federal grant programs including one for an Empowerment Zone. Windsor has a Strategic Plan, adopted in 2003, that guides its economic development activities, and in this document there is only one reference to the US side of the border, that being to the need for 'building links with Detroit/South East Michigan beginning with a joint meeting.'[12] There is little other evidence of cross-border interaction in the area of economic development. The primary regional structural entity is the Windsor–Essex Country Development Commission. Again, this should perhaps not be surprising given the differences in the size, role, and economic structure or base of the two cities.

Cities along the US–Mexico border   Here the population figures would suggest that the two primary pairings joint or cooperative initiatives might have great potential. The San Diego MSA and Tijuana have populations of 2.8 and 1 million, respectively, and for the El Paso MSA and Ciudad Juárez these figures are 680 000 and 1 million. But several factors have acted to limit the nature of the interaction that has been possible. First, the US–Mexico border is quite a different affair than is that between the USA and Canada. Illegal migration and flows of drugs have made the border into a heavily policed barrier to free interaction. This in spite of Mexico's creation of frontier zones that have pushed the tightest border controls several miles south of the border itself. In 1996 the US Congress introduced reform of its illegal immigration laws, including the infamous Section 110 which mandated that all foreigners be registered when entering or leaving the USA. This legislation was aimed specifically at Mexicans, but was subsequently dropped. The frontier zones have made casual tourism much easier, but the nature of some of the cross-border activity does put constraints on the legitimate economic interaction that would typically be possible. Second, the nature of the Mexican border towns and cities was to some extent defined in the period of prohibition during the 1920s and 1930s in the USA when Americans crossed into Mexico for alcohol, gambling, prostitution, and other diversions that were banned at home. These activities are usually more prone to control by organized crime entities than are other activities, hence a climate or culture of crime and corruption still colors both Tijuana and Ciudad Juárez. Symptomatic of this is the campaign being carried out by Amnesty International against 'the murdered women of Chihuahua,' 370 women who it argues have 'disappeared' since 1993. This, too, makes legitimate economic interaction uncertain and difficult. Third, subsequent economic development has largely been based on expansion of production in *maquiladora* industrial sites which use low skilled, low wage labor to do assembly for US and other manufacturing firms. This type of production does not provide a base for activity that will support a partnership of equals, but rather one in which the Mexican city provides a service that may only have a minimal relationship to the economy of the US city across the border. Fourth, Tijuana and Ciudad Juárez lack the decades of investment in transportation and communication infrastructure and the decades of development of private sector economic development that characterizes the two US cities. Both San Diego and El Paso are cities with a heavy military presence and while this has some negative consequences, it does have many positive spin-offs and expenditure stability consequences.

Even more so than with the USA and Canada, the US–Mexico border is marked by substantial cultural, political and economic differences that impede close cooperation in any but the most superficial ways, such as the San Diego Dialogue project mentioned in Chapter 3. For example, San Diego found its international positioning to be hampered by the limitations of its airport, Lindbergh Field, which is situated so that it has an awkward flight path for landings and departures and is in a location which will not allow for expansion to accommodate trans-Pacific type aircraft. In the early 1990s the city had at first initiated a plan with Tijuana to develop a true bi-national airport. This airport would have had longer runways and would have given full customs and immigration access to both countries. Unfortunately, the Mexican government, which was at the time trying to implement a plan for privatization, rejected the idea.[13] Because of this difficulty in implementing a cross-border initiative, San Diego has had to explore other options such as expanding other smaller civilian airports or gaining access to a military air base that may be closed.

El Paso has seen its economic situation decline steadily for many decades. In fact, it has lost its justification for being in its geographic location since the loss of importance of El Camino Real, the Spanish colonial 'royal road' that linked Mexico City with Santa Fe. Now there is little reason for a city of El Paso's size to be located where it is, at the corner of Texas, New Mexico, and Chihuahua. The main transportation line between Mexico and Texas is that from Monterrey to San Antonio with the border crossing at Laredo/Nuevo Laredo, 400 miles to the east. Two hundred miles to the west is the crossing at Nogales for the traffic from the west coast of Mexico. Border crossings by their nature do not do much for the cities which host them. The traffic is largely flow-through traffic that may generate some low-level transshipment activity, but little else. This is especially true for cities such as El Paso given the opposition from politically potent US trucking interests in keeping Mexican trucks from being able to drive more than a few miles into the USA. Almost all cities along the US–Canada and US–Mexico borders have tried to leverage this bridge city function into assembly and service sector activities, with varying degrees of success.

In spite of the economic, locational and historic difficulties facing this cross-border region, there has been an effort to generate some forms of interaction. El Paso and Ciudad Juárez have joined with Las Cruces, New Mexico, to create the Paseo del Norte region. Progress has been made in some of the more pressing areas, such as designing a regional water sharing plan and efforts to work together on environmental quality. But in other areas in which bureaucratic structures are dramatically different and make cooperative action difficult, little of lasting presence has been accomplished. Samuel Schmidt has given us an excellent analysis of the difficulties that are posed by differing approaches in Texas and Chihuahua to land use planning, public sector decision-making, sweeping staffing changes that accompany each election, especially on the Mexican side of the border, the differing tax systems and structures of municipal finance in each country, and occasional diplomatic flare-ups at the national level, among many other factors.[14] When these factors are added to the income and economic structure differences between

El Paso and Ciudad Juárez, the stagnation of the entire region, the pressing problems of unemployment and poverty, and the local incidence of national problems such as flows of illegal migrants and drugs, it becomes clear that any comprehensive and lasting structures of planning for economic development or competitiveness are, at least for the foreseeable future, extremely difficult.

Some conclusions from the North American experience   It is clear from the experiences of North American cities that creation of effective cross-border structures of interaction are very difficult to achieve. Indeed, it is not even clear that the cities that provided us with the most promising potential for this consistently wanted to implement and maintain these structures. It does not take much spatial distance for cooperative efforts to seem to be a low priority item in the list of possible initiatives of a city mayor. The 140 miles that separate Seattle and Vancouver and the 100 between Buffalo and Toronto have in practice contributed to the lack of interaction in each case. But even when there is no distance between partner cities, as is the case with Detroit and Windsor, El Paso and Ciudad Juárez, and San Diego and Tijuana, effective and mutually beneficial interaction is difficult.

Another factor that is apparent in North America, but especially in the US, is the lack of a continuing commitment to whatever cross-border activity that may be created. Any initiative is the project of one mayor and, whether successful or not, his or her successor usually has the need to give an individual stamp to city policy. There are many instances of a mayor who is internationally or regionally focused being followed by one who is solely interested in neighborhoods or brownfield development or crime and drugs and so forth. Thus even if one of the two partner cities wants to continue the initiative the other usually loses interest and the initiative dies. We have also noted that it is often difficult for a mayor to see the future of the city as being nested in a larger regional or cross-border economic space. Mayors typically have four-year terms, and many are not able to be reelected for additional terms. Regional or cross-border initiatives may be too slow to develop and to bring positive results to be accommodated by the electoral pace of local politics.

Differences in local cultures, institutional structures, political practices and aspirations, and also the understanding in one partner city of those of the other city can be a powerful deterrent. In Mexico, until the recent election of President Fox, the government has been very state-oriented with state companies and central direction dominating economic decision-making. In Canada, most governments have seen the need to establish a path for themselves that was explicitly independent of that of the USA. The international policy adopted by the current administration of President George Bush is one that does not tolerate hesitation or independence on the part of other national governments. This has resulted, at all levels of government, in tension and conflict that has always made cooperative ventures difficult at best. In addition, there are differences among the three countries with regard to the role of government in social and economic policy. In this environment, cities cannot expect that they will be able to gain the support and resources from superior levels of government for whatever initiatives that they may have chosen to pursue.

Europe
The Association for European Border Regions (to be discussed shortly) has designated scores of cross-border regions that include literally every kilometer of border both in the EU and in contiguous European areas, such as Norway and Switzerland. They also include cities on both sides of the major seas of Europe: the Baltic, the English Channel, the Adriatic, the Irish Sea and so forth. Some involve Europe's largest cities while others are a stretch of sparsely populated terrain. Some are composed of actively engaged and highly cooperative cities and towns while others exist solely on paper. It is the European instinct to establish these structures in part to create ties between peoples who have lived for centuries in conflict and war, in part to achieve mutually beneficial policy objectives, and in part to serve as more or less official entities that can apply to various sources for allocations of development funding. There is nothing quite like this in the North American urban experience. A full examination of these urban regions would be a book in itself; in this chapter we will limit ourselves to just two of the most relevant and interesting of them. Together they will suggest what is being accomplished in Europe in the area of cross-border city interaction.

Öresund   One of the most promising inter-urban structures in Europe consists of the Danish city of Copenhagen and Sjaelland, the island on which it is situated, and the Swedish province of Skåne, dominated by its largest city Malmö and its university town Lund. It must be stressed that what is sought here is a much tighter and deeper interaction than was envisioned for Seattle and Vancouver – Öresund is to become a true cross-border urban agglomeration. Geography is an ally here as the principal cities are separated by a body of water that has been spanned by a bridge and tunnel structure that accommodates both motor vehicles and trains. Again in contrast with Seattle and Vancouver, all levels of government in both countries are strongly in support of this initiative. The Danish and Swedish national governments have stated that 'Öresund is a model for development toward a "Europe of regions" within the framework of the EU and a model for development in the entire Baltic area.'[15] Situated in the northern periphery of the EU economic space,

Copenhagen has long sought to carve out a role for itself. During the past two decades it has adopted strategy of developing as a 'gateway city' to the EU for Asian and North American companies with its airport, Kastrup, as the focal point; it has argued to its national government that a region or a small nation cannot be successful economically unless its principal city receives the resources needed to make it successful; it has sought to promote itself as the principal city of the Baltic region with direct access to the rest of the EU (that is, to become a 'bridge city' between the Baltic and the EU); and, finally, it is pinning its hopes on the strength of the Öresund economic region to overcome the disadvantages of its peripheral location. Malmö and Lund are attracted to this latter conceptualization largely because of the proximity to Copenhagen and the much longer distance to Stockholm – 15 miles versus 300.

In spite of this spatial proximity, considerable distances still remain – distances in culture and social practice. Those who know the region recognize the power of linguistic and cultural differences that differentiate the two contiguous provinces of Sjaelland and Skåne. The two nations have, through centuries, developed different legal and regulatory systems and different institutional practices. In a generally very favorable review of this project, a survey of local companies by two consulting firms found that this region is one of Europe's most attractive locations for investment and a 'metropole of international class.'[16] Nonetheless, the survey also found considerable differences between Danish and Swedish responses: Swedish respondents expressed significantly greater concerns than did Danish respondents about the barriers posed by technical standards and regulation, administrative barriers, telecommunications costs and to a very significant degree culture and language. Danish firms have concerns over differing value-added taxation and transport. To a degree that is surprising to outsiders, this suggests that the two sides of the border may be living in two different 'imagined communities.'

Regio Tri-Rhena   Of the more than 100 designated regions of Europe, perhaps the most instructive for the purposes of this chapter is that of the upper reaches of the Rhine River. *Regio Tri-Rhena* (RTR) is the name given to the southernmost area consisting of the area encompassing Basel, the French cities of Mulhouse, Belfort and Colmar, and the German cities of Freiburg and Lörrach.[17] RTR dates from 1971 with its first initiative being planning for a rail connection, although this was not realized until 1997. The economy of RTR has been undergoing a process of integration that has proceeded with a rationale that is independent of that of the EU. The fact that Switzerland is not a member of the EU seems to have had little impact on this local integration process. One of the most powerful factors is the existence of personal income differences that have induced workers to force the process. Of the workers in the Basel region, 45 000 are resident in either Alsace or Baden-Württemburg. In 1990, 24 900 French workers commuted from Alsace to Baden-Württemburg and 30 500 commuted to jobs in Switzerland. Given that wages were highest in Switzerland and lowest in France, reverse commutes have been much lower.[18]

While Öresund is situated on the periphery of the European economic space, RTR is in the heart of it, centrally located in the famous 'blue banana' region that extends from Southeast England up the Rhine and into northern Italy. This location has enormous advantages with regard to population density, transportation infrastructure, proximity to markets and so forth. In order that this advantage may be realized RTR has had to minimize the consequences of two quite different languages, three national cultures, and three sets of national and subnational institutions, practices and procedures. In actuality RTR has put in place an impressive and extensive set of cross-border initiatives. Three of the strongest industries in the region are chemical/ pharmaceutical, machine tool/automobile, and 'other industries.' In support of this strength has developed a tri-national engineer education program at technical schools in Basel, Mulhouse and Lörrach, with programs in mechanics, electronics and information technology, as well as business administration and communication. Bilingual instruction materials for students aged 8–15 have been developed, as has cooperation among the universities and technical schools in the three countries. There are 40 000 students enrolled in the universities at Basel, Freiburg, Mulhouse/Colmar and Belfort/Montbéliard. Those in bio-technology can enroll in courses offered at any of these universities. Technology centers include BioTechPark in Freiburg, Bio-pôle in Colmar and Inovations-zentrum in the canton of Basel-Land. These initiatives have been fostered under the umbrella of BioValley, which coordinates these activities and has been a central funding entity for them all, especially with project funding from the European Union.

The transportation infrastructure consists of the usual highways, canals and connections to high-speed rail lines in France and Germany. Perhaps the major initiative in this area has been the EuroAirport which serves Basel, Freiburg and Mulhouse. Clearly this has a future that is limited to being a regional airport (according to traffic, numbers five in France and three in Switzerland). Nonetheless, it is the *sine qua non* of RTR becoming a player on the European regional field. With its strengths in bio-pharmaceutical and automotive products, RTR still faces strong competition from other regions, one of which is Öresund and another of which is that of nearby Lyon–Chambéry–Grenoble.

RTR has received funding from the EU INTERREG/PAMINA program for things such as a framework for zoning, joint environmental projects and cross-border dynamics. In addition, funds have been obtained from national and subnational sources for a variety of tri- and bi-national cooperative initiatives. This has all been done under the supervision and leadership of the Council of the RegioTriRhena. The Council has established working groups in transport policy, education and training, regional policy, environment and culture, among others. Membership on the Council consists of officials from local communities and departments as well as those from the three national governments. RTR may not be the most dynamic of the 115 regions of Europe, but it does provide an example of what can be accomplished when local authorities and leaders work together to promote cross-border regional cooperation that benefits all of them. In this case it is also a cooperation that is based on the region's three largest cities, Basel, Mulhouse and Lörrach.

It should be noted that in 1995 a new structure for regional cooperation was created with the Karlsruhe Accord with which RTR became nested in the larger region that extends northward from Basel down the Rhine through Alsace and Lorraine, in France, and Baden-Württemburg, the Rhine Pfaltz, and the Saar, in Germany, to Luxemburg. Whether this larger region will have the cohesiveness of RTR is yet to be determined.

Continental and global structures

Given the lower intensity of inter-city cooperative structures in North America, it should come as no surprise that there is apparently no comprehensive structure that includes cities of Canada, the USA and Mexico. Individual cities do occasionally establish linkages of a twinning or sister-city nature, but that is the extent of it in North America. European cities are quite engaged in continental structures as we have seen in the discussion of EuroCities. In this section of the chapter we will examine some other structures in which specifically European cities participate, an agency of the European Union, and two inter-continental entities. There are literally dozens of these entities and we examine these since they are the most important and because they offer examples of ways in which such organizations can be successful and useful to cities in the enhancement of their economic competitiveness and function; some be less exemplary in this regard.

The Assembly of European Regions   The Assembly of European Regions (AER) was established in 1985 as 'a political organization of the regions of Europe and the speaker for their interests at the European and international level.'[19] The current membership includes 250 member regions from 30 countries, nine interregional organizations, including the Association of European Border Regions (to be discussed next), 'working communities' for Alpine regions, the Danube and the Pyrenees, and the Association of European Regions with Industrial Technology, the Association of European Wine-Growing Regions and the Assembly of European Fruit and Vegetable Growing and

Horticultural Regions. Thus, AER is in some sense an umbrella organization for Europe's regions and their economic interests.

Membership is, of course, voluntary and it should be noted that in many countries very few regions are members, and often membership is of primarily rural or agricultural regions. For example, in Denmark only the small city regions of Fyn and Vejle participate but not regions including Copenhagen or even Aarhus. In Germany only four regions are members: Baden-Wüttemberg, Bavaria, Lower Saxony and Thüringen. This includes the cities of Stuttgart, Munich, and Hannover but membership is more important for the agricultural interests than for these large cities. This is the case in many of the countries and diminishes the role of AER in the resolution of urban economic and social problems.

The Association of European Border Regions This is the oldest of the organizations we will examine in this section of the chapter. The Association of European Border Regions (AEBR) was established in 1971 in Bonn, with just 10 member regions.[20] The AEBR has designated 115 border regions that, as was noted above, cover all of the land borders and several sea borders of Western, Central and Eastern Europe, of which 85 are currently participating members. In addition, 14 large multinational regions have been identified, of which five are members. While the latter are clearly beyond the interest of city governments, the smaller ones are often dominated by one large city; hence, the city has the additional option of seeking its objectives through action at the level of the region. During its first decade, ABER worked on its organization and on issuing proposals for cross-border cooperation in conjunction with the European Parliament. In its second, ABER issued in 1981 the 'European Charter of Border and Cross-border Regions,' working in conjunction with the European Council. This leads to the development of the EU Community Initiative INTERREG, through which funds are disbursed for the purpose of increasing cooperative ventures across national borders.

The objectives of ABER are all focused on the development of mutually beneficial cooperative interactions between or among contiguous regions separated by a national border, to embed these regions in Europe-wide networks, to seek funds from national and EU sources, and to discuss problems of cross-border regional interaction and to find solutions to them. This is all supported by a program of research and in 2003 alone ABER issued eight publications on such cross-border topics as labor markets, maritime cooperation, security and economic and social cohesion, as well as issuing recommendations to bodies of the EU. The members of AER are national or subnational entities such as German Länder and French départements, but ABER members are structured to include only the immediately relevant territory. For this reason the objectives of the entities can be more closely focused on the interests of the participating cities.

EU Committee of the Regions   The Treaty on European Union, usually referred to as the Maastricht Treaty, established the Committee of the Regions (CoR) in 1994 for the purpose of ensuring that 'regional and local identities and prerogatives are respected.'[21] The CoR is composed of 222 members who represent the 15 member nations on a population basis. Germany, France, Italy, and the UK each have 24 members and Luxembourg is the smallest with six. With the recent addition of the ten nations from the Baltic, Central Europe, and the Mediterranean, the membership has increased to 344. The CoR includes the possibility that its members may be town council members or mayors of large cities. This makes it explicit that large cities can use the CoR to assist them in achieving their objectives with regard to economic and social issues, infrastructure, security and other policies. For example, Europe is still working on putting in place a network of high-speed rail lines. Two or more large cities may want very much to see their proposal for such a link approved. Through the CoR they can enlist the assistance of other smaller cities that will be served by the line and their regional governments as well.

The CoR does not have decision-making power, but it can issue opinions on proposals of the European Commission that are of importance to cities and regions. The Treaty also mandates that the Commission and the European Council must consult with the CoR on issues that concern its members. The CoR can also formulate its own proposals and present them to the Commission, the Council and the European Parliament. For these purposes the CoR has created six commissions whose task it is to prepare proposals and other materials for five annual CoR plenary meetings. These commissions treat the following issues: territorial cohesion, economic and social policy, sustainable development, culture and education, constitutional and governance issues and external relations. Clearly these issues are of primary interest to city governments.

The International Union of Local Authorities   IULA is neither a European nor a North American organization; its membership includes all of the major industrial countries in the world plus 16 countries in Africa, all countries of Central America, North America and Europe, the principal Asian countries and seven countries from Latin America. In each case the member is the national association of local authorities or other similar organizations of the city governments of the nation. Founded in 1913, it now has participants in over 100 countries and has decades of action on the behalf of its city members. As mentioned earlier, at a conference held in Paris, IULA merged with another organization,

United Towns Organization, to form United Cities and Local Governments, with its headquarters in Barcelona. At this conference, the program reflects the interests of the organization: first, local sustainable development, including poverty alleviation, social inclusion, multicultural cities and city management in a globalizing world; second, decentralization and local democracy, in particular, including women in local decision-making, public–private partnerships, and citizen participation; and third, cooperation and diplomacy, that is, city development strategies, fighting AIDS, information and communication technologies and local capacity building.

Being a global organization, IULA has had policy objectives that have gone beyond those of the large cities in industrialized countries, such as those that motivate EuroCities, for example. This can be seen from the list of its policy interests, which have been focused on: UN representation, poverty and development, sustainable development, decentralization, urbanization, cities' alliances, women, capacity building and children. In almost all of these interests IULA has sought to have influence with other global entities, such as the United Nations but also the World Bank, the World Associations of Cities and Local Authorities Coordination and the World Urban Forum.

The new United Cities and Local Government will take over these mandates and, one must anticipate, will continue the work of IULA. Yet to be determined is the extent to which the new organization will be of benefit to large cities in the industrialized world and the extent to which it will come to see its role as being more narrowly that of stimulating healthy growth and development of communities from villages to mega-cities throughout the Third World.

Metropolis   Metropolis is an effort to bring academic research to bear on issues that are of primary concern to large cities throughout the world.[22] Established in 1995, it has grown to a membership of entities in over 20 countries as well as several international organizations, such as the European Commission, UNESCO and the OECD. The issue that has been chosen to focus on is migration policy, with almost all large cities being powerfully affected by the movement of people from rural areas or from countries with lower incomes and fewer economic opportunities. Annual conferences have been held in Milan (1996), Copenhagen (1997), Zichron Yaacov, Israel (1998), Washington (1999), Vancouver (2000), Edmonton (2001), Montreal (2002), Vienna (2003) and Geneva (2004). The 20 member countries include, in addition to those of the conference cities, Argentina, Australia, New Zealand and 11 European countries. A sampling of the member countries indicates that only a small number of cities are active participants: in Norway (Oslo), in Italy (Rome, Turin and Bologna), in Austria (Vienna) and in the Netherlands (Rotterdam); but in Canada there are five members that encompass virtually all of the major cities – Vancouver, Toronto, Montreal, plus the Prairie and Atlantic regions, with the head office being in Ottawa. In addition to universities and migration research centers, in each country government ministries of migration or social policy, or local governments or labor, participate. In the United States, the Carnegie Endowment for International Peace is the lead participant.

The research agenda of Metropolis comprises six aspects or domains of migration policy: citizenship and culture, economics, education, physical infrastructure, political and public services and social issues. A rich and comprehensive list of research projects on such aspects as exclusion, racial discrimination, language training, occupational training and the economic impact of immigration have been completed and placed at the disposal of municipal authorities in member cities and countries, and to all others through dissemination in scholarly or specialist journals and periodicals.

While Metropolis is neither an entity of city governments nor one that is comprehensive in its membership, it does nonetheless demonstrate how a substantial number of large cities can come together, in partnership with agencies of other levels of government and with academic research centers, to gain an understanding of some of the most pressing social problems facing them.

FINAL COMMENTS

At the beginning of this chapter we noted that inter-city cooperative initiatives have had a mixed reception. While there is an underlying understanding that city governments can learn from the experiences of their counterparts elsewhere, and while it is also understood that cities can work together, for example, to exert pressure on decision-makers in other levels of government, still many city leaders either mistrust this interaction or see little value in it. Some programs, such as sister-city exchanges, often have little benefit to the economy of either city and are frequently seen as sops given to local ethnic communities. Given the historic, political and operational differences on the two continents, this reluctance to participate in inter-city ventures is a feature of North American cities (particularly those in the USA) but is offset by an equally pronounced interest in doing just this in Europe. In this chapter we have examined a variety of initiatives of this nature that have ranged from those that are national in scope to those that are global; we have focused primarily on the experience of cities in North America and Europe, primarily because of the interest and limited knowledge of the authors. In this examination we think we have found several things that are of interest to specialists in the study of urban economies.

First, these inter-city ventures serve a variety of perceived needs. Metropolis is primarily a structure that supports research into urban problems and brings the findings of that research to metropolitan leaders and practitioners. The Assembly of European Regions serves to exert pressure in support of city initiatives on agencies of the European Union. The three Canadian and US organizations, the FCM, the NLC and the USCM, essentially do the same thing in these countries. EuroCities appears to function as an organization that more comprehensively meets the needs of its members.

Second, the political and social cultures of each continent shape the organizations that are established and also the use big city mayors are likely to make of them. In Europe, the mayor is nested in a set of public–private sector entities with mandates and bureaucracies that continue to function no matter who is mayor. Thus, a continuity of effort is in most cases assured. By contrast, North American mayors, especially in the USA, tend to wipe the policy slate clean upon their installation and want to introduce their own mark on the policies of the city government. The weakness of the associated structures and the strength of the mayor means that initiatives in the areas of internationalization, competitiveness enhancement and cooperation with other similar cities are typically allowed to die and to be replaced by programs directed at neighborhoods or some local social pathology, or vice versa. This lack of continuity in the USA hinders cities in their economic development efforts and certainly puts inter-city cooperation on the back burner.

Third, from the standpoint of the sort of city that has been studied in this book, mostly large internationally-engaged cities in Europe and North America, not all of the organizations will have much to offer. Much of the focus of IULA has been on the issues that are of importance to Third World cities and much of its effort to encourage policy initiatives has been aimed at the UN. Even the NLC and CUSM in the USA have memberships that are heavily weighted toward smaller cities and toward cities in rural parts of the country. At least the FCM has its caucus of mayors of large cities.

Fourth, the issues of competition and cooperation enter the scene differently in Europe and North America. In the mandates of the three North American associations, economic development or competitiveness enhancement do not have a prominent place. The leaders of US cities, in particular, appear to be dominated by the notion of competition among similar cities and cooperation is far from their minds. They appear to view this sort of cooperation and discussion to be a zero-sum game, and they do not want to risk being, or being seen to be, the loser in the exchange. Due to a variety of factors, such as domestic political structures, the affection felt for cities and for city life, the need to overcome past mentalities that have resulted in conflict, the exigencies of the integration process since the 1950s, and an acceptance of a stronger role of the state in economic matters, European city leaders have more fully embraced inter-city initiatives and interaction.

NOTES

1. 'Paris and Berlin pledge more regional co-operation,' *Financial Times*, 29 October 2003, p. 4:3.
2. http://www.hud.gov/library/bookshelf18/hudmission.cmf.
3. Dunfield, 2003.
4. *Eurocities: Documents and Subjects of Eurocities Conference*, 1989.
5. Eurocities Policy Advisory Group, 1994.
6. Ibid., p. 6.
7. Ibid., p. 8.
8. 'Eurocities Mayors' declaration,' 2002.
9. Artibise, 1995; and Urban Affairs Annual Review, No. 44, 1995, pp. 221–50.
10. Barry, 2003, pp. 10–15.
11. Planning and Development Department, *Master Plan of Policies*, Detroit: City of Detroit, 1992, pp 112–3.
12. City Planner's Office, 2003, p. 11.
13. Erie, 2001, p. 36.
14. Schmidt, 1995, in Kresl and Gappert.
15. *Øresund – en region bliver til: Rapport udarbejdet af den danske og svenske regering*, 1999, p. 11.
16. Reported in Söderström, 1999, p. 96.
17. See Regio Tri-Rhena website: http://www.regiotrirhena.org.
18. Estrose, 1996, pp. 81–2.
19. See Assembly of European Regions website: http://www.are-regions-europe.org.
20. See Association of European Border Regions website: http://www.aebr.net.
21. See website for EU Committee of the Regions: http://europa.eu.int/institutions/cor/index_en.htm.
22. See Metropolis website: http://www.metropolis.net.

7. Strategic planning for competitiveness enhancement

In the previous chapters of this book we have examined the enormous challenges and threats that confront the decision-makers of urban economies, both in the United States and in other countries. The fundamental confrontation is with the issue of their competitiveness but, as we have seen in earlier chapters, they have opportunities to improve their situation through participation in regional or international structures of cooperation; they can promote themselves through urban diplomacy; technology can be both a beneficial factor and impose threats to existing economic activities, and they can improve the effectiveness of their governance. All of these issues come together in the process that is the subject of this final substantive chapter – planning for competitiveness enhancement.

Cities do much planning, but little of it is directly relevant to the enhancement of competitiveness. Land use, social housing, transportation infrastructure, accommodation of the needs of whatever economic interest presents a demand, cleaning up industrial sites, waterfront development, urban renewal and so forth, have captured a great deal of the time and attention of local authorities. Some of this is remedial work to make up for past inattention or the negative consequences of past economic activities. All of these actions make the city more attractive and viable than it would be without them. Good housing, efficient transportation, urban amenities and attractive urban spaces are all aspects of a competitive urban economy. But in themselves, they do not address the specific economic competitiveness needs of that city. Hence, we are devoting this chapter to a focused discussion of planning for competitiveness.

The strategic planning process is quite complex and requires that several issues be dealt with effectively. The list of these issues is indeed a long one, and in this chapter we will discuss each of the following:

1. How can the strategy of the planning exercise be set? (It should be noted parenthetically here, that while the word strategy is used throughout this chapter, the strategy chosen may be multi-faceted so that strategies might in some cases seem to be more appropriate.)
2. How can planners determine the best means of achieving the strategy of the plan?

3. Which entities can assist the effort, and which can hinder the planning process?
4. What can local governments control or affect or realistically hope to accomplish?
5. What do state and national governments control or affect?
6. How can local actors be most effectively mobilized?
7. How can costs be contained?
8. How can local government be made most effective?
9. What criteria should be used to assess success? How long should the evaluation period be?
10. What links to external entities, such as other similar cities, will be found to be useful?

After examining each of these issues we will offer a model for urban strategic planning that is designed to meet the requirements of some of the most important of them, and we will link it to recent research on creativity and innovation. Then we will make explicit the international dimensions of this issue. Finally, we will offer some comments on the process of strategic planning for competitiveness enhancement.

THE ISSUES INHERENT IN URBAN PLANNING FOR COMPETITIVENESS ENHANCEMENT

Each of the issues enumerated above must be examined by planners if their initiative is to be successful. Most of them are standard for any planning exercise, but if they are not treated specifically from the standpoint of competitiveness enhancement, the results will usually be disappointing. A Google search for 'strategic planning' will give access to many sites of consultants and agencies on which the essentials are discussed, but there is also a published literature on this subject that is of some interest. In the late 1980s and early 1990s, some planners were attracted to the approach of the Committee for Economic Development and its three-part process 'diagnosis–vision–action.'[1] To assist in implementation, there was the model for the public sector of Public Technology, Inc. that consisted of seven steps from gaining community involvement through to monitoring or assessment of the results.[2] The three central steps are identification of key strategic issues, developing strategies, and developing an action plan. What is left vague in these approaches is the methodology that will be used to accomplish these steps. One danger is that the process will be essentially inward looking, rather than explicitly comparative with the understanding of the city's strengths and weaknesses being developed in relation to competing cities.

A popular 'text book' on the subject argues that the goal of strategic planning should be quality jobs, economic stability and economic and employment diversity.[3] To achieve this, the successful strategy is a composite of four distinct approaches: (1) locality development (the built environment), (2) business development (demand), (3) human resource development (supply) and (4) community-based employment development (the neighborhood). Presumably, the diagnosis stage (of the CED approach) would give the planners the understanding needed to attach priorities to each of the four but, again, the methodology of doing this is left unspecified. While it is true that narrowly targeting specified industries is risky in a complex and rapidly changing global economy, it is nonetheless also true that different industries will impose different demands on each of the four approaches. How are priorities to be attached to each? This will be discussed below, but it must be recognized that some specificity in targeting is unavoidable and that decisions will have to be made with regard to exactly what is to be done with regard to each of the four.

This literature is very useful in providing an overview of the process of strategic planning for competitiveness enhancement. In the examination of the ten issues that were listed above, what follows has been compiled not from those sites but from the authors' own experience and study. Hence, references to the literature will be minimal as much of this is simply perceived as common sense.

Strategy Setting

This would at first glance appear to be a fairly straightforward thing to establish. But as was noted in Chapter 2, the specific strategy of the planning effort may be hotly contested as the several participants in the process may have different visions as to how this should be done. The strategic plan for competitiveness enhancement itself should be considered an attempt to alter the future economic development of the city through purposeful action. This action should be done according to a well thought-out strategy that is based on a realistic understanding of the assets at hand, the capacity for realizing certain initiatives, the capabilities of local actors and institutions, and the aspirations of the residents of the city. That is, the strategic plan must be grounded in reality and enthusiastically endorsed by all of the required participants. Unfortunately, these two rather obvious conditions have not always been met in practice. First, it may be that the mayor or head of the planning process will impose a strategic objective that he or she simply believes to be the preferred objective. This may be because it is in conformity with the 'favorite of the day' among planning consultants who will be brought into the process, or local interest groups may press for an objective that meets their specific needs. Second, the planning process may be conducted by a small group of insiders with little public consultation and debate. This is usually the approach that takes less time and energy and that generates the known and desired end result, but it also usually means that the planners have an enormous and often futile task of gaining the active participation of the rest of the community. In either event, the planning process is far less likely to be successful than if the two conditions had been met. The trick, of course, is to be able to accomplish them both while still having a process that can be effective and timely in its execution.

What are the Best Means?

Once the strategy has been decided upon, the next step is determination of what has to be done for it to be successfully realized. Each strategy will require a different set of urban assets. Clearly, some strategies will require a labor force with specific skills or with a specific educational attainment. Niche manufacturing and bio-pharmaceutical are both reasonable strategies for some cities, but each imposes its own distinctive demands on the work force. Some strategies will be best achieved with the participation of large multinational firms while others will be of the 'third Italy' type which typically involves many small firms. Each of these two industrial structures will be different in their access both to technology and to capital. Each will have different expectations of the involvement of local government and agencies. For some types of work force, labor will have to be attracted and retained through the provision of recreational or cultural amenities, or health facilities, or quality schools, or restaurants and a historic district, or a certain stock of housing. Some industries place heavy demands on air transport facilities and connections, or interstate-quality highways or a communications infrastructure. For some research-based sectors it may be necessary to ensure that local universities and research institutes or laboratories are effectively and cooperatively linked, rather than present but isolated.

One could go on at great length in this vein but the more pressing question is that of ensuring that the most effective means will be used to achieve the strategy. The most promising approach is that of making an assessment of specifically which means are suited for each strategy and from this will emerge a set of urban assets or institutional changes/developments that must be in place and that will constitute much of the most important work of the local authorities. This will be discussed more explicitly later in this chapter.

Who Can Help and Who Can Hinder?

It is highly unlikely that a city government will be able to accomplish its planning task relying only on its own resources; other entities, local and distant, will have to be involved in the process. It must also be remembered that a new strategy for competitiveness will present threats and challenges to other entities. Entrenched businesses may work against the plan as there may be nothing in it for them and indeed it may privilege other sectors that may compete for the same labor or may refocus infrastructure, and so forth. Other cities will be negatively affected by the success of the plan and may see their position in the urban hierarchy deteriorate as a consequence. Therefore, the question of who can help and who can hinder is an important one and must be addressed.

As will be discussed shortly, the state and national governments have roles to play and disgruntled firms that see themselves being marginalized may seek to gain support from them in an effort to slow down or even to sabotage the planning effort. Any plan will place demands for change on regulatory bodies, transportation authorities, tax and expenditure agencies and so forth. The trick here is to avoid being blind-sided by one of these entities. Just as state governments are torn between the needs of urban and rural constituencies, so that cities may not be able to obtain the support they need for some initiatives, the local chamber of commerce and similar private sector groups may be torn between the demands of member firms in the privileged and the marginalized sectors of the economy.

What Can Local Government Accomplish?

Cities are situated in structures of governance in which there are both superior and inferior levels of government, each of which has its own constitutionally or legislatively determined capabilities and responsibilities. Above are the national and state or provincial governments. The relationship with county government is less clear as many larger cities are in two or more counties, although most are not. Then below in the structure are boroughs and a variety of special-purpose entities such as school districts, business development districts and so forth. In addition, there are regional authorities for public services such as, among others, transportation, police, fire, water and economic development. Private sector entities such as the chamber of commerce, arts organizations and civic clubs are also part of the picture. Within this structure the city will find entities that can help or hinder its efforts, as was just noted, but there is also the more neutral fact that certain things can only be done by certain entities. Michael Porter's 'diamond' makes it clear that local and superior levels of government and the private sector all have roles to play in enhancing competitiveness.[4]

Clearly the city can take the lead position in the process of designing the economic strategy for the urban region. It can also encourage the participation of local actors, and develop mechanisms of liaison with entities outside that region. Much of the built environment, zoning, schools, some of the transportation infrastructure, urban amenities such as parks, cultural and recreational facilities, public safety and health facilities are substantially under its control. Resources can be invested in making neighborhoods attractive, safe and congenial places to live and to spend leisure time. City boosterism is often maligned but it can play a powerful role in giving the community a sense of single purpose and an enthusiasm about the city's prospects. Business investments are decided on hard factors such as the profitability of that facility, but when several possible sites are of roughly equal profitability, soft factors such as amenities, local spirit and attractive places for workers and staff to live can be the determining factors.

What is the Role of Superior Levels of Government?

Unfortunately, cities do not control decisions made about taxes, inter-regional transportation projects, education, the macroeconomic environment, trade policy, immigration, foreign policy and a host of other important aspects that impinge on the city's economic activity. They can, of course, lobby with their state government and can, individually or as part of a larger group of cities, try to influence the decisions of the national government. While European cities have had, as was shown in the previous chapter, a long history of working together to achieve common objectives, cities elsewhere, especially in the United States, have not been quite as active. In many countries with democratic political systems, state/provincial and national governments are torn between the demands of rural and of urban voters. A delicate balance between the two groups must be achieved and city governments are constrained in the demands they can place on the other levels of government. One thinks, again, of New York City and upstate New York, and of Chicago and down-state Illinois as prime examples. In several US states two or more large cities may be in competition with each other for the attention of the state legislature and governor. In Canada, British Columbia, Alberta, Ontario and Quebec all have more than one large city, although the provincial urban hierarchy is quite clear. Thus, while the potential of superior levels of government to do good for the city is clear, so too is the difficulty the city often has in realizing that potential in competition with other rural or urban claimants.

In Europe in the early 1990s, the argument was presented by cities such as Amsterdam, Barcelona and Copenhagen that the health and vitality of the largest city was crucial for the health and vitality of the entire 'national' (Netherlands, Catalonia and Denmark) economy. It was argued that this was due in part to the fact that the city's economy dominated the larger economy, and in part because of positive spread effects throughout the national economic space emanating from the economic activity of an internationally competitive urban economy. In North America, given the weak economic impact of state and provincial borders, this argument has carried less weight. Many large cities, such as New York, Chicago, Philadelphia, Cincinnati, St. Louis, Kansas City, Portland (Oregon) and Memphis, have an economic reach that extends into more than one state, and some, namely Detroit, Seattle, Buffalo, San Diego and El Paso, reach into another nation. So for many cities it is difficult if not impossible to get effective assistance for their efforts to enhance their competitiveness from the national or state/provincial levels of government.

An additional difficulty in this area arises from the fact that in large nations the regional components of the national economy are so diverse in their needs for interest rate policy or counter-cyclical fiscal policy or international trade policy that no single approach to the specific policy will meet the needs of most of the cities. This is shown clearly in the efforts of the European Central Bank to design a monetary policy for Euroland and the difficulty the member nations have in coming into compliance with the requirements of the growth and stability pact. Amsterdam may be over-heating while Turin or Madrid is in recession; the same is true in the USA or in Canada.

Mobilization of Local Actors

No strategic plan will have credibility with the larger community unless there is broad participation in its design and in the discussion that generates it. Furthermore, elected officials and their private sector colleagues have only limited capability to implement the plan and to realize its strategy, therefore they must engage individuals in all sectors of the local community and all of its major institutions, such as universities, infrastructure agencies, social agencies, cultural institutions, and so forth. As Charles Landry wrote: 'Cities have one crucial resource – their people. Human cleverness, desires, motivations, imagination and creativity are replacing location, natural resources and market access as urban resources.'[5] Involvement in the process is clearly the single most effective mechanism in realization of the ends of the plan. As will be made clear shortly, it is of crucial importance that the planning process be as open to new thinking and that those involved in it should be other than 'the usual suspects.' Many diverse constituencies have a stake in the outcome of the process and have skills and political clout that are indispensable to design and implementation of a successful strategic planning exercise.

How Can Cost be Managed?

Given the current obsession with tax reduction and the widespread animosity toward the public sector, no strategic plan will be accepted in the local community unless the local authorities present a convincing argument that they have designed a plan that is both cost-effective and no more than necessarily intrusive. Furthermore, unless this can be achieved the city will appear to be less than otherwise attractive to the economic interests the city will wish to attract or retain. Thus efficiency is always one of the primary considerations in any question of strategic planning. Managers tend to focus on things such as competitive bidding, appropriateness of materials and so forth. Economists focus on decision-making and on the allocation of resources, including labor and time. Since the author of this chapter is an economist, the latter will be the concern here – without intending to diminish the importance of the former. The first concern here is that there must be absolute clarity as to both the strategy and the means of the plan. Second, the strategy and the means must be the results of objective analysis of the city's true situation and must be rationally linked to each other. Third, there must be a detailed mapping of the responsibilities of each participant in the process so that wasteful turf battles can be avoided and each participant can have his or her effort most effectively focused. Any confusion about strategy, means or tasks will result in inefficiency in effort and will increase the costs of implementing the plan. This, in turn, will make it less appealing to various constituencies in the local community.

Effective Local Government

Partly, this is a concern over structure in that some metropolitan governance structures facilitate metro-wide planning while others make it virtually impossible. On the face of it, Pittsburgh with most of the metro area within Allegheny county would have a relatively easy time of it. The Allegheny County Commission has the potential of getting all of the participants in the same room with a clear understanding as to who is in charge. Individual towns can always bolt and go off on their own, but there are disadvantages of their doing this. Buffalo, on the other hand, has two counties, two airport commissions and four international bridge commissions, the city, the Western New York Development Authority and some private sectors actors. Once they were all in the same room there was no clear-cut locus of authority. Chicago has one large city and scores of smaller towns and no central authority. In fact the city managed to obtain a corridor of land between it and O'Hare International Airport so the city would have authority over it and so that the surface rail connection could be implemented. New York is nested in the Port Authority of New York and New Jersey for airport and metro-wide transportation planning. Other cities have their own individual problems and structural solutions to them. Not all of them work effectively. No matter how well designed the strategic plan is, unless there is a structure of governance that is capable of getting all of the relevant entities to the table and of inducing them to act in a productive and coordinated way, successful implementation is doubtful.

A second problem for cities in the United States in particular is the fact that there is little long-term consistency in the approach taken to strategic planning and little long-term continuity in the individuals who are involved in the process. The typical pattern is for everything to be refocused and re-structured each time a new mayor is elected. In European cities, senior development and planning staff are employed for decades and the plans and policies they pursue are developed in conjunction with the local chamber of commerce and business community. So when a new mayor is elected he/she often has little political capacity to make a sudden change in the city's priorities. In the United States the incoming mayor typically has little attach-ment to the existing strategy for economic development or competitiveness enhancement and, wanting to impose his/her mark on the priorities of the mayor's office, strikes off on a new course. The existing work has then been done for naught. In addition to putting the planning process on hold for a few years, this has obvious implications for cost containment, or the lack of it, in the sense of the efficient utilization of resources. Thus, effective and consist-ent local governance is one of the continuing problems for US cities.

What External Linkages/Relationships Should be Developed?

We have already examined in a previous chapter the possibilities that exist for municipal diplomacy and for structured relationships with other cities and regions, so little need be said here on this subject. But we have just noted the explicit identification of entities that can both help and hinder the city in realization of the goals of its plan. In addition to generating good publicity regarding the assets of the city, municipal diplomacy can be of assistance in development of mutually beneficial relations with other cities or groups of cities. The specific content of the plan will indicate exactly which sorts of inter-city linkages would be of benefit. Both the strategy and the means of the plan will create opportunities for mutually beneficial contacts and cooperative ac-tion with other cities and entities. Some cities will be facing or have faced the same challenges and may have useful experiences and solutions to share. Other entities such as the International Union of Local Authorities or EuroCities can extend those contacts beyond the immediate national space. This is of special importance as cities on other continents or in other nations will be far less likely to be in direct competition with the city in question. In fact for some activities such as inter-modal transportation, foreign cities will be natural partners and will have some interest in making certain that the subject city gets it right. It is also the case that multinational companies looking for specific urban assets may be able to direct local authorities to other cities in which they have facilities that have been successful in developing those assets.

What Will be the Criteria for Success?

The success of the plan will, of course, be contingent upon two elements: the achievement of the strategy, and the efficiency with which this is done. This does not mean that the plan should be rigidly adhered to in the face of changing reality. It is in the nature of this process in this situation that new threats from new competitors and from new objective developments ranging from policy changes at another level of government or in another nation to technological advances will present local planners with the need to respond effectively. Thus the strategy of the plan may have to be altered, and the means along with them, but the changes must be the result of the same deliberative process that generated the plan in the first place.

There is also the need to establish clearly the short-run and the long-run criteria for judging the success of the plan. In the short run the community will expect to see some positive impact on the standard objectives of economic policy – reduced unemployment, increased economic activity, increased investment and such visible indicators such as improvement of the living conditions of the citizenry and especially of those who are homeless and with low incomes. These may not be explicit objectives of the plan but once the plan has been adopted the community will be looking for progress in these areas. No planning process can ignore these natural concerns of the community. In the longer run the stated objectives of the strategy will be what must be achieved. These will be the more difficult objectives of quantitative expansion or qualitative restructuring.

While there are some things that can be done to answer these ten questions, it is most important to recognize that each response should be tailored to the specific strategic direction the city chooses to pursue. As an aid to determination of that direction, we offer the following model.

A MODEL FOR STRATEGIC PLANNING FOR URBAN COMPETITIVENESS ENHANCEMENT

One approach to the process of strategic planning for competitiveness enhancement is given in Table 7.1. Descending from 'ultimate objective' to

Table 7.1   A model of urban economic strategic planning options

Ultimate objective: ECONOMIC VITALITY IN AN INCREASINGLY INTERNATIONALIZED ENVIRONMENT

Basic goal	Quantitative expansion				Qualitative restructuring			
Strategies	Export promotion	Bridge city	Regional center	Headquarters national	Develop niches	Access Point city	R&D center	Headquarters: international
Means								
I	X				X		X	
II	X	X	X					
III	X				X		X	
IV						X		
V				X		X	X	X
VI		X		X		X		X
VII			X	X	X	X	X	
VIII	X	X	X					X

I   = Development and support of small and medium sized firms
II   = Development of alliances with other cities
III = Establishment of effective links between firms and universities and research centers
IV   = Establishment and expansion of international linkages
V   = Construction of infrastructure: housing and urban amenities
VI   = Construction of infrastructure: transportation
VII = Construction of infrastructure: communication
VIII = Development of adequate specialized business services

Source: Kresl, 1992.

173

'means' we go from the most general to the most specific. The Ultimate Objective may appear to be utterly banal but it does focus on the international situation in which the city finds itself and the reference to vitality does suggest that a long-term dynamic process is at issue. The first real decision for local authorities is whether the plan should consist of an effort simply to expand in future years the existing nature of the local economy. That is, should the goal be that of doing more of the same and doing it better, or should the local economy be qualitatively restructured so as to abandon some of its traditional activities and to develop what are perceived to be the city's strengths for the future? Some cities can revitalize existing economic activities and work from their historic strengths; however, others have historic strengths that have no future. We can all think of cities that have taken one path or the other in face of a challenge to their historic economic specialization and role in the urban hierarchy. While Chicago has diversified its economy away from steel and heavy manufacturing, it still has important manufacturing strength in higher value-added areas. The steel industry both in Pittsburgh and Buffalo has suffered decline, and while Pittsburgh has restructured itself by developing robotics, medical technology and electronic instrumentation, Buffalo still languishes in search of its future. Toronto has restructured its economy away from manufacturing into finance, headquarters activity and some high-technology production. Miami has become less reliant on tourism and more so on finance and other services related to Latin America.

Each city will have to examine its situation in light of its assets and the options that are available to it. That is to say, it will have to select a strategy for development of its response to the challenges it faces. The third line in Table 7.1 gives sets of strategies that are consistent with each of the two goals. There are four strategies for each goal, but they are meant to be illustrative of the options that present themselves to city planners. It would be easy to add several other strategies to the table. In this example, the qualitative expansion goal can be met through promotion of production and export of existing production, through development of an existing advantage of linking two national economies (the bridge city), through increasing its status as a regional center, or through assisting existing firms in becoming more prominent in the national economy. Each of these strategies builds on existing strengths and capabilities, and each will have a distinctive impact on the shape of the city's future economy – its production, employment, role in the urban hierarchy, attractiveness to specific categories of workers and so forth. The qualitative restructuring city will have to rely less on past accomplishments than on the potential for development of new activities. The four strategies indicated suggest that the city has an option to develop niches in emerging sectors such as information technology and bio-pharmaceutical. The requisite skilled labor can be attracted to the city, and inducements can be offered that will develop a cluster of firms in the targeted sector. Montreal has been relatively successful during the past two decades in doing exactly this. Or the city can develop as an 'access point city' in which it serves as a point of entry and a base of operations for a continent for firms from other continents. Toronto has tried to do this, as have several West Coast cities from Vancouver to Los Angeles. Linking universities to laboratories and firms can enhance the city's role as a center of research and development and, finally, the city can, perhaps in conjunction with point-of-access status, develop into an international headquarters location. Again, each of these strategies will work to shape the economic, social and cultural identity of the city.

The demands of, for example, research and development, bridge-city status and export promotion are clearly distinct and different from each other. This is represented in the fourth line, means, in which the requirements for each strategy are identified. Again, this is meant to be illustrative rather than inclusive. For example, some will require that investment be made in various aspects of infrastructure and others will require strengthening of certain institutions. As was noted above, for the means to be put in place it may be necessary for the city to develop cooperative relationships with other levels of government, regulatory agencies, or with firms. An excellent current example of this is the case of Pittsburgh and US Airways, as the city tries to retain its status as a regional hub for that airline. Not only must the city negotiate with the airline, it must get the state and Allegheny County to agree to a variety of tax incentives as well as regulatory and other changes.

The advantage of this approach is that it makes clear to city planners what their options are and what decisions have to be made. Settling on the goal is crucial. But once this has been done, the strategy should be consistent with it. The strategy may, of course, be a comprehensive one that is composed of more than one of those that would be listed in Table 7.1 as it would be developed for a particular city. Further analysis would be required for a full understanding of what means would actually be required for each strategy, but once this is done the community would know exactly what had to be accomplished and would then be in a position to allocate tasks to each of the constituent groups.

Finally, the Kresl–Singh model of urban competitiveness that was presented in Chapter 2 would be of considerable use to the local planners in assessing accurately the relative strengths and weaknesses of their city in relation to other cities with which they would be in competition for the same functions, or investments, or firms. This would suggest in general what the city should be doing to enhance its overall competitiveness, but it would also indicate those means in which the city might be relatively deficient. Table 7.2 was developed for this purpose and is presented here where it is most relevant for the analysis. The 24 cities are listed vertically according to there relative

Table 7.2 City rankings by explanatory variable, 1977–92

	Primary determinants										Secondary determinants						
	$Y	RC/MVA	F100	BA	EARM	Cult	K	Export	Pop	Transp	RC/N	LocSun	FRP	F20	N	Cult81	Rank
San Francisco	11.0	7	4	3	5	18	6.0	1	10.0	2	3	1	22.0	18	2	5	1
Seattle	23.0	13	20	10	7	13	22.0	4	7.0	5	13	0	13.5	21	8	15	2
Miami	8.0	6	7	14	3	10	2.5	8	8.0	12	23	1	13.5	22	3	21	3
Phoenix	9.0	12	19	19	4	24	1.0	15	1.0	22	16	1	5.0	23	7	23	4
Tampa	6.0	18	10	21	8	23	2.5	23	5.0	24	24	1	14.0	20	6	24	5
Atlanta	3.0	9	5	11	12	21	10.0	18	3.5	14	12	0	2.0	14	5	22	6
Boston	1.0	4	2	5	13	14	4.0	12	15.0	13	2	1	20.5	15	21	4	7
Los Angeles	12.5	23	8	2	9	22	6.0	3	6.0	23	22	1	24.0	16	4	2	8
Dallas-Ft. W.	17.0	22	12	7	11	2	23.5	13	3.5	10	21	1	3.0	13	11	10	9
San Diego	14.0	3	3	13	2	9	6.0	16	2.0	18	5	1	20.5	24	9	16	10
Denver	20.0	1	11	15	1	1	16.0	24	12.0	9	1	1	10.0	19	17	18	11
New York	2.0	20	1	1	10	17	11.0	2	19.0	1	20	0	17.0	4	1	1	12
Minn.-St. P.	7.0	11	16	12	17	11	8.0	11	11.0	21	9	0	23.0	12	16	9	13
Cincinnati	12.5	15	13	24	24	4	14.5	17	16.0	19	10	0	7.0	1	14	17	14
Philadelphia	5.0	8	9	6	16	15	17.5	9	17.0	4	11	0	6.0	2	10	6	15
Houston	24.0	16	6	9	6	8	23.5	7	9.0	6	17	1	4.0	11	15	8	16
Kansas City	15.0	10	18	22	19	3	12.5	22	13.0	20	8	1	1.0	10	18	20	17
Cleveland	21.0	24	23	16	21	7	14.5	14	23.0	8	19	0	8.0	9	12	7	18
Detroit	16.0	14	24	8	14	12	20.5	5	22.0	11	7	0	16.0	17	23	13	19
Chicago	19.0	17	21	4	15	19	20.5	6	21.0	3	14	0	13.5	3	22	3	20
Milwaukee	18.0	21	17	23	23	5	19.0	21	20.0	7	15	0	13.5	6	20	11	21
St. Louis	10.0	19	22	18	22	16	12.5	19	18.0	16	18	0	18.0	8	19	19	22
Pittsburgh	22.0	2	15	20	20	6	17.5	20	24.0	17	4	0	9.0	7	24	14	23
Baltimore	4.0	5	14	17	18	20	9.0	10	14.0	15	6	0	19.0	5	13	12	24

Primary determinants

$Y	Growth in per capita money income, 1979–87
RC/MVA	Research centers/manufacturing value added, 1987
F100	Growth in the percentage of firms with more than 100 employees, 1977–82
BA	Number of individuals with a university degree, 1990
EARM	Share of Engineering, accounting, research and management workers in total labor force, 1987
Cult	Growth in number of cultural institutions, 1981–5
K	Increase in the capital stock for the state, 1977–87
Export	Exports as a share of total output, 1993

Secondary determinants

Pop	Growth in population, 1980–90
Transp	Quantity of transportation services
RC/N	Research centers/labor force, 1987
LocSun	Location in the 'sun belt,' 1 = yes, 0 = no
FRP	Fiscal, regulatory and political climate
F20	Percentage of firms with more than 20 employees, 1980
N	Growth in the labor force, 1979–87
Cult81	Number of cultural institutions, 1981

Source: Kresl, 1992.

177

competitiveness, with San Francisco being the most competitive and Baltimore the least. Arrayed horizontally across the top of the table are the variables that have been ascertained empirically to be those that determine urban competitiveness. The first eight variables on the left are primary determinants that determine overall competitiveness, while the second eight on the right are secondary determinants of two of the first eight, increase in per capita income and the share of 'Engineering, accounting, research and management' (EARM) workers in the labor force.

Using a table similar to this, but designed with the situation of the individual city in mind, local authorities will be able to determine empirically which aspects of their economy are weaknesses that should be strengthened and which are strengths that should be maintained. For example, reading across horizontally it is clear that for this period of time Miami was ranked third most competitive but that it was relatively weak in its cultural institutions, in the education of its work force, and in its transportation infrastructure. Los Angeles was relatively weak in its research sector, its transportation infrastructure, and in 'Fiscal, regulatory and political' (FRP). A city as poorly ranked as Pittsburgh was, nonetheless, highly ranked in its research sector and its cultural institutions. The reader can do this for the other cities. The benefit of this approach is that it is both empirical and comparative, thus giving an objective evaluation of what the city must work on if it is to enhance its relative economic competitiveness, in general improving on its weaknesses and maintaining its areas of strength. Again, this is both empirical and comparative and as such should minimize the danger of self-delusion. The specific strategic plan that is adopted will also, as will be shown below, highlight certain of the determinants as being of particular importance for what is specifically being emphasized in the plan – certain urban functions or certain economic sectors.

THE URBAN MILIEU: CREATIVE OR OTHERWISE

Considerable attention has been given in recent decades to research on the creative process – not just what creativity is but also where it is found and how it can be nurtured. Most of this work is ultimately based on the research of two psychologists, Mihaly Csikszentmihalyi and Howard Gardner. Two urbanologists, Charles Landry and Peter Hall, have made use of this work in their study of cities. In this section of the chapter we will examine what this research on creativity can contribute to the enhancement of urban competitiveness.

Csikszentmihalyi is particularly important because he stresses that '(w)e cannot study creativity by isolating individuals and their works from the social and historical milieu in which their actions are carried out.' He has constructed a model in which there are three interacting 'main shaping forces,' the creativity triangle. First, there is the field consisting of a set of social institutions 'that selects from the variations produced by individuals those that are worth preserving.' Second, there is the stable cultural domain 'that will preserve and transmit the selected new ideas or forms to the following generations.' Third, there is the individual 'who brings about some change in the domain, a change that the field will consider to be creative.'[6] Thus, creativity involves not only coming up with something that is new and import-ant – it must also be recognized as such by those who comprise the field in which the individual is working. Botticelli and Bach are only two of many individuals who have been determined to be very creative but who were not recognized as such by the field at the time of their creativity. In the Soviet Union, Lysenko was esteemed above Mendel because in that society ideology and politics trumped science.

Of more interest to us is the emphasis placed on the domain that facilitates the work of the creative individual by compiling and preserving the creative contributions of previous individuals. In the context of our study, the city is the place in which these aspects of the domain are situated. Csikszentmihalyi does not elaborate on this, concerned as he is with the creativity of the individual, but he does note that the development of the domain is influenced by economic and political forces.[7] Government since its earliest manifesta-tion has provided an environment which has promoted creative activity. In market economies, such as the United States, this support is also provided by both public and private-sector entities. Unfortunately, government does not always act in positive ways, as the actions of the Nazi and Soviet govern-ments have shown. But if the creative powers of the individual in the political space of a city are to be realized, then the actions of government can be crucial in this process.

Gardner has used Csikszentmihalyi's individual-domain-field model but has added to it the notion of multiple human intelligences. Specifically, he finds that in addition to the two intelligences regularly focused on in schools, logical and mathematical, humans are also characterized by personal, bodily, musical, artistic, spatial and linguistic intelligences. The creative individuals he studied, Freud, Einstein, Picasso, Stravinsky, Eliot, (Martha) Graham and Gandhi all had different areas of strength and weakness. He also stresses the importance of what he calls 'asynchrony,' or 'a lack of fit, an unusual pattern, or an irregularity within the creativity triangle (individual-field-domain).' An individual may find him/herself in tension with the field or there may be tension between the field and the domain 'as when classical music was moving sharply in an atonal direction, while the audiences and critics contin-ued to favor tonal music.'[8] There is a degree of asynchrony that is fruitful, but asynchrony may also be excessive or insufficient. Gardner generalized from these and other studies of creative individuals in his seminal construction of the 'Exemplary Creator (EC).'[9] This individual comes from a place that is some distance from the center of power and influence but which is open to contact with the center. The family tends to be bourgeois – not highly educated but understanding the advantages of learning. At some stage of development EC 'discovers in the metropolis a set of peers who share the same interests: together, they explore the terrain of the domain.' Inevitably, the creative individuals will encounter other individuals 'with whom they must intersect;' each will have one or more mentors, and 'will also spawn colleagues, rivals, and followers.'[10]

Both Csikszentmihalyi and Gardner studied creative individuals and dealt with phenomena, such as infancy and relationships with parents at crucial times in childhood, that have nothing at all to do with the issue of urban competitiveness. But Csikszentmihalyi does discuss the role of government on the domain, and Gardner mentions mentors and rivals and a creative tension between the various elements in the creativity triangle. Both of them focus on the milieu within which creative activity is most likely to take place and it is this aspect of their work that is relevant to the strategic planning of local authorities. What can local authorities do to establish an environment which will generate creative solutions to their problems or challenges?

As a consequence of the work of Csikszentmihalyi and Gardner, the notion of the 'creative city' has been joined by those of the innovative city, the intelligent city and so forth. Peter Hall has given us a survey of the creative city/milieu work of Hägerstrand and Törnquist, and Taine, and the studies of the innovative milieu of Schumpeter, Aydalot and Castells.[11] This literature is too extensive to be examined here, but the central focus of these writers is the capacity of an urban economy to nurture the local capacity to respond effectively to the challenges of an evolving economy and to the demands it places on local institutions, structures, and imagination. In a competitive environment some cities will be able to do this relatively well while others will not. Charles Landry, in his book *The Creative City*, takes advantage of his work with Comedia, a British firm that consults on urban problems, to promote development of a creative milieu as an aid to city problem-solving.[12] He gives many examples of cities in Europe, but in Africa and Asia as well, which have been successful in this regard, once a problem has been identified. What to do if the city is considered to be a cultural wasteland? What to do with abandoned industrial sites? What to do to make a city a 'wired city?' Hall, on the other hand, uses the notions of creative and innovative milieux to highlight the successes of the great cities of the past – fifth century BC Athens, *fin-de-siècle* Vienna, Weimar Berlin and so forth. Thus, while both Landry and Hall are of interest to us, neither speaks directly to the question of how the city can enhance its competitiveness and how it can plan strategically to do so. In addition to stressing the importance of creativity and innovation, Landry is primarily of use after an exercise, such as that of the Kresl–Singh model, has identified the strategy/ies and the means that will comprise the basis for the strategic plan. For example, how can the city establish itself as a 'point of access' city, or how can it become a center of research and development? He also suggests ways in which some of the ten questions raised at the beginning of this chapter can be dealt with: questions such as, how can local actors be mobilized? And how can the various levels of government be integrated most effectively into the plan?

Another writer who has added to our understanding of this aspect of the urban economy is Richard Florida. In his recent book, *The Rise of the Creative Class*, he articulates a view that is held widely among specialists in urban economies:

> States and regions across the country continue to pour countless billions into sports stadiums, convention centers, tourism-and-entertainment centers and other projects of dubious economic value. The payback would be far greater if these regions channeled only a fraction of such funds into creative capital, for example, by supporting new biotechnology and software research or by investing in the arts and cultural creativity broadly. Such investments generate substantial and ongoing returns by attracting top scientific, technical and creative talent, generating spin-off companies and attracting firms from other places. By adding to the stock of creative capital, they increase wealth and incomes substantially and generate jobs for people across the classes.[13]

Rather than simply arguing his case persuasively, Florida relies on an empirical analysis in which he first defines the creative class and then uses census data to create a series of indices that he uses to rank cities of various populations according to their creativity. A listing of the indices will suggest the constituents of a creative city milieu: high-tech index (local high-tech output), innovation index (patents per capita), gay index (gay/lesbian population as a share of the total), bohemian index (numbers of artistically creative people), talent index (educational attainment) and melting pot index (percentage of population that is foreign born). In addition, the creative class index includes components of high-skill professional occupations, of working class occupations, of service sector occupations and agriculture. He then composes two composite indices: the composite diversity index, combining the gay, bohemian and melting pot indices; and the creativity index, combining the innovation, high-tech, gay and creative class indices.

Florida goes far beyond the notion that the key to the future of a city is, for example, its information-communication or biotechnology sector and the skilled labor that sector requires. A moment's consideration of his indices makes it clear that according to him, the key is in the city's openness to alternative lifestyles, immigrants from other cultures, and artists and other cultural workers, as well as highly educated technology workers. Also, the required labor for the creative milieu can be found in all sectors of the work force. Clearly it is the interaction of all of these individuals that produces the creative stew from which the ideas, innovations and creative solutions to the city's problems and challenges is to be gained. One thinks of course of Thorstein Veblen's contrast between the engineers, who were always seeking new technologies and processes so that things could be produced more efficiently, and the captains of industry, who were always trying to slow down technological progress so as to maximize profits.[14]

If one examines some of the cities that in recent history have had periods in which there was a blossoming of creativity in art, music, architecture, science, and other areas of artistic and intellectual endeavor, such as *fin-de-siècle* Vienna, Paris before the First World War, the Harlem Renaissance, Weimar Berlin and New York in the 1950s and 1960s, one finds a consistent set of elements that are present and, one can argue, contributory if not necessary for the creative milieu. In general they are in conformity with Florida's indices. First, in each instance there was significant inward migration of talented individuals from outside the city's boundaries. Individuals came to Vienna from all over the Austro-Hungarian Empire, to Paris from all of Europe, to Harlem from the US south, the Caribbean, from Paris and from Africa, and to New York from the rest of the world. Second, many of the creative individuals were outsiders in some way. Jews in Vienna, blacks in Harlem, gays and bohemians in Berlin, Paris and New York. Since they did not 'fit' into, or were not accepted by, the dominant society they had to create their own social and cultural space and it was understandably quite different from the dominant one. Third, they also reacted against the accepted practices or tastes of the current field and domain, in Csikszentmihalyi's model. They fashioned something that was new and often something that presented a discontinuity with what was accepted; this new approach usually had lasting impacts on the area of activity, impacts that lasted decades.

When we consider application of this understanding to the planning processes of cities, it is clear how this conceptualization can be seen as unpredictable in terms of its output or contribution to the planning process, and threatening to the established group of decision-makers. This is, of course, true and it is also the key to its success. The natural predilection is for local leaders to try to control the process too tightly and to rely on individuals with whom they have a working relationship. The thinking of such a group tends to be incremental or marginalist rather than discontinuity-seeking. Cost minimization takes precedence over charting a course in new directions, a course that may entail a bit of uncertainty. The Schumpeterian notion of creative destruction being the key to future growth and vitality has great relevance here.

THE INTERNATIONAL DIMENSION

Cities throughout the industrialized world have seen their traditionally satis-factory economic bases diminished or, as has often been the case, demolished through the process of global restructuring and deindustrialization. The glo-bal market share of the industrialized countries in heavy manufacturing industries, such as steel, automotive goods, and shipbuilding, has dropped significantly during the past quarter century, as has that in other sectors such as textiles and electronics. Throughout the world countries that had long been mired in political and economic systems that were geared more toward tight control, favoritism and corruption than efficiency, transparency, progress and democracy have turned the corner and are on a path that promised long-term improvement in their situation. This is the case in a large number of coun-tries, especially in Latin America, Asia, and Central Europe; Africa and the countries of the former USSR have not yet taken that first important and lasting step. The cities in countries that have emerged from their earlier condition have all sought to find some niche for themselves in the global economy. This is the first aspect of the challenge to cities in industrial countries. The second aspect is the result of the changes that have taken place in the global trading world itself. As trade liberalization has progressed both at the global level, through the GATT and now the WTO, and at the regional level, through initiatives such as NAFTA, the EEC/EU, and scores of other regional and bilateral trade agreements, the impediments to the free move-ment of goods and services have been greatly diminished – GATT tariff barriers were over 40 per cent in 1950 and are now less than 5 per cent. When the effects of changes in technology are added to trade liberalization, each city in the industrial world is increasingly vulnerable to the threat of imports of goods and services from industrial cities that are increasingly situated in new, relatively frictionless economic spaces. We will now examine each of these two aspects individually.

The Challenge of Global Restructuring

The stabilization and transformation of many countries in the Third World and the transition of countries in Central Europe have involved developing systems of government, or movements toward them, that are increasingly based on laws, transparency, economic rationality and a sense of the national interest rather than just that of the national leader. This is a positive develop-ment to be sure; but for urban economies in the developed world it presents them with a new set of threats and challenges, and challengers. First was the lure for companies of potential production sites with low-skill, low-wage labor. Lower labor costs are most directly translated into lower costs of

production in labor-intensive industries such as clothing and shoe manufacturing, electrical product assembly and niche production in many other
industries such as automotive goods and even aerospace. After a few years of
job loss, countries in the developed/industrialized world responded with protectionist measures such as the Multi-Fiber Agreement (1974) which
established mutually agreed upon constraints on the extent to which the
market share of Third World products in the developed countries could rise.
Most states and clothing and textile cities in the American South protested
strongly against the 'theft' of their jobs by Third World countries using low
wages, no-union policies, lax but cost-saving agreements on worker safety,
and low or non-existent health and retirement benefits. They forgot, of course,
that they had used exactly the same techniques to lure the jobs from New
England states decades ago in the first place. Some cities made a successful
transition to new more promising industries, such as Charlotte, North Carolina, did with financial services. Other cities have chosen to continue to seek
quota or anti-dumping protection for existing activity rather than make the
transition to newer ones.

A second wave of deindustrialization came when Third World countries
such as Brazil and South Korea were able to offer lower cost opportunities
for basic heavy industry such as steel, and when in the automotive sector
South Korea began to export cars and farm equipment, and other countries
such as Turkey, India and Indonesia began to supply their own markets and
those of other Third World countries with automobiles. Manufacturing in
both North America and Europe has experienced a steady deterioration and
decline in jobs since the 1970s. In Europe the EU has been forced to devote
much of its structural funds to declining industrial regions, as cities in the
English Midlands, in the Ruhr, and along the French–Belgian border have
seen activity fall, unemployment rise, and incomes decline. In North America
manufacturing in Canadian cities such as Montreal and Hamilton and in the
industrial cities of the Northeast and Upper Midwest – Chicago, Pittsburgh,
Cleveland, Buffalo and many others – has come on hard times and these
cities have, with varying degrees of success, been forced to change the nature
of their basic economic orientation. Once again, as is indicated by the recent
implementation by US President Bush of tariffs of up to 30 per cent on
imports of steel, protection is the first response of many producing companies
and cities in the developed world.

One response of cities subject to deindustrialization and restructuring that
appeared to offer some hope was that of promoting the service sector and
new technology-related activities. Toronto focused on developing its role as
the corporate headquarters and the financial services center of Canada. Montreal has promoted its 'virage technologique' for 25 years and has focused on
information-communication, multi-media and electronic commerce. Pittsburgh

moved from steel to electronic instrumentation and medical technology. Chicago has shifted from basic steel to high technology niches in that industry and has increased its importance as a regional economic center. Most of the large cities have promoted their universities and research infrastructure and, to make themselves more attractive to this component of the labor force, their cultural institutions and other urban amenities. Cultural tourism and exposure to the unique pleasures of large cities have brought revenues and employment to many cities. Unfortunately, these responses have not always been sufficient as the appeal of Third World locations proved to be as attractive to many service activities as they did to manufacturing. Many companies now do their accounting and billing in the Caribbean, south India has become a center of computer software development, and in the financial sector back-office work was transferred from the city center to the suburbs to Central Europe or Asia. Now, some of the largest financial firms are transferring some of their analytical work from MBAs in US metropolitan areas to MBAs in India where the salary is but a minor fraction of what would be expected in New York, Chicago or Los Angeles. Thus, the drain of jobs from cities in the developed world to cities in the Third World seems to be a phenomenon without end as the lost jobs move up the chain from low skill assembly jobs to highly skilled professional jobs.

Economists would argue that there is an equilibrium that will be reached at which there will be a new and stable division of labor between developed and Third World cities. Each will find areas in which it can specialize and will also identify niches in industries in which it is possible to develop and to maintain a comparative advantage. This long-term scenario will be of little solace to local authorities who have to encounter the dissatisfaction of their residents who are faced with unemployment and/or stagnating wages. The challenge to local authorities and planners in cities in North America, Western Europe, Japan and Australia is to do careful analysis as to what those more promising activities are. As was suggested above, in Table 7.1, for some cities improving performance in existing areas may be the answer while for others a qualitative restructuring will be the best approach.

The Challenge from Other Industrialized Cities

Challenges to the economic lives of cities in the industrialized world are not confined to those emanating from Third World cities. The competition among cities in North America, Japan, Australia and Europe is just as strong. In spite of the discussion just given in Chapter 6 of ways in which cities can cooperate, there is no sense glossing over the fact that many of these cities are in strong competition for the same international events, corporate headquarters, plant location, transportation functions and so forth. Most recently Boeing decided to move its headquarters with the top 500 employees to a city other than Seattle. It wanted a site that was not too closely identified with aircraft assembly and design since the company was more than that and it also wanted a location with better air connections to more of its customers. Three cities were in the running in the last stage: Denver, Dallas and Chicago, and the site selection committee visited each of the cities. Many factors were involved, of course, but when the committee made its visits each city took a different approach. Denver played the sports card, with football quarterback John Elway in attendance; Dallas touted local culture with a mariachi band; Chicago gave a grand soirée at the Art Institute with music provided by members of the Chicago Symphony Orchestra. Chicago won the competition. It is of interest to us that high culture won over sports and local culture, albeit one of many determining factors, but of more importance is the fact that the cities were engaged in a battle amongst themselves for this prestigious corporate headquarters decision. The same was true when Atlanta won the Summer Olympics a decade ago and Toronto lost. The location of the BMW and Mercedes–Benz auto plants in the US drew competitive bids from several cities as does almost every locational decision for a major economic activity. There are scores of these sorts of competitions among cities throughout the global economy.

When confronting the competition from cities in a similar state of development, standard economic arguments, such as factor endowments, often have little relevance. Within the United States or Canada factors of production such as skilled labor or capital are highly mobile and can be induced to travel hundreds or thousands of miles for new employment. Clearly this is the case with capital, which is internationally mobile. With regard to skilled labor, many cities have been successful in creating the urban amenities and employment opportunities that have enabled them to change their economic specialization in fairly short time. These cities have discovered that, to use a line from a recent movie, 'if you build it they will come.' Challenging jobs in an expanding economy, good housing and educational facilities, cultural institutions, and access to recreational areas and activities are the keys to attracting and retaining the desired skilled labor force. For competition among developed world cities there is a different dynamic than that between developed and Third World cities. Here there are several important factors that should be kept in mind:

- *Functions* The strategies that were elaborated in Table 7.1 can also be interpreted as functions for the city in the national or international urban hierarchy. Clearly some cities, most notably Saskia Sassen's three Global Cities – New York, London and Tokyo, will function as global decision and command centers. Others will be nationally or regionally oriented cities. These functions will be the result of decades of competitive struggle with other cities for that same position. There was once a classic struggle among the eastern port cities of the USA for supremacy. Boston and Philadelphia each had a turn at it but in the long run New York won out. Similarly cities have vied against each other for dominance in the aerospace, automobile, insurance, steel, entertainment, chemical and other industries. Some have been successful in becoming centers of research and development or financial services. Others have drifted without being able to create a valued and distinctive position for themselves in the urban hierarchy. This is not to say that it is impossible for a city to be successful with a widely diversified economic structure, but it is almost impossible to direct the invariably scarce resources at hand, in terms of individuals, funds and policy initiatives, toward an objective if the targets are too numerous.

- *Niches* In the industrialized economies, in many instances both old and new economic sectors are moving toward comparative strength in some subsector, or niche, in production. While the traditional steel industry in the United States is having great difficulty meeting the competition from Third World producers in rolled sheet, rails, bars and other standard forms, many producers are highly competitive world-wide in high-technology specialty steels. Many of these producers have developed and patented their own technology. Some other industries such as chemicals and pharmaceuticals are almost predicated on the notion of niche specialization. A niche may be something that is developed by refocusing assets that are to be found locally, with some additional assets and coordination adding to their value. But it is more likely that, as was indicated in Table 7.1, a niche will have the character of a new or restructured activity – a new departure for the city's economy. Given the mobility of capital and highly skilled labor, the particular niche to be developed will most likely be more related to the opportunities that exist in one or more industries than on the city's traditional production strengths. There is the obvious danger in this of bureaucrats selecting a niche that has little or no long-term viability; hence, objective analysis and cooperation with experts who may have nothing to do with the city should be relied upon for guidance.
- *Clusters* This is a concept, as we saw in Chapter 4, that has gotten enormous play in recent years. While it goes back at least as far as Alfred Marshall and his 'industrial districts,' economic geographers recently have embraced clusters as the central focus of much of their analysis about urban economies. The effects on urban and regional development of negative and positive externalities, of spatially confined pools of resources such as skilled labor, of urban or regional branding,

of face-to-face contact, of transportation economies and so forth have been recognized for decades. Examples such as the Third Italy or Silicon Valley have been extensively studied by economic planners.[15] The alluring notion of communicating to Manhattan or San Francisco by Internet, e-mail, fiber optic lines and satellite has not proven to be feasible except for a very few specialized activities. Clusters are of importance in many industries such as bio-pharmaceutical and information technology, but in other industries they are of decreasing importance. There have been recent reports from companies such as the Ford Motor Company and Levis Jeans that they see their future as entities that concentrate on research, design, marketing and customer relations with manufacturing and assembly being done elsewhere in the world on contract. Levis has just closed its last North American plant. Ford sees its vehicles being assembled by a firm such as Magna International from parts made in the USA and Canada, Mexico, Asia and Europe. The clustering in Detroit and other centers of the automotive industry will occur at the convenience of the contractors, and in fact it may not continue. So clustering is important for some cities specializing in some activities but not for all cities.

- *Start-ups*   It should be remembered that if a city can lure an economic activity from another city, it is to be expected that after a few years the firm will respond to a better offer from some other city. If the idea is to build a long-term economic base, research tells us that firms that are local start-ups are far more likely to remain in place than are many, though not all, firms in industries in which cost competitiveness is a primary factor in their survival.[16] The founders of start-ups have personal allegiances and affinities for the city or region that tend to keep them in place. Hence science parks, incubators, entrepreneur-university linkages, and tax and other incentives for start-ups can all have very positive impacts.

- *Character*   By character, we mean a strong urban identity that indicates to outsiders basic attributes of the local economy and society that give the city a 'brand.' Most strong cities have some clear identity to others: New York is the center of so much, Chicago has always been brash, San Francisco has sophistication, while Detroit, New Orleans, and Atlanta have images that make them less attractive to mobile skilled labor or investors. Many city identities may appear to be clichés but these are the consequences of events that have taken place over several decades. It is easy to disparage city boosterism and public relations campaigns because there is often little or no substance behind them. Yet Paul Krugman refers to the effort of local boosters as 'self-fulfilling prophecies' and suggests how important they can be.[17] Once positive attributes have been nurtured, making them known throughout the relevant economic space is the logical and necessary next step. In addition to having the message about the city's attributes received by economic actors hundreds of miles distant, a realistic message also has powerful impacts within the city itself and its metropolitan region. Local firms and individuals in all capacities develop a better sense of how they fit into the city and what it is that will make them want to remain and to participate in the city's future.

There are other issues that confront cities in their strategic planning for competitiveness enhancement, but these seem to be the most important.

FINAL THOUGHTS

In this chapter we have argued that a strategic planning exercise is of vital importance for cities concerned with their competitiveness and their economic future. An effective plan will result in the most efficient utilization of the available resources or assets, and it will mobilize the community and key individuals around a common set of desired results and means to achieve those results. The methodology offered here will facilitate that process. It also indicates how carefully that strategy must be determined and what specific means are attached to that strategy or set of strategies. Finally, it suggests how finely nuanced the plan will be for each individual city. There is no single approach that works for many or all cities, and local authorities should avoid following the path, so to speak, with the latest trend in thinking about competitiveness and economic development. If done properly, the results can be very positive and will be invaluable for a city trying to navigate through the sea of globalization-induced threats, challenges and opportunities to create the economic future to which its residence realistically can aspire.

NOTES

1. Committee for Economic Development, 1986.
2. D.L. Sorkin and others, 1984. For an application of this approach see Luke *et al.*, 1988.
3. Blakely and Bradshaw, 2002, Ch. 6.
4. Michael E. Porter, *The Competitive Advantage of Nations*, New York: The Free Press, 1990.
5. Landry, 2000, p. xiii.
6. Csikszentmihalyi, 1988, p. 325.
7. Csikszentmihalyi, 1996, p. 44.
8. Gardner, 1993, pp. 40–41.
9. Gardner, 1993, pp. 360–63.
10. Gardner, 1993, p. 376.

11. Peter Hall, 2001, Chs. 1 and 9.
12. Landry, 2001.
13. Florida, 2002, p. 320.
14. Veblen, 1963.
15. Best, 2000.
16. Haug, 1991.
17. Krugman, 1991, pp. 30–33.

8.   What lies ahead?

The previous chapters have made it clear that during the past 30 or so years we have entered into a new era of engagement and activism at the level of the city or the urban economy. In part this is due to the exigencies of the globalization process, and in part to the less interventionist or less intrusive postures that have been adopted by national and subnational governments. Technological change, freer trade and market liberalization have both given urban economies new possibilities for economic activity and made them more vulnerable to competition from counterparts thousands of miles away. Superior levels of government now do less to manage local economies than was earlier the case, and they have chosen to do less on behalf of negatively affected local constituencies. Whatever the cause, local authorities have become increasingly engaged in the activities we have detailed in this book: analysing their individual competitiveness, designing strategic plans for enhancement of that competitiveness, establishing initiatives in municipal diplomacy, creating new inter-urban structures, and restructuring municipal governance. City leaders in the public and private sectors recognize that their active engagement in these areas will be crucial and perhaps decisive in shaping the economic futures of their urban economies and in determining the degree to which their residents have economically satisfying or disappointing futures.

MAJOR ISSUES CONFRONTING URBAN ECONOMIES IN THE NEAR FUTURE

If anything, the coming quarter century promises to be one in which the pace of developments and the need for proactive response and anticipation at the level of the urban economy will be greater than we have experienced thus far. In this final chapter we will examine six factors that we are convinced will be crucial for urban leaders and for the future of their respective economies. This set of six factors is a combination of aspects of the economy of the next decade or two that city leaders will have to take into account in their strategic planning and aspects of traditional thinking that may not be as relevant to the future as they have to the recent past. The context is that which we have developed thus far – one of rapid change, of increased inter-urban contact (whether through competition or cooperation), growing responsibility for their own future, changing structures of production and so forth. The list of issues we will discuss could be made much longer, of course, but the following will give municipal leaders enough to think about.

Cities and the Supply of and Demand for Urban Assets

In an economy in which government intervention and guidance are currently being supplanted by what Harry Johnson referred to as 'interrelated networks of markets,' impersonal market forces and interactions are of primary importance. Markets are always composed of individuals or firms with demands for various goods and services and their counterparts who undertake to supply those same goods and services. The counterpart of this is that primary agents of urban economies should see their cities as suppliers of an array of factors of production, urban amenities, infrastructure and supportive policies to a very large number of relatively foot-loose firms which have specific demands for sets of these urban assets. Here the interaction of the demand for and supply of urban assets does not result in an equilibrium price, as is usually the case in market analysis, but rather in a stream of production activities that extends into the not too distant future. This stream of production activities will provide jobs of certain qualities, incomes and a rate of growth of these variables that will determine whether the urban leadership, private and public sector, has performed in a way that realizes the potential of that urban economy to position itself among its competitor cities. However, it must be remembered that firms that are attracted to a set of urban assets may be attracted to another somewhat more advantageous set or to charges that may be lower. The environment in which these decisions are made and in which the cities function is a highly competitive one, and no city can rely on past successes or relationships, important though these may be in some individual cases, to sustain it in its future. Hence each city leader must see this as a dynamic if not unstable process. Regular scrutiny of the relationship with major employers in the urban region will be required if unfavorable plant location decisions are to be avoided, as will regular evaluation of the nature and quality of the assets the city has to offer. Much of this was discussed in the previous chapter in which we examined strategic planning. Clearly firms in different industrial sectors will have different requirements for urban assets. The city has to make the choice between making the best use of what it has, on the one hand, or, on the other, re-configuring the set of assets it presents to target firms. Each choice will have as a consequence a structure of output, a structure of skill requirements for the labor force and, of course, demands for infrastructure and various municipal services, policy initiatives and investments. While this may seem at first glance to be an imposing burden on the local government, failure to act proactively and with clear vision may relegate the urban economy to the side lines and to secular decline. All industrial nations offer numerous examples of cities that have suffered just such a marginalization, after decades of economic vitality. Clearly the issues of municipal governance that were discussed in Chapter 5 must be dealt with effectively.

City leaders have to go beyond conceiving of their city's economic future as being dependent upon low taxes, good infrastructure, a good supply of labor and good government. Each of these may be totally irrelevant to firms in the sectors they want to build up. There has been a justified reaction against development plans that are highly targeted toward what are generally taken to be 'sun rise' industries; the preferred approach has become that of supporting the general climate for investment and growth. But if the city appears to have a developing advantage in some sector of production and if the firms in that sector can articulate what assets they need to be most successful, then it is relatively safe and relatively intelligent for city leaders to do what they can to provide those specific assets. The model presented in Chapter 7, in Table 7.1, suggests the sort of approach that could be taken, linking the chosen strategy with the means required to achieve it.

What remains to be stressed is the need for the metropolitan leaders to ensure that the assets of their location are effectively promoted throughout an economic space that can be global even for rather small cities. Many firms function in networks of supply and production that extend throughout the world. While the large multinational firms are easy enough to contact with regard to the specific assets the city has to offer, many smaller firms are equally international in their operations but may not want to devote the resources to making a complete search of possible sites for new facilities. Here the city leaders must take the initiative through the usual sorts of publicity – trade or commercial fairs, internet sites, embassy resources, hired agents and so forth. Firms that are looking for places to invest or establish facilities will make their selection from the alternatives they have before them – there may be no necessity for them to contact more that a small number of the most accessible cities in their search for a specific set of local assets. The city that lacks proximity or renown for specific urban assets will not even enter the competition let alone do well in it.

The Need to be Attractive to the High Tech Labor Force and Companies

There has been a lot of hype about high technology production and its proper role in the urban economy. There is always a danger that something will be promoted beyond its usefulness, and there are reasons to be wary of the arguments of high tech salesmen. Now almost every city of any size includes some aspect of high technology in its strategic plan, be it, among other things, information communications technology, or bio-pharmaceutical, or nanotechnology. At first glance one would think this would be like a game of musical chairs in which not all end up with a place to sit; and there is, of course, a bit of truth in this. But there are several aspects of high technology production that suggest that a high technology strategy may work for a very large number of cities. First, not all of this work is done on a very large scale. Many of the most innovative firms are rather small, often start-ups by university researchers and assisted by local small firm development initiatives. To be sure, many of these successful firms are acquired by large multinational firms but: (1) the original site often continues operation for decades, and (2) it was obviously a fertile environment for innovation and over time other start-ups are begun. So, looked at as a long-term process of innovation a city with the right environment can continue to see high technology production as part of its future.

Second, neither ICT nor bio-pharmaceutical are narrowly defined sectors with one or two main lines of activity. Each, and the other high technology sectors in manufacturing, transportation and logistics, services, defense and so forth, is characterized by scores or hundreds of niches in which individual firms can make innovative contributions. So there is room for thousands of firms in each of these sectors and it is up to local entrepreneurs to discover where they can establish themselves successfully and for local authorities to give the support they require at the initial phase of their development.

Third, it is true that much work in the high technology sectors is done by low skill, low pay workers in assembly and fabrication, however, management, design and research are dominated by the educated and well paid workers all cities would like to have in their community. These latter workers, among other things, pay more in taxes, do more to renovate the housing stock, demand improvements in the local infrastructure, contribute to cultural organizations, and generate retail and restaurant revenues. Firms in these sectors also provide employment for young workers graduating from local universities and technical schools, thereby halting the outward migration of the sons and daughters of residents that troubles so many places, including US states such as Pennsylvania. So having a stock of high technology workers creates the conditions that induce additional workers with these desirable characteristics to stay or to move into the city.

Fourth, firms that are innovative and that are linked to universities and research activities have been shown to be more likely than those that do not have these characteristics, to have high exports and output growth and to be relatively competitive and productive.[1] On the surface, exports would seem to be an objective of the national economy rather than for producers in a city;

after all, everything sent out of the metropolitan area can be considered to be an export of sorts. But city leaders should do what then can to promote exports by their local firms because: (1) export markets provide markets when the national market is in recession, (2) exports bring local firms in contact with a wider variety of competitors and consumers and this brings knowledge of the needs of this larger constituency of demanders as well as new, or at least different, ways of doing the same thing in production, research, distribution and management and (3) firms producing in a niche of an industry may need foreign sales in order to achieve economies of scale and to grow beyond a certain level of output. Higher rates of productivity are so uncontroversial that they require no comment. If high technology firms achieve both higher productivity and higher degrees of penetration of foreign markets, this can only work to the advantage of both those firms and host urban economy.

Policies to deal with this aspect of urban strategic planning must focus on both aspects of the issue: the highly skilled labor force and firms in high technology economic activities. Obviously, the two are inseparable, and if one or the other is slighted when it comes to policy initiatives it is most likely that the effort to promote the other will not succeed. Incentives to encourage start-ups, to develop beneficial linkages between universities, research laboratories and high technology firms, to offer tax incentives to firms to invest or do research and development, and so forth, must be accompanied by efforts to enhance the cultural, recreational and entertainment assets, the housing stock and the health and educational systems that are demanded by a high skill work force. These policies were stressed in Chapters 2 and 7 and nothing more needs to be written here.

The Question of the Urban Economy and Absolute or Comparative Advantage

This may sound like a rather arcane academic debate, but in fact it has powerful implications for many urban economies. The standard argument about the wisdom of free trade, that is to say specialization in production and exchange of those goods and services with other economies was developed by David Ricardo in 1817, with a extensive list of assumptions about the world in which free trade would occur. Since Ricardo it has been standard procedure for economists to assume a two country world, a world in which each country, even though it may be blessed with absolute advantage in all lines of production is damned with a similarly extensive absolute disadvantage. In this model the exchange rate and prices will adjust so as to give each country some activity in which it can have a comparative advantage. That is, each country will have a product in which it has a comparative advantage and can participate in mutually beneficial specialization and exchange. However, when there are multiple economies in a situation in which exchange rates and prices are not at all flexible or are not sufficiently flexible this mutually beneficial adjustment of output may not occur and while in the aggregate production, and exchange seem to work out as anticipated, any one of the economies can find that it has no product in which it has a comparative advantage. It will import all goods and services and export none and, absent the price adjustment mechanism, it will face an extended period of time in which it is marginalized and stagnates. This is exactly the situation in which an urban economy can find itself. In a large national economy there will be no exchange rate adjustment and whatever price adjustments there are may not be sufficiently flexible or of a sufficient magnitude to generate the necessary comparative advantage.

This is the situation in which urban economies find themselves, and it only increases the importance of their making the right decisions in a timely manner. As Camagni reminds us the only adjustment mechanism operative may be the outward migration of workers seeking the satisfying employment that the economy of the city in which they find themselves has failed to provide.[2] Monetary wages are often determined by national union, or union-influenced, contracts that allow for little or no adjustment to local conditions. Smaller cities or even large cities in large national economies will have little impact on, or little to say about, the exchange rate of the national currency. In this situation, comparative advantage in which each economy specializes in something for export fails to work and gives way to absolute advantage. In this latter situation it need not be the case that each economy will find something in which it can specialize and sell in other markets. Without an export specialization, the urban economy will drop out of the national or international division of labor and will stagnate or will spiral down to lower and lower levels of output and income. This is a familiar story for many of the older industrial economies in North America and Europe. Such a situation can be sustained only through inflows of resources from outside the urban economy, such as inter-governmental transfers, the sale of local assets to outsiders or inward transfers from individuals such as family living and working elsewhere. While Camagni suggests that such a condition cannot be maintained in the long run, it is in fact true that it can be and has been for example with the lagging provinces in Atlantic Canada or in other long-term depressed regions of the USA or Europe. For the traditional comparative advantage model of specialization and exchange to work, there must be factor immobility so flows of goods and services would bring the needed adjustment, but even here this would work only if wages could fall to a level that would make some good(s) and/ or service(s) marketable in the outside world.

The unsettling possibility that this opens is that of a city that struggles for decades to find a niche for itself without being successful in its attempt to do so. Some cities in the US industrial heartland, such as Pittsburgh and Buffalo, or in the English Midlands, or in the Ruhr and French–Belgian border area have been characterized by exactly this experience. Obviously, all metropolitan leaders must continually be aware of this possibility for their own city. Each of the now struggling cities in the regions just mentioned was at an earlier date a wealthy, thriving center of economic activity.

THE IMPORTANCE OF CLUSTERS

The concept of the cluster has been to economic geographers what globalization has to economists: a phenomenon of considerable historical relevance, a concept of great analytical usefulness and, finally a notion that is quickly becoming a cliché. In this book we have avoided both terms to the extent that has been possible. With regard to globalization, we have chosen to focus on its components, trade and market liberalization and rapid changes in technology, and to put them in the context of internationalization of economic relationships and processes. Clusters have a powerful relevance to many industries, but the point needs to be made that the establishment of one or more clusters is not something that assures an urban economy that it will be successful in its strategic planning for competitiveness. While the Third Italy, Baden-Wüttemburg and Silicon Valley are clear examples of the importance of clustered activity, there are many other examples that illustrate the clusters may not have long-term durability or that they can fail in their initial implantation.

In his seminal statement of the phenomenon of the industrial district, Alfred Marshall stressed the advantages to firms that locate their operations in close proximity to each other of having access to a local labor pool with specialized skills and knowledge, of the development of firms in related activities, and specialization among the firms so as to make more efficient use of expensive machinery.[3] This is a district which is composed of many small sized firms, each of which gains from economies of specialization and scale that would not be attainable absent location in such a cluster. One of the features of the cluster is the transmission of tacit knowledge from worker to worker which occurs most effectively and which there is less 'distance-decay' of knowledge than in non-clustered situations.[4] Marshall wrote in 1890, but it is in the most recent two decades that the large volume of literature on industrial districts and clustering has been written.

In the economy of the early 21st century several developments have taken place that have reduced the importance of clustering. First, there is the size and nature of the firm itself. In many of the industries in which clustering might offer advantages, firm size has grown dramatically, from the firm of the individual entrepreneur and a few workers to multinational firms with thousands of workers and tens of production locations. In this structure firms have internalized the knowledge transfer efficiencies that were offered by the cluster. Bell Laboratories and Hewlett-Packard are examples of companies that have done precisely this. Wolfe and Gertler have demonstrated that there is little evidence that 'direct, non-market interaction and knowledge sharing between local firms in the same industry is rampant.' Furthermore, they find that 'a large component of the knowledge inputs to local production – at least in certain sectors – is drawn from well outside the region.'[5] A similar point is made by Simmie who shows that, for firms in the UK, while non-innovative firms concentrate on local and regional markets for 54 per cent of their sales, innovate firms rely on these markets for only 22.4 per cent of sales and for national and international markets for 66.8 per cent of their sales. This runs counter to another argument about clusters – that 'local clustering allows rapid perception of new buyer needs.'[6] While Simmie does not provide the relevant descriptive information about the firms, his results would be all the more compelling the more they related to firms producing intermediate goods that are sold to final goods producers. Finally, while the Silicon Valleys of the world continue to demonstrate the value of face-to-face contact and while the city continues to have a powerful advantage for this mode of knowledge transfer, to a growing extent improvement in telecommunications have reduced the advantage of clusters in this regard in many areas of this activity.

The picture we get of the contemporary firm is that to a far greater degree than was true in the days of Marshall or even the latter decades of the 20th century, comparatively large firms are internalizing within the firm transfers of knowledge that used to be a feature that was identified with clusters and that these firms are linked through sophisticated telecommunications networks to entities throughout the world. Clusters will remain important for many sorts of economic activity, but city leaders must be alert to the need to examine the cluster model carefully and to seek to implement it only after careful consultation with representatives of firms operating in that sector. How other changes in factors such as technology, firm structure, the emergence of new actors in Third World countries, and location of activities throughout the global economy will affect the economic advantages of clustering in the years to come cannot, of course, be assessed at this time. Nonetheless, this staple of economic geographic thinking will have to be taken with a bit of skepticism.

Sharing the Gains – Convergence or Divergence, and Intra-urban Income

Increased economic efficiency, which is what market liberalization and technological change promise, results in increased total output. Historically, the pressing question that follows is that of how this increased output is distributed among regions, social classes and members of various racial and gender categories. Those who have reservations about globalization invariably note that income and wealth have, in recent decades, generally been disproportionately concentrated in the hands of those who are wealthy, white and male. A quick review of history will confirm that when the distribution of income and wealth are perceived by the mass of the population to be done unfairly, frustration, dissention and ultimately revolution are the result. While few would suggest that revolution is on the cards for cities in the developed world, it is clear that frustration and dissention, as well as alienation and a host of urban pathologies, are in evidence in many places.

In the EU the record of recent decades indicates that at the national level there has been income convergence during the 1980s but divergence in the decade that followed, while among regions there was divergence throughout the period.[7] A large part of this latter phenomenon is due to growing divergence between rural and urban per capita income which is confirmed by the persistent migration of people from the countryside to the city. This story is repeated in the USA and other countries throughout the world and, as has been noted earlier in this book, modern technologies and emerging industries favor the urban environment as the location for their activities. There is little city leaders can do to redress this imbalance, in fact in their efforts to enhance the competitiveness in relation to other cities they exert pressure in national capitals, and for EU cities in Brussels, for a restructuring of funding priorities away from rural and agricultural programs toward those that favor urban infrastructure, the consequences of immigration, urban pathologies, and so forth. In fact, it has been shown that there is a direct relationship between decentralization of power from the national to the local level and regional inequalities.[8] In this way urban leaders only exacerbate the income divergence problem – but what other options do they realistically have?

The other side of the issue, however, is that of income divergence within the neighborhoods, races and classes that make up the population of the city itself. It is here that city leaders can have a beneficial impact on an aspect of their community that could otherwise generate the crime, urban decay, abandonment of the city center and bad reputation that can make progress on economic development exceedingly difficult if not impossible. As Clark and Blue put it, there are two parts to the resolution of race and class segregation and income inequality. First, is the legal approach of introducing and enforcing fair housing laws and other laws against discrimination. Many cities have gone beyond this prohibition of segregation and discrimination by situating subsidized housing for low-income residents in the midst of middle class housing. This has an impact in the short run but does nothing to make this integration of race and class sustainable in the long term or to enable those targeted residents to be able to continue to live in these units without a subsidy, perhaps *ad infinitum*. Thus, this approach in law is a necessary but not a sufficient step. Second, one can work on the ability of minorities and low-income residents to insinuate themselves into the main community of the city. This requires that they be able to earn the income that will make this possible. Clark and Blue demonstrate that 'income and education may be the important variables in creating greater levels of integration.'[9]

This would appear to be just common sense, but as a policy prescription it takes on additional importance when we consider the nature of the economy of the first decades of the 21st century. This economy has been portrayed in this book as one which is likely to be increasingly focused on technology, high levels of skill acquisition and knowledge. Some writers, such as Stephen Graham, argue that

> I(nformation) T(echnology) can empower historically isolated individuals and groups ... IT has the potential to provide low-income, urban residents with: the requisite skills to participate in the informational economy; new opportunities to facilitate the communication and networking among individuals necessary for community building; the means to more effectively participate in public discourse; and data and information to understand and attack the problems they face.[10]

At the same time that support for the education and technical training of disadvantaged youth and workers is becoming so crucial in dealing with some of the major problems facing cities, governments at all levels are being pressed to lower taxes and to reduce support for these human capital development programs.[11]

City leaders clearly face a difficult situation, with some sectors of the community clamoring for lower taxes and with state and federal governments reducing their support of urban initiatives. But the picture is fairly clear: urban social pathologies have a negative impact on a city's economic development, and investment in the human capital programs that will give racial minorities and low-income residents the education and income they need to reduce their marginalized status without ongoing subsidization. Once again, those cities that can manage to accomplish this successfully with have a far greater likelihood of realizing their strategic objectives, while those that are not able to do this will suffer disappointment.

The Enhanced Speed of Change and its Demands on Institutional Flexibility

The essential characteristic of technological change is speed, speed in production, in transportation, in communication, in decision-making, in structural change, in skill and knowledge decay and so forth. Rapid change has been a feature of the global economy for the past two centuries and the exponential rate of technological advance is putting enormous burdens on all economic actors to develop the capacity to deal with it. During the last half of the 20th century, the global economy consisted of a small set of industrially developed rich countries and a far larger number of largely ex-colonial countries that were characterized by primary goods production, low income, poor infrastructure, dependency and political immaturity and/or instability. For cities in the industrialized world it was a rather comfortable period. They specialized in heavy industry and the full array of services, agriculture was protected and farm incomes were decent, small towns thrived and the migration from them to the cities was manageable, and change in this order was slow and not terribly threatening. After the oil price shocks of 1973 and 1979, older industrial districts began to deteriorate; in the USA the industrial heartland became the rust belt; in Europe the English Midlands, the Ruhr and the French–Belgian border area, among others, began or accelerated a similar deterioration.

De-industrialization became the concept of the day, soon to be followed by that of global restructuring. These latter concepts were indications of a fundamental shift in the structure of the global economy. Corporations became more aggressive in seeking cost reduction as a way to enhance profit margins. Increased information and technological change in transportation and communication made it possible for firms to separate and spread more widely their design, administration, production and distribution functions to take advantage of lower costs for some activities in the formerly stagnant, primary-goods-exporting ex-colonial countries of the Third World. Slow, measured change by firms that had some commitment to location became replaced by foot-loose multinational corporations that would abandon a site that had been used for decades or a century or more for a location in Asia or Latin America at the drop of a hat with the incentive being a few percentage points of reduction in labor or operating costs. The symbol of the age is the US football team, the Baltimore Colts, which left Baltimore under cover of darkness, at 3 o'clock in the morning, to announce the move from its new home in St. Louis. It seemed as though nothing could any longer be held to be lasting or not subject to challenge and threat.

The present situation is charged with the phenomenon of outsourcing and hollowing out. In the extreme this would have a firm such as a major automobile manufacturer doing product design, marketing and administration.

All production would be let out to the lowest bidder, with no preference as to whether that producer were in Detroit, Los Angeles, China or India. The firm is hollowed out in that its activities are little more than the equivalent of a shell of what had been done in the past, and the outsourcing process transfers the jobs that had existed in Detroit or other US, Canadian or European, production centers to locations and producers in low-cost countries in the Third World or in Economies in Transition (largely Central Europe and China, and perhaps some day Russia). Firms are in competition with each other in this race to find opportunities to gain a cost advantage. The actual magnitude of the impacts of outsourcing on the structure and level of activity in urban economies is subject to heated debate in all industrial countries. Critics of globalization and political candidates see in outsourcing and hollowing out phenomena that are predictable, negative consequences of the relaxation of national controls over economic flows of goods, services, capital and investment. Mainstream economists argue that while there are short-term difficulties for industrial economies, they are insignificant in their magnitude and are just the first step in a process that ultimately will see growing incomes in Third World countries generate demands for goods and services produced in industrial economies.

Whatever the short- or long-term actual consequences of outsourcing and hollowing out, this is simply the way in which the contemporary economic system operates, and there is nothing city leaders can do to change it. The only viable response open to them is to redesign or reconsider the way in which they relate to firms and to try to adapt to the new situation. The first thing they can do is understand that the ebb and flow of industrial activity and investment is a reality. While most cities will lose some activities, they have to focus on the other end of the process – they have to attract firms to replace those that depart or they have to make the local environment congenial to the start-up of new firms locally. A decade ago when Siemens moved its facility out of the center of Stuttgart, Germany, to a location in the periphery, city officials saw this as a positive development as it gave them scarce land which could be used for a much needed recreational or science park. Second, municipal governance structures must be structured in such a way as to allow for minimal decision and implementation times for policy initiatives. It must be clear just where the authority for decision-making is lodged and the local actors must be organized so they can be mobilized for policy implementation. In many cities it is not clear who is in charge and precious time is lost in sorting out the various agency agendas and mandates. Third, effective strategic planning must result in broadly accepted objectives, it must be flexible in the face of constant change, and it must result in clear identification of the means required for achievement of the objectives of the plan and the allocation of tasks.

FINAL THOUGHTS ON THE FUTURE THAT WILL CONFRONT URBAN ECONOMIES

History is replete with forecasts of or comments about the future that proved to be not only false but also embarrassing for those who made them. Forecasts in August 1929, November 1941, January 1973 or August 2001 are only the most graphic and notorious of scores of examples of our inability to reliably look into the future. The best we can do is to identify what are most likely to be the forces or phenomena that will exert an influence, of undeterminable power, on actors into the not too distant future. That is all we will attempt to do in this final section of the book. The discussion of each of these factors will be rather brief as they have all been discussed in this or in earlier chapters.

- Cities throughout the world will experience continued challenges to their economic structures and their place in the global urban hierarchy as the world economy moves through a transition to a new division of labor. Workers in Third World economies are as intelligent and trainable as their counterparts in the already industrialized world. Once they have put effective educational systems in place for the mass of the population, have achieved political stability and instituted transparent and predictable systems of laws and enforcement each of these countries will begin to attract investment, production and jobs from developed economies. This period of transition will continue for decades. This is not to say that the liberal economic forecast of factor price equalization and specialization according to comparative advantage will foreseeably lead to development and equal incomes and prospects for all; this does not even happen within developed countries. However, these forces will be at work and will have significant impacts on the lives of scores of millions of people in both the developed and third worlds. Therefore, cities in the developed world should expect to be confronted by a need to adapt and continually reshape their economies as they will have no choice but to make room for these new arrivals.
- The pace of trade liberalization may be slowed by the political reactions of people in all countries to its consequences. In the next decade or so, the advances in the opening of markets to international trade will involve concessions from the industrialized countries in areas in which they have resisted concessions because of the political reaction from those who will be negatively affected. The two primary areas in which these concessions will have to be made are reductions in financial support for agriculture and the trade-off of exports of high tech goods from industrialized countries for imports of labor intensive goods from

the Third World. In all industrial countries, farmers have been increasingly vocal and politically engaged in their resistance to their loss of market share to Third World producers. The WTO has just acted against US cotton subsidies and against protectionist EU sugar policy. These successes could embolden Third World countries to press their cases in other sectors of agriculture. The Bush administration has just had the WTO find against its 30 per cent tariff on imports of steel. The increasing vulnerability of farmers and blue collar industrial workers in Europe and North America is certain to generate political pressures against further trade liberalization schemes. In the US presidential race, Democrat John Kerry has indicated that he will not support the Central American Free Trade Agreement and that he will re-examine the trade agreements, primarily the North American Free Trade Agreement and the granting of most-favored nation status for China. In all cases, it is the approach that has been taken to labor and environmental standards that is at issue. If John Kerry's approach fails, one should anticipate Ross Perot-type populist sentiment to grow, with 'outsourcing' replacing 'the sucking sound of jobs going South.' While cities are by definition urban places, many of them, such as Chicago and Minneapolis, are strongly linked to the vitality of their agricultural hinterlands. Whether via the route of agricultural conflict or via the deterioration of their manufacturing sectors, a halting or reversal of recent trade liberalization initiatives would have a powerfully negative impact on the economies of the cities of the industrialized world.

- Technological change must be expected to continue at a rapid, and perhaps increasing, pace. As international competition for markets increases, firms and governments are forced to devote larger shares of revenues to research and development. This suggests that new technologies and new product development will continue at a rapid if not increasing pace. Clearly, this in itself has its disruptive impacts. But what may be of greater importance is the emergence of China, India, Brazil and other Third World countries as centers of technological advance. Hundreds of thousands of young people from these countries have pursued higher education in industrialized countries as well as their own. This means that the control over technological advance, both its direction and its pace, will to a significant extent shift from industrialized to other countries. This will generate an environment that is even more challenging and threatening to city leaders in North America, Europe and Japan.

- If national, state and provincial governments continue to be pressed by electorates to reduce taxes this will mean that expenditures of these governments and their transfers to municipal governments will have to be reduced. The consequence will, of course, be less expenditure on social welfare programs, education (especially at the K-12 grades), urban renewal, income maintenance and even, perhaps, public safety except for the broad category of 'homeland security.' This sets up a conflict between the skills and stability needs of the contemporary economy and the increasing disparity between inner city minority residents and more affluent whites, both in the city center and the suburbs. The burden on municipal governments to maintain their urban assets and to reduce the incidence of urban social pathologies will only grow, and when the burden becomes too great the city will find its competitiveness and attractiveness to firms will deteriorate. In Canada, the recently elected minority government of Liberal Paul Martin and the leader of its partner, Jack Layton of the New Democratic Party, both argued during the campaign for increased transfers from the national government to the cities. There is little to suggest that the winner of the US presidential race in 2004 will be similarly inclined. Thus, at least in the USA there appears to be little relief for the aforementioned burden of the country's municipal governments. Should this be the case one should expect to see increased militancy on the part of disadvantaged inner city minorities. This will only add to the difficulties with which city leaders will be faced as they try to maintain or to enhance their city's economic competitiveness.

- Demographically, there are several developing situations that promise to become even more important for urban economies than they already are. First, the rural to urban migration continues except for some poorly performing and relatively unattractive cities that have lost population in recent years. Second, many cities are situated in countries in which the population is ageing to the extent that in these countries sometimes severe fiscal difficulties are foreseen as retirement and health care expenses rise but revenues from a declining percentage of the population is workers and tax payers. In many Third World countries just the reverse is the case. Whether from the push of relatively unattractive prospects at home or from the pull of inducements from industrialized countries, we may expect to see a migration of young, energetic but not necessarily skilled workers from Third World countries adding to the inward migration from rural areas. Both of these migratory flows have the promise of long-term benefit, but at the cost of short-run expense and increasing social, ethnic and racial tension. Third, rising levels of education, especially in some Third World countries, promise to bring the positive returns one would hope would be the natural consequence of investment in human capital. The challenge to cities is that of making themselves attractive, in terms of housing, recreation, culture and stimulating jobs so they can capture a sufficient share of these talented young workers on whom the future of all cities will be grounded. These demographic factors have been discussed above, so these brief comments will serve to remind the reader, and city leaders, of their importance.

- On the positive side, city officials have gained considerable experience with networking and inter-urban interaction, and with public-private sector cooperation during the past couple of decades. This was the subject of Chapters 3 and 6, on municipal diplomacy, and structures and networking, respectively. Given the needs for proactive planning and initiative at the level of the municipality and the urban region this recently gained competence and awareness will be put to good use during the (perhaps difficult) next couple of decades. Where city leaders have participated in these ventures, they have come to understand that they need not think that they will be forced to deal with these problems individually, but will be able to share concerns about common problems, to discuss responses to changes over which they have no control, to study solutions and responses that have or have not worked, and to form cooperative ventures and structures. Cities that choose to go it alone will find themselves in a world of uncertainty in which the risk is high, as are likely to be the pay-offs or losses from what they decide to do. Cities need a bit of entrepreneurship and risk-taking, but it must be remembered that what is at stake are the economic futures of the city's residents. Entrepreneurship in this case is best leavened with prudence. Firms and other private sector actors are the natural allies in this effort and successful cities will be the ones that have got this right.
- Furthermore, as energy costs rise urban area dwellers may be forced to reconsider the wisdom of continued sprawl, use of the private automobile as the sole means of transportation, investment in public transportation and, as Ken Livingston, the mayor of London, is arguing, building vertically rather than horizontally. Significant change will not be immediate as the constraints of decades of urban development based on cheap energy will make change costly, in the short run, and difficult to gain acceptance. Access to water may also make it costly, if not impossible, to continue to expand urban populations in arid areas such as the US West and Southwest. Conflict between agricultural users and cities, and among states sharing the same river, lake or aquifer is increasing and all of the possible resolutions of this conflict, except perhaps desalinization of ocean water, can promise relief only in the short term. These energy and water issues will force both a gradual restructuring of, and limit the possible expansion of, affected

urban areas. Many cities that had been privileged in the years of ample low cost energy and water will find themselves disadvantaged in the new resource supply and cost environment.

As a final comment, we would argue the need for increasingly effective and competent municipal and urban regional governance. Schumpeter's 'creative waves of destruction' are more powerfully operational and effective in today's globally-open economy than they have ever been. Its impacts on firms, communities, the labor force, governments at all levels and the well-being of individual households will in many cases be profound. The challenges of governance will be greater than ever before and enlightened public servants and statesmen and stateswomen, more than run-of-the-mill politicians, will be needed to lead city halls around the world. The challenges to all cities are clear and we hope that in this book we have clarified some of them, suggested approaches to their resolution and given guidance to public and private sector leaders in individual cities.

NOTES

1. Simmie, 2004, p. 1104.
2. Camagni, 2002, p. 2402.
3. Marshall, 1959, pp. 222–31.
4. Howells, 2002, p. 880.
5. Wolfe and Gertler, 2004.
6. Simmie, 2004, pp. 1105–7.
7. Cappelen *et al.*, 1999, p. 134; and Hart, 1998, p. 166.
8. Gil Canalete *et al.*, 2004, p. 91.
9. Clark and Blue, 2004.
10. Graham, 2001.
11. Wolf-Powers, June 2001.

Bibliography

Academy of Social Sciences (2003).

Aeppel, Timothy (2000), 'Think small,' *Wall Street Journal*, 1 January.

Agarwal, P.K. (2000), 'It's the new economy, stupid,' *Government Technology*, July.

Altshuler, Alan and David Luberoff (2003), *Mega-Projects: The Changing Politics of Urban Public Investment*, Washington, DC: Brookings Institution Press.

Altshuler, Alan, William Morrill, Harold Wolman and Faith Mitchell (eds) (1999), *Governance and Opportunity in Metropolitan America*, Washington, DC: National Academy Press. *American Cities and the Global Economy: Challenges and Opportunities*, Thousand Oaks, CA: Sage Publications.

Anas, Alex, Richard Arnott and Kenneth A. Small (1998), 'Urban spatial structure,' *Journal of Economic Literature*, **XXXVI**, 1426–64.

Andersen, Hans Thor and Ronald van Kempen (eds) (2001), *Governing European Cities*, Aldershot, UK: Ashgate.

Andrew, Caroline, Katherine A. Graham and Susan D. Philips (eds) (2003), *Urban Affairs*, Montreal: McGill-Queen's University Press.

Andrew, Caroline, Pat Armstrong and André Lapierre (eds) (1999), *World Class Cities: Can Canada Play?*, Ottawa: University of Ottawa Press.

Arizona Republic (1995), 5 February.

Artibise, Alan (1995), 'Achieving sustainability in Cascadia: An emerging model of urban growth management in the Vancouver–Seattle–Portland Corridor,' in Peter Karl Kresl and Gary Gappert (eds), *North American Cities and the Global Economy*, Thousand Oaks, CA: Sage Publications.

Assembly of European Regions, www.are-regions-europe.org.

Association of European Border Regions, www.aebr.net.

Bachman, S.L. (2003), *Globalization in the San Francisco Bay Area*, Los Angeles: Pacific Council on International Policy.

Bairoch, Paul (1988), *Cities and Economic Development: From the Dawn of History to the Present*, translated by Christopher Braider, Chicago: University of Chicago Press.

Barlow, Maude, and Tony Clarke (2001), *Global Showdown: How the New Activists Are Fighting Global Corporate Rule*, Toronto: Stoddart.

Barry, Donald (2003), 'Managing Canada–US relations in the post-9/11 era: do we need a big idea?,' Washington: Center for Strategic and International Studies, Policy Paper on the Americas, **XVI**, Study 11, November.

Bartlett, Randall (1998), *The Crisis of America's Cities*, Armonk, New York: M.E. Sharpe.

Begg, Iain, Barry Moore and Yener Altunbas (2002), 'Long-run trends in the competitiveness of British cities,' in Iain Begg, *Urban Competitiveness: Policies for Dynamic Cities*, Bristol: Policy Press.

Begg, Iain (ed.) (2002), *Urban Competitiveness: Policies for Dynamic Cities*, Bristol: Policy Press.

Berners-Lee, Tim (1999), *Weaving the Web*, New York: Harper.

Best, Michael H. (2000), 'Silicon Valley and the resurgence of Route 128: Systems integration and regional innovation,' in John H. Dunning (ed.), *Regions, Globalization, and the Knowledge-based Economy*, Oxford: Oxford University Press, 459–84.

Bhagwati, Jagdish (2002), 'Coping with antiglobalization,' *Foreign Affairs*, **81** (1).

Blakely, Edward J. and Ted K. Bradshaw (2002), *Planning Local Economic Development: Theory and Practice*, 3rd edn, Thousand Oaks, CA: Sage Publications.

Borja, Jordi and Manuel Castells (1997), *Local and Global: Management of Cities in the Information Age*, London: Earthscan Publications.

Borjas, George J. (1999), *Heaven's Door: Immigration Policy and the American Economy*, Princeton: Princeton University Press.

Bourne, Larry S. (2000), 'Urban Canada in transition to the twenty-first century: Trends, issues, and visions,' in Trudi Bunting and Pierre Filion (eds), *Canadian Cities in Transition*, 2nd edn, Don Mills, Ontario: Oxford University Press.

Bradford, Neil (2002), *Why Cities Matter: Policy Research Perspectives for Canada*, Ottawa: Canadian Policy Research Networks.

Brooks, Janet Rae (2003), 'Turin sees its olympic moment as investment in future,' *Salt Lake Tribune*, 10 March.

Brotchie, John, Peter Newton, Peter Hall and John Dickey (1999), *East–West Perspectives on 21st Century Urban Development*. Aldershot, UK: Ashgate.

Buchanan, Patrick J. (2002), *The Death of the West*, New York: St Martin's.

Bueno de Mesquita, Bruce (2002), 'Domestic politics and international relations,' *International Studies Quarterly*, **46** (1), 1–10.

Camagni, Roberto P. (1995), 'The concept of *innovative* milieu and its relevance for public policies in European lagging regions,' *Papers in Regional Science*, **74**, (4), 189–208.

Camagni, Roberto P. (2002), 'On the concept of territorial competitiveness: sound or misleading?', *Urban Studies*, **39** (13), 2395–411.

Camarota, Steven A. (2001), *Immigrants in the United States – 2000: A Snapshot of America's Foreign-Born Population,* Washington, DC: Center for Immigration Studies, January.

Capello, Roberta (1994), 'Towards new industrial and spatial systems: the role of new technologies,' *Papers in Regional Science,* **73** (2), 189–208.

Cappelen, Aadne, Jan Fagerberg and Bart Verspagen (1999), 'Lack of regional convergence,' in Jan Fagerberg, Paolo Guerrier and Bart Verspagen (eds), *The Economic Challenge for Europe,* Cheltenham, UK and Northampton, MA, USA: Edward Elgar, 134.

Cartier, Carolyn (2002), 'Transnational urbanism in the reform-era Chinese city: Landscapes from Shenzhen,' *Urban Studies,* **39** (13), 1513–32.

Castells, Manuell (1989), *The Informational City: Information Technology, Economic Restructuring and the Urban Regional Process,* Oxford: Blackwell.

Centre d'études prospectives et d'information internationales (1998), *Compétitivité des nations,* Paris: Economica.

Center for Strategic and International Studies (2003), *Policy Paper on the Americans, Vol. XIV, Study 11,* November.

Chanda, Nayan (2002), 'Coming together: Globalization means reconnecting the human community,' *YaleGlobal,* 19 November.

Chernotsky, Harry I. (2004), 'Fragmenting federalism and local economic policy,' paper presented at the 45th Annual Convention of the International Studies Association, Montreal, 20 March.

Chernotsky, Harry I. and Jennifer Watson Roberts (1996), 'America's shifting global agendas: a case study of local foreign policy,' paper presented at the 37th Annual Convention of the International Studies Association, San Diego, 16 April.

Chesire, Paul (1990), 'Explaining the recent performance of the European Community's major urban regions,' *Urban Studies,* **27** (6), 311–33.

Cheshire, Paul, Gianni Carbonaro and Dennis Hay (1986), 'Problems of urban decline and growth in EEC countries: or measuring degrees of elephantness,' *Urban Studies,* **23** (2), 131–49.

Chicago Tribune (2002), 21 July.

Cities for Peace, www.ips-dc.org/citiesforpeace.

City Planner's Office (2003), *Community Strategic Plan: 2003 Action Plan,* Windsor: City of Windsor.

Clark, David E. and William J. Hunter (1992), 'The impact of economic opportunity, amenities and fiscal factors on age-specific migration rates,' *Journal of Regional Science,* **32** (3).

Clark, Robert P. (2001), *Global Life Systems: Population, Food, and Disease in the Process of Globalization,* Lanham, MD: Rowman and Littlefield.

Clark, William V. and Sarah A. Blue (2004), 'Race, class, and segregation

Patterns in US immigrant gateway cities,' *Urban Affairs Review*, **39** (6), 274–81.

Clarkson, Stephen (2002), *Uncle Sam and Us: Globalization, Neoconservativism, and the Canadian State*, Toronto: University of Toronto Press.

CMEA, 'Brief history of European town-twinning,' at www.ccre.org/docs/jumelages/origins.html.

Cohen, Malcolm S. and Mahmood A. Zaidi (2002), *Global Skill Shortages*, Cheltenham, UK and Northampton, MA, USA: Edward Elgar.

Commission on Global Governance (1995), *Our Global Neighborhood*, New York: Oxford University Press.

Committee for Economic Development (1986), *Leadership for Dynamic State Economies*, New York: Committee for Economic Development.

Conway, Maureen and Josef Konvitz (2000), 'Meeting the Challenge of Distressed Urban Areas,' *Urban Studies*, **37** (4), 749–74.

Council of European Municipalities and Regions (2003), 'Enhancing democracy in the European Union: A stronger involvement for local and regional government,' *A White Paper on European Governance*, Brussels: Council of European Municipalities and Regions.

Crahan, Margaret E. and Alberto Vourvoulias-Bush (eds) (1997), *The City and the World: New York's Global Future*, New York: Council on Foreign Relations.

Cross, Malcolm and Robert Moore (eds) (2002), *Globalization and the New City*, New York: Palgrave.

Csikszentmihalyi, Mihaly (1988), 'Society, culture, and person: a systems view of creativity,' in Robert J. Sternberg (ed.), *The Nature of Creativity: Contemporary Psychological Perspectives*, Cambridge: Cambridge University Press.

Csikszentmihalyi, Mihaly (1996), *Creativity*, New York: HarperCollins.

Czarniawska, Barbara (2002), *A Tale of Three Cities*, New York: Oxford University Press.

Daniels, P.W. and J.R. Bryson (2002), 'Manufacturing services and servicing manufacturing: Knowledge-based cities and changing forms of production,' *Urban Studies*, **39** (5–6), 977–92.

Day, George S. and David J. Reibstein, with Robert Gunther (1997), *Wharton on Dynamic Competitive Strategy*, New York: John Wiley and Sons.

Deas, Iain and Benito Giordano (2002), 'Locating the competitive city in England,' in Iain Begg, *Urban Competitiveness: Policies for Dynamic Cities*, Bristol: Policy Press.

Deseret News (2000), 17 October.

DiGaetano, Alan and John S. Klemanski (1999), *Power and City Governance*, Minneapolis: University of Minnesota Press.

Dreier, Peter, John Mollenkopf and Todd Swanstrom (2001), *Place Matters:*

Metropolitics for the Twenty-first Century, Lawrence: University Press of Kansas.

Drennan, Matthew P. (2002), *The Information Economy and American Cities*, Baltimore: Johns Hopkins University Press.

Drolet M. and R. Morissette (2002), 'Are knowledge-based jobs better?,' *Canadian Economic Observer* (Statistics Canada).

Drucker, Peter F. (1989), *The New Realities*, New York: Harper and Row.

Drucker, Peter F. (1999), *Management Challenges for the Twenty-First Century*, New York: HarperBusiness.

Drucker, Peter F. (2003), *A Functioning Society*, New Brunswick, NJ: Transaction Publishers.

Dunfield, Allison (2003), 'Martin promises new deal for cities,' *The Globe and Mail*, 12 November.

Economist (2001), 31 March.

Edisis, Adrienne T. (2003), 'Global activities by US states: Findings of a survey of state government international activities,' paper prepared by the Elliott School of International Affairs, George Washington University, July.

Encyclopaedia Americana, 2000.

Erie, Stephen P. (2001), 'Global gateways and infrastructure challenges: The case of Southern California,' in Earl H. Fry and V. Wallace McCarlie (eds), *Globalization and the Information Technology Revolution: Their Impact on North America's Federal Systems*, Provo, UT: Brigham Young University.

Erie, Steven P. (2003), *Enhancing Southern California's Global Gateways*, Los Angeles: Pacific Council on International Policy.

Erie, Steven P. (2004), *Globalizing LA: Trade, Infrastructure, and Regional Development*, Stanford: Stanford University Press.

Estrose, Christian (1996), *La cooperation transfrontalière au service de l'aménagement du territoire*, Paris: Conseil Economique et Social.

Eurocities: Documents and Subjects of Eurocities Conference (1989), Barcelona: Organising Committee of the Eurocities Conference, 21 and 22 April.

Eurocities Mayors' Declaration (2002), Brussels: Eurocities, 29 November.

Eurocities Policy Advisory Group (1994), 'Towards an expanded European urban policy,' Brussels: Eurocities, June.

European Union Committee of the Regions, www.europa.eu/int/institutions/cor.

Fagerberg, Jan and Bart Verspagen (1996), 'Heading for divergence: regional growth in Europe reconsidered,' *Journal of Common Market Studies*, **34** (3), 431–48.

Fairbanks, Robert B. and Patricia Mooney-Melvin (eds) (2001), *Making Sense of the City*, Columbus: Ohio State University Press.

Federation of Canadian Municipalities (2001), *Early Warning: Will Canadian Cities Compete?*, Ottawa: Federation of Canadian Municipalities.

Federation of Canadian Municipalities (2002), *Communities in an Urban Century: Symposium Report*, Ottawa: Federation of Canadian Municipalities.

Federation of Canadian Municipalites (2003), press release.

Feinberg, Richard (2001), *San Diego, Baja California and Globalization: Coming from Behind*, Los Angeles: Pacific Council on International Policy.

Feldman, Maryann P. and David B. Audretsch (1999), 'Innovation in cities: Science-based diversity, specialization and localized competition,' *European Economic Review*, **43**, 409–29.

Fenn, W. Michael (2003), 'Emerging trends in urban affairs – A municipal manager's view,' in Andrew, Graham and Philips (eds), *Urban Affairs*.

Financial Times, various issues.

Florida, Richard (2002), *The Rise of the Creative Class*, New York: Basic Books.

Fortier, François (2001), *Virtuality Check: Power Relations and Alternative Strategies in the Information Society*, London and New York: Verso.

Fowler, Edmund P. and David Siegel (eds) (2002), *Urban Policy Issues: Canadian Perspectives*, 2nd edn, Don Mills, ON: Oxford University Press.

Francis, Diane (2002), 'Why size doesn't matter,' *National Post*, 28 September.

Freedom House (2003), 'Global freedom gains amid terror, uncertainty,' press release, at www.fredomhouse.org, 18 December.

Friedman, Thomas L. (1999), *The Lexus and the Olive Tree*, New York: Farrar Straus Giroux.

Friedmann, John (1995a), 'The world city hypothesis,' in Knox and Taylor (eds), *World Cities in a World-System*, Cambridge: Cambridge University Press.

Friedmann, John (1995b), 'Where we stand: A decade of world city research,' in Knox and Taylor (eds), *World Cities in a World-System*, Cambridge: Cambridge University Press.

Friedmann, John (2002), *The Prospect of Cities*, Minneapolis: University of Minnesota Press.

Fry, Earl H. (1980), *Financial Invasion of the USA*. New York: McGraw-Hill.

Fry, Earl H. (1995), 'North American municipalities and their involvement in the global economy,' in Peter Karl Kresl and Gary Gappert (eds), *North American Cities and the Global Economy*, Thousand Oaks, CA: Sage Publications.

Fry, Earl H. (1998), *The Expanding Role of State and Local Governments in US Foreign Affairs*, New York: Council on Foreign Relations Press.

Fry, Earl H. (2000), *The North American West in a Global Economy*, Los Angeles: Pacific Council on International Policy.

Fry, Earl H. and Wallace McCarlie (2002), *Mapping Globalization Along the Wasatch Front*, Los Angeles: Pacific Council on International Policy.

Fujita, Masahira and Jacques-François Thisse (2002), *Economics of Agglomeration*, Cambridge: Cambridge University Press.

Gardner, Howard (1993), *Creating Minds*, New York: HarperCollins.

Garreau, Joel (1981), *The Nine Nations of North America*, Boston: Houghton Mifflin.

Garreau, Joel (1991), *Edge City: Life on the New Frontier*, New York: Doubleday.

Gaspar, Jess and Edward L. Glaeser (1998), 'Information technology and the future of cities,' *Journal of Urban Economics*, **43**, 136–56.

Gertler, Meric (1995), '"Being there": Proximity, organization, and culture in the development and adoption of advanced manufacturing technologies,' *Economic Geography*, **71** (1), 20–21.

Gil Canalete, Carlos, Pedro Pascual Arzoz and Manuel Rapún Gárate (2004), 'Regional economic disparities and decentralisation,' *Urban Studies*, **41** (1).

Glaeser, Edward L. and Jesse M. Shapiro (2002), 'Cities and warfare: The impact of terrorism on urban form,' *Journal of Urban Economics*, **51** (1), 136–56.

Glaeser, Edward L. and Jesse M. Shapiro (2003), 'City growth,' in Katz and Lang (eds), *Redefining Urban and Suburban America*.

Globe and Mail (2003), 4 December.

Gold, Harry (2002), *Urban Life and Society*, Upper Saddle River, NJ: Prentice-Hall.

Goldsmith, Stephen (1997), *The Twenty-First Century City*, Washington, DC: Regnery.

Gongliff, Mark (2003), 'US jobs jumping ship,' *CNN/Money*, 2 May.

Gordon, Peter and Harry W. Richardson (1998), 'World cities in North America: Structural change and future challenges,' in Fu-Chen Lo and Yue-Man Yeung (eds), *Globalization and the World of Large Cities*, Tokyo: UN University Press.

Gotham, Kevin Fox (2002), 'Marketing Mardi Gras: Commodification, spectacle and the political economy of tourism in New Orleans,' *Urban Studies*, **39** (10), 1735–56.

Graham, Stephen (2001), 'Information technologies and reconfigurations of urban space,' *International Journal of Urban and Regional Research*, **25** (2), 424–5.

Green, Charles (2001), *Manufacturing Powerlessness in the Black Diaspora*, Walnut Creek, CA: Altamira.

Greenstein, Rosalind and Wim Wiewel (eds) (2000), *Urban-Suburban Interdependence*, Cambridge, MA: Lincoln Institute of Land Policy.

Haberman, Martin (2003), 'Who benefits from failing urban school districts?' *EducationNews.org*, March.

Hall, Peter (1996), *Cities of Tomorrow*, updated version, Cambridge, MA: Blackwell.

Hall, Peter (1998), 'Globalization and the world cities,' in Fu-Chen Lo and Yue-Man Yeung (eds), *Globalization and the World of Large Cities*, Tokyo: UN University Press.

Hall, Peter (2001), *Cities in Civilization*, New York: Fromm International.

Hall, Peter (1999), 'Planning for the mega-city: A new Eastern Asian urban model,' in Brotchie, Newton, Hall and Dickey, *East-West Perspectives*.

Hall, Peter and Ulrich Pfeiffer (2000), *Urban Future 21*, London: E. and F.N. Spon.

Handley, Susan (ed.) (2001), *The Links Effect: A Good Practice Guide to Transnational Partnerships and Twinning of Local Authorities*, London: Local Government International Bureau.

Hart, Mark (1998), 'Convergence, cohesion and regionalism: contradictory trends in the new Europe,' in Brian Graham (ed.), *Modern Europe: Place, Culture and Identity*, London: Arnold, p. 166.

Haug, Peter (1991), 'The location decisions and operations of high technology organizations in Washington State,' *Regional Studies*, **25** (6), 525–41.

Held, David, Anthony McGrew, David Goldblatt and Jonathan Perraton (1999), *Global Transformations*, Stanford: Stanford University Press.

Hobbs, Heidi (2004), 'Fragmenting federalism and the reinvigoration of local foreign policy activism,' paper presented at the 45th Annual Convention of the International Studies, Montreal, 20 March.

Hodge, Gerald and Ira M. Robinson (2001), *Planning Canadian Regions*, Vancouver: University of British Columbia Press.

Hohenberg, Paul M. and Lynn Hollen Lees (1995), *The Making of Urban Europe, 1000–1994*, Cambridge: Harvard University Press.

Hohenberg, Paul M. and Lynn Hollen Lees (eds) (1985), *The Making of Urban Europe 1000–1950*, Cambridge: Harvard University Press.

Hopkins, A.G. (ed.) (2002), *Globalization in World History*, London: Pimlico.

Howells, Jeremy R.L. (2002) 'Tacit knowledge, innovation and economic geography,' *Urban Studies*, **39** (5–6).

Ikenberry, G. John (ed.) (2002), *America Unrivaled: The Future of the Balance of Power*, Ithaca, NY: Cornell University Press.

Inter-American Development Bank (2001), *Competitiveness: The Business of Growth – Economic and Social Progress in Latin America*, Baltimore: Johns Hopkins University Press.

International Herald Tribune (2002), 13 March; (2003), 29 October.

International Trade Administration, 'Export sales of US Metropolitan Areas, 1993–1999.' at www.ita.doc.gov/TSFrameset.html.

Jacquemin, Alexis and Lucio R. Pench (eds) (1997), *Pour une compétitivité européenne*, Brussels: De Broeck University.

Japan Automobile Manufacturers' Association (2002), 'Japan Automobile Manufacturers: Global companies meeting new challenges with advanced technologies,' at www.jama.org.

Jensen-Butler, Chris, Arie Shachar and Jan van Weesep (eds) (1997), *European Cities in Competition*, Aldershot, UK: Avebury.

Kalypso, Nicolaidis and Robert Howse (eds) (2001), *The Federal Vision: Legitimacy and Levels of Governance in the United States and the European Union*, Oxford: Oxford University Press.

Kantor, Rosabeth Moss (1995), *World Class: Thriving Locally in the Global Economy*, New York: Simon & Schuster.

Katz, Bruce and Robert E. Lang (eds) (2003), *Redefining Urban and Suburban America*, **1**, Washington, DC: Brookings Institution Press.

Kearns, Ade and Ronan Paddison (2000), 'New challenges for urban governance,' *Urban Studies*, **37** (4), 845–50.

Kemp, Roger L. (ed.) (2001), *The Inner City: A Handbook for Renewal*, Jefferson, NC: McFarland.

Kincaid, John (1997), *American Cities in the Global Economy*, Washington, DC: National League of Cities.

Klinkenbourg, Verlyn (2003), 'Trying to measure the amount of information that humans create,' *New York Times*, 12 November.

Knox, Paul L. and Peter J. Taylor (eds) (1995), *World Cities in a World-System*, Cambridge: Cambridge University Press.

Kotkin, Joel (2000), *The New Geography*, New York: Random House.

Kresl, Peter Karl (1992), *The Urban Economy and Regional Trade Liberalization*, New York: Praegar.

Kresl, Peter Karl (1995), 'The determinants of urban competitiveness: A survey,' in Peter Karl Kresl and Gary Gappert, *North American Cities and the Global Economy* (Urban Affairs Annual Review 44), Thousand Oaks: Sage Publications.

Kresl, Peter Karl and Gary Gappert (1995), *North American Cities and the Global Economy* (Urban Affairs Annual Review 44), Thousand Oaks: Sage Publications.

Kresl, Peter Karl and Balwant Singh (1995), 'The competitiveness of cities: the United States,' *Cities and the New Global Economy*, Melbourne: OECD and the Australian Government, 425–46.

Kresl, Peter Karl and Balwant Singh (1999), 'Competitiveness and the urban economy: twenty-four large US metropolitan areas,' *Urban Studies*, **36** (5–6), 1017–27.

Kresl, Peter Karl and Pierre-Paul Proulx (2000), 'Montreal's place in the

North American economy, *American Review of Canadian Studies*, **30** (3), 1017–27.

Krugman, Paul (1991), *Geography and Trade*, Cambridge: MIT Press.

Ladner, Joyce A. (2001), *The New Urban Leaders*, Washington, DC: Brookings Institution Press.

Lambooy, Jan G. (2002), 'Knowledge and urban economic development: An evolutionary perspective,' *Urban Studies*, **39** (5–6), 1019–36.

Landry, Charles (2000), *The Creative City*, London: Earthscan Publications.

Lang, Robert E. (2003), *Edgeless Cities*, Washington, DC: Brookings Institution Press.

Las Vegas Review-Journal (2003), 4 January, 17 July.

Le Galès, Patrick and Alan Harding (1998), 'Cities and states in Europe,' *West European Politics*, **21** (3).

Le Galès, Patrick (2002), *European Cities: Social Conflicts and Governance*, Oxford: Oxford University Press.

Lee, Chong Moon, William F. Miller, Marguerite Gong Hancock and Henry S. Rower (eds) (2000), *The Silicon Valley Edge*, Stanford: Stanford University Press.

Lever, William F. (2000), 'The knowledge base and the competitive city,' in Iain Begg, *Urban Competitiveness: Policies for Dynamic Cities*, Bristol: Policy Press.

Light, Ivan (2002), 'Immigrant place entrepreneurs in Los Angeles 1970–1999,' *International Journal of Urban and Regional Research*, **26** (June), 215–28.

Light, Ivan, Rebecca Kim and Connie Hum (2002), 'Globalization's effects on employment in Southern California, 1970–1990,' in Malcolm Cross and Robert Moore (eds), *Globalization and the New City*, New York: Palgrave, 151–67.

List, Friedrich (1966), *The National System of Political Economy*, New York: Augustus M. Kelley.

Lo, Fu-Chen and Peter J. Marcotullio (eds) (2001), *Globalization and the Sustainability of Cities in the Asia Pacific Region*, Tokyo: UN University Press.

Lo, Fu-Chen and Yue-Man Yeung (eds) (1998), *Globalization and the World of Large Cities*, Tokyo: UN University Press.

Los Angeles Times (1999), 12 July; (2001), 8 July; (2002), 7 February; (2003), 1 June, 27 July, 8 August.

Luke, Jeffrey S., Curtis Ventriss, B.J. Reed and Christine M. Reed (1988), *Managing Economic Development*, San Francisco: Jossey-Bass.

Lyon Economic Development Agency, www.lyon-aderley.com.

Madden, Janice Fanning (2003), 'The changing spatial concentration of income and poverty among suburbs of large US metropolitan areas,' *Urban Studies*, **40** (3), 481–503.

Malecki, Edward J. (2002) 'Hard and Soft Networks for Urban Competitiveness,' *Urban Studies*, **39**, (5–6), 929–46.

Manning, Bayless (1977), 'The Congress, the Executive and intermestic affairs: Three proposals,' *Foreign Affairs*, **55** (2), 306–24.

Marcuse, Peter and Ronald van Kempen (eds) (2002), *Of States and Cities*, Oxford: Oxford University Press.

Marshall, Alfred (1959), *Principles of Economics*, London: Macmillan.

Marshall, Tim (2000), 'Urban planning and governance: Is there a Barcelona model?,' *International Planning Studies*, **5**, 299–320.

McFetridge, Donald G. (1995), 'Competitiveness: Concepts and Measures,' occasional paper number 5, Ottawa: Industry Canada.

McIsaac, Elizabeth (2003), 'Immigrants in Canadian cities: census 2001 – what do the data tell us?', *Policy Options*, **24** (May), 58–63.

Metropolis, www.metropolis.net.

Micklethwait, John and Adrian Woolridge (2000), *A Future Perfect*, New York: Crown Business.

Miller, David Y. (2002), *The Regional Governing of Metropolitan America*, Boulder: Westview Press.

Milwaukee Journal Sentinel (2003), 11 December.

Moavenzadeh, Fred, Keisuke Hanaki and Peter Baccini (eds) (2002), *Future Cities: Dynamics and Sustainability*, Dordrecht: Kluwer Academic Publishers.

Mollenkopf John H. and Manuel Castells (eds) (1991), *Dual City: Restructuring New York*, New York: Russell Sage Foundation.

Mollenkopf, John and Ken Emerson (eds) (2001), *Rethinking the Urban Agenda*, New York: Urban Foundation Press.

Montreal International, www.MontrealInternational.org.

Moon, M. Jae (2002), 'The evolution of e-government among municipalities: Rhetoric or reality?', *Public Administration Review*, **62** (4), 424–33.

Mooney, Chris (2001), 'Localizing globalization,' *The American Prospect*, 2 July, 23–6.

Morris, Frederic A. (2003), *Boeing and Beyond: Seattle in the Global Economy*, Los Angeles: Pacific Council on International Policy.

Musgrave, Richard (1959), *The Theory of Public Finance*, New York: McGraw-Hill.

National Post (2002), 28 September.

National League of Cities (1993), *Global Dollars, Local Sense: Cities and Towns in the International Economy*, Washington DC: National League of Cities.

National League of Cities (1995), *Leading Cities in a Global Economy: Local Officials Guide*, Washington, DC: National League of Cities.

Negrey, Cynthia and Mary Beth Zickel (1994), 'Industrial shifts and uneven development: Patterns of growth and decline in US metropolitan areas,' *Urban Affairs Quarterly*, **30** (1), 27–47.

Nevarez, Leonard (2003), *New Money, Nice Town*, New York: Routledge.

Neusy, André-Jacques (2003), 'White paper, presented at the Global Health Challenges in World Cities conference, New York City, 6–8 March.

New Economy Task Force (1999), *Rules of the Road: Governing Principles for the New Economy*, Washington, DC: Progressive Policy Institute.

New York Times (2001), 30 May; (2003), 5 January, 22 and 27 July, 11 November, 7 December; (2004), 1 January, 3 January.

Nye, Joseph S., Jr. (2002), *The Paradox of American Power*, New York: Oxford University Press.

Nye, Joseph S., Jr. and John D. Donahue (eds) (2000), *Governance in a Globalizing World*, Washington, DC: Brookings Institution Press.

Ohmae, Kenichi (1990), *The Borderless World: Power and Strategy in the Interlinked Economy*, Cambridge: Harvard Business School Press.

Ohmae, Kenichi (1995), *The End of the Nation State*, New York: Free Press.

Olds, Kris (2001), *Globalization and Urban Change*, Oxford: Oxford University Press.

Olivier, Charles (2002), 'Labyrinth of incentives,' *Financial Times*, 2 December.

Øresund – en region bliver til: Rapport udarbejdet af den danske og svenske regering (1999), Copenhagen: Statens publikationer, May.

Orfield, Myron (1997), *Metropolitics: A Regional Agenda for Community and Stability*, revised edition, Washington, DC: Brookings Institution Press.

Orfield, Myron (2002), *America Metro Politics*, Washington, DC: Brookings Institution Press.

Oster, Sharon (1999), *Modern Competitive Analysis*, 3rd edn, New York: Oxford University Press.

Pagano, Michael A. (2003), 'Cities' fiscal challenges continue to worsen in 2003,' *Research Brief on America's Cities*, Washington, DC: National League of Cities, November.

Pastor, Manuel, Jr. (2001), *Widening the Winner's Circle from Global Trade in Southern California*, Los Angeles: Pacific Council on International Policy.

Pastor, Manuel, Jr., Peter Dreier, J. Eugene Grigsby III and Marta Lopez (2000), *Regions That Work: How Cities and Suburbs Can Grow Together*, Minneapolis: University of Minnesota Press.

Peirce, Neal R. (1993), *Citistates: How Urban America Can Prosper in a Competitive World*, Washington, DC: Seven Locks Press.

Pengfei, Ni (ed.) (2003a), *Blue Book of City Competitiveness No. 1, Report on Chinese Urban Competitiveness*, Beijing: Chinese Academy of Social Sciences.

Pengfei, Ni (2003b), *China Urban Competitiveness: Theoretical Hypothesis and Empirical Test* (English text), Beijing: Chinese Academy of Social Sciences.

Pew Global Attitudes Project (2003), 'Views of a changing world,' Washington, DC: Pew Research Center for the People and the Press, June.

Piller, Charles (1999), 'Silicon Valley immigration debate ignores many locals,' *Los Angeles Times*, 12 July.

Pittsburgh Post-Gazette (2003), 4 December.

Planning and Development Department (1992), *Master Plan of Policies*, Detroit: City of Detroit.

Pollard, Jane and Michael Storper (1996), 'A tale of twelve cities: Metropolitan employment change in dynamic industries in the 1980s,' *Economic Geography*, **72** (1), 1–22.

Popkin, Joel and Company (2003), 'Securing America's future: The case for a strong manufacturing base,' report prepared for the NAM Council of Manufacturing Associations, June.

Population Reference Bureau, www.prb.org.

Porter, Michael E. (1995), 'The competitive advantage of the inner city,' *Harvard Business Review*, May/June.

Porter, Michael E. (1990), *The Competitive Advantage of Nations*, New York: Free Press.

Progressive Policy Institute (1999), 'Introduction,' *Rules of the Road, Governing Principles of the New Economy*, Washington, DC: PPI.

Ranney, David (2003), *Global Decisions, Local Collisions*, Philadelphia: Temple University Press.

Regio Tri-Rhena, www.regiotrirhena.org.

Robinson, Jeffrey (2000), *The Merger: The Conglomeration of International Organized Crime*, Woodstock, NY: Overlook.

Robinson, Jennifer (2002), 'Global and world cities: A view from off the map,' *International Journal of Urban and Regional Research*, **26** (3), 531–54.

Rocky Mountain News (2001), 31 March.

Rogerson, Robert J. (1999), 'Quality of life and city competitiveness,' *Urban Studies*, **36** (5–6), 969–86.

Rosenau, James N. (1999), 'Toward an ontology for global governance,' in Martin Hewson and Timothy J. Sinclair (eds), *Approaches to Global Governance Theory*, Albany, NY: State University of New York Press.

Rugman, Alan, and Karl Moore (2001), 'The myth of globalization,' *Ivey Business Journal*, 1 September, 65.

Rusk David (1995), *Cities Without Suburbs*, 2nd edn, Washington, DC: Woodrow Wilson Center Press.

Samers, Michael (2002), 'Immigration and the global city hypothesis: Toward an alternative research agenda,' *International Journal of Urban and Regional Research*, **26** (2), 389–402.

Samuelson, Robert J. (2004), 'Calling the next tech challenge,' *Washington Post*, 26 March.

San Diego Dialogue (2000), *The Global Engagement of San Diego/Baja California*, San Diego: San Diego Dialogue. November.

San Diego Union-Tribune (2003), 24 June.

Sappenfield, Mark (2003), 'Around the globe, new "Silicon Valleys" emerge,' *Christian Science Monitor*, 29 December.

Sassen, Saskia (1991), *The Global City: New York, London, Tokyo*, Princeton: Princeton University Press.

Sassen, Saskia (1998), *Globalization and its Discontents*, New York: New Press.

Sassen, Saskia (ed.) (2002), *Global Networks, Linked Cities*, New York: Routledge.

Saxenian, AnnaLee (2002), *Local and Global Networks of Immigrant Professionals in Silicon Valley*, San Francisco: Public Policy Institute of California.

Schmidt, Samuel (1995), 'Planning a US–Mexican bi-national metropolis: El Paso, Texas–Ciudad Juárez, Chihuahua,' in Peter Karl Kresl and Gary Gappert (eds), *North American Cities and the Global Economy: Challenges and Opportunities*, in *Urban Affairs Annual Review*, 44, 187–220, Thousand Oaks, CA: Sage Publications.

Schultze, Claus J. (2003), 'Cities and EU governance: Policy-takers and policy-makers,' *Regional and Federal Studies*, **13**, 122–3.

Schutte, Hellmut (1994), *The Global Competitiveness of the Asian Firm*, New York: St. Martin's Press.

Schweke, William and Robert Stumberg (2000), 'The emerging global constitution: why local governments could be left out,' *Public Management*, January, 4–10.

Scott and George C. Lodge (eds), *U.S. Competitiveness in the World Economy*, Boston: Harvard

Scott, Allen J. (ed.) (2001), *Global City-Regions: Trends, Theory, Policy*, Oxford: Oxford University Press.

Scott, Allen J. (2002), 'Competitive dynamics of Southern California's clothing industry: The widening global connection and its local ramifications,' *Urban Studies*, **39** (8), 1287–1306.

Scott, Bruce R. and George C. Lodge (eds) (1985), *US Competitiveness in the World Economy*, Boston: Harvard Business School Press.

Scott, Bruce R. (1985), 'US competitiveness: Concepts, performance, and implications,' in Bruce R. Scott and George C. Lodge (eds), *US Competitiveness in the World Economy*, Boston: Harvard Business School Press.

Sellers, Jeffrey M. (2002), *Governing from Below: Urban Regions and the Global Economy*, Cambridge: Cambridge University Press.

Shachar, Arie and Daniel Felsenstein (1992), 'Urban economic development and high technology industry,' *Urban Studies*, **29**, (6), 839–55.

Shatz, Howard J. (2003), *Business Without Borders? The Globalization of the California Economy*, San Francisco: Public Policy Institute of California.

Shuman, Michael H. (1998), *Going Local: Creating Self-Reliant Communities in a Global Age*, New York: Free Press.

Simmie, James (2004), 'Innovation and clustering in the globalised international economy,' *Urban Studies*, **41**, (5–6), 1104–7.

Simmie, James and William F. Lever (2002), 'Introduction: The knowledge-based city,' *Urban Studies*, **39**, 855–7.

Simons, Henry C. (1948), 'A positive program for laissez faire: some proposals for a liberal economic policy,' reprinted in his *Economic Policy for a Free Society*, Chicago: University of Chicago Press.

Singh, R.B. (ed.) (2001), *Urban Sustainability in the Context of Global Change,* Enfield, NH: Science Publishers.

Sklair, Leslie. (2002), *Globalization: Capitalism and its Alternatives*, 3rd edn, Oxford: Oxford University Press.

Smil, Vaclav (2002), 'Energy resources and uses: a primer for the twenty-first century,' *Current History* (March).

Smith, Adam (1937), *An Inquiry into the Nature and Causes of the Wealth of Nations,* New York: The Modern Library.

Smith, David A., Dorothy J. Solinger and Steven C. Topik (eds) (1999), *States and Sovereignty in the Global Economy*, London: Routledge.

Sobrino, Jaime (2002), 'Competitividad y ventajas competitivas: revisión theórica y ejercicio de aplicación a 30 ciudades de México,' *Estudios Demográficos y Urbanos*, **17** (2), 311–61.

Sobrino, Jaime (2003), 'Competitividad territorial: ámbitos e indicadores de análisis,' Mexico City: Centro de Estudios Demográficos y de Desarrollo Urbano de El Colegio de México, unpublished paper.

Söderström, Lars (1999), 'Ett nationalekönomiskt perspektiv,' in *Integration och utvekkling i Öresundsregionen*, Lund: Lunds Universitet, 7 February.

Soja, Edward W. (2000), *Postmetropolis: Critical Studies of Cities and Regions*, Oxford: Blackwell.

Soldatos, Panayotis (2003), *Le rôle international des villes à l'aube du millénaire*, Bruxelles: Bruylant.

Solomon, Daniel (2003), *Global City Blues*, Washington, DC: Island Press.

Sorkin, D.L. and others (1984), *Strategies for Cities and Counties: A Strategic Planning Guide*, Washington: Public Technology.

Soros, George (2002), *George Soros on Globalization*, New York: Public Affairs.

Southall, Aidan (1998), *The City in Time and Space*, Cambridge: Cambridge University Press.

Spalding, Mark J. (ed.) (1999), *Sustainable Development in San Diego and Tijuana*, La Jolla: Center for US–Mexican Studies, University of California, San Diego.

Statistics Canada (2001), census data.

Statistics Canada (2002), census data.

Statistics Canada (2003), *The Daily*, 31 July.

Taylor, Melissa and James Carroll (2002), *The Changing Population in the US: Baby Boomers, Immigrants, and Their Effects on State Government*, Lexington, KY: Council of State Governments.

Taylor, P.J., G. Catalano and D.R.F. Walker (2002a), 'Exploratory analysis of the world city network,' *Urban Studies* **39** (13), 2377–94.

Taylor, P.J., G. Catalano and D.R.F. Walker (2002b), 'Measurement of the global city network,' *Urban Studies*, **39** (13), 2367–76.

Thorns, David C. (2002), *The Transformation of Cities*, New York: Palgrave Macmillan.

Thürer, Daniel (2003), 'Federalism and foreign relations,' in Raoul Blindenbacher and Arnold Kollers (eds), *Federalism in a Changing World*, Montreal: McGill-Queen's University Press.

Toffler, Alvin (1970), *Future Shock*, New York: Random House.

Toffler, Alvin (1980), *The Third Wave*, New York: Bantam Books.

Toronto City Summit Alliance (2003), *Enough Talk: An Action Plan for the Toronto Region*, Toronto: Toronto City Summit Alliance.

Toronto Star (2003), 13 December.

Treverton, Gregory F. (2001), *Making the Most of Southern California's Global Engagement*, Los Angeles: Pacific Council on International Policy.

Treverton, Gregory F. (2003), *A Tale of Five Regions: Meeting the Challenge of Globalization in the US West*, Los Angeles: Pacific Council on International Policy.

Uldrich, Jack (2002), 'Why nanotechnology will arrive sooner than expected,' *Futurist* (March–April).

UNAIDS/WHO (2003), *AIDS Epidemic Update*, New York: United Nations, December.

UNCTAD (2002), *World Investment Report 2002: Transnational Corporations and Export Competitiveness: Overview*, New York: United Nations.

UN Department of Economic and Social Affairs, Population Division (2001),

World Urbanization Prospects, the 1999 Revision, New York: United Nations.

UN Department of Economic and Social Affairs, Population Division (2002), *International Migration Report 2002*, New York: United Nations.

UN Department of Economic and Social Affairs (2004), *World Urbanisation Prospects: The 2003 Revision*, New York: United Nations.

UN Development Program (2000), *Human Development Report*.

UN-Habitat 2001, press release, 4 June.

UN-Habitat, www.unhabitat.org.

UN Human Settlements Program (2001), *The State of the World's Cities Report 2001*, New York: United Nations.

UN Population Division (2002), *International Migration Report*, New York: United Nations.

Urban Affairs (1995), Annual Review No. 44, 221–50.

Urban Studies (1999), **36** (5/6), May.

USA Today (2002), 17 December.

US Bureau of the Census, *County and City Data Book*, Washington: Government Printing Office.

US Bureau of the Census, *State and Metropolitan Data Book*, Washington: Government Printing Office.

US Conference of Mayors (2001), 'US metro economies: A decade of prosperity,' report compiled by Standard and Poor's DRI unit.

US Department of Commerce (2002), census data.

US Department of Housing and Urban Development, www.hud.gov/library/bookshelf18/hudmission.cmf.

US National Association of Manufacturers (2003), 'Annual Labor Day Report,' at www.nam.org.

Van den Berg, Leo, Erik Braun and Willem van Winden (2001), *Growth Clusters in European Metropolitan Cities*, Aldershot, UK: Ashgate.

van Geenhuizen, Marina and Peter Nijkamp (1998), 'The local environment as a supportive operator in learning and innovation,' in J.-M. Fontan, J.-C. Klein and D.-G. Tremblay (eds), *Entre la Métropolisation et le village global*, Sainte-Foy: Presses de l'Université du Québec, 303–17.

Van Hecke, Steven (2003), 'The principle of subsidiarity: ten years of application in the European Union,' *Regional and Federal Studies*, **13**, 55–71.

Veblen, Thorstein (1963), *Engineers and the Price System*, New York: Harcourt Brace and World.

Ville de Lyon, 'Partner cities,' www.marie-lyon.fr/international/villes_partenaires.

von Hoffman, Alexander (2003), 'Small businesses, big growth,' *New York Times*, 4 September.

Wall Street Journal (1995), 11 April; (2001), 9 July; (2003), 8 July, 23 July.

Wang, Chia-Huang (2003), 'Taipei as a global city: A theoretical and empirical examination,' *Urban Studies*, **40** (2), 309–34.

Washington Post (2000), 18 January; (2001), 9 July; (2002), 11 November; (2003), 23 July.

Washington Times (2003), 28 January.

Watson, Douglas J. (1995), *The New Civil War: Government Competition for Economic Development*, Westport, CT: Praeger.

Wessel, David (2004), 'If a city isn't sunny – and air conditioned – it should be smart,' *Wall Street Journal*, 26 February.

Westerbeek, Hans and Aaron Smith (2003), *Sport Business in the Global Marketplace*, New York: Palgrave Macmillan.

Wolfe, David A. and Meric S. Gertler (2004), 'Clusters from the inside and out: local dynamics and global linkages,' *Urban Studies*, **41** (5–6), 1090.

Wolf-Powers, Laura (2001), 'Information technology and urban labor markets in the United States,' *Journal of Urban and Regional Research*, **25** (2), 434.

Wood, Peter (2002), 'Knowledge-intensive services and urban innovativeness,' *Urban Studies*, **39** (5–6), 993–1002.

World Cities Energy Partnership, www.wcep.org.

World Commission on Environment and Development (1987), *Our Common Future*, Oxford: Oxford University Press.

World Economic Forum (2003), 'Executive summary,' *Global Competitiveness Report, 2002–2003*, New York: Oxford University Press.

World Economic Forum, *Global Competitiveness Report*, New York: Oxford University Press, annually.

World Tourism Organization (2003), *Tourism Highlights: Edition 2003*, Madrid: World Tourism Organization.

World Trade Organization (2003), *World Trade Report 2003*, Geneva: World Trade Organization.

YaleGlobal (2003), 30 January.

Yeung, Yue-man (2000), *Globalization and Networked Societies: Urban–Regional Change in Pacific Asia*, Honolulu: University of Hawaii Press.

Yusuf, Shahid and Weiping Wu (2002), 'Pathways to a world city: Shanghai rising in an era of globalization,' *Urban Studies*, **39** (7), 1213–40.

Index